Israel/Palestine

Israel/Palestine

Border Representations in Literature and Film

Drew Paul

EDINBURGH
University Press

Edinburgh University Press is one of the leading university presses in the UK. We publish academic books and journals in our selected subject areas across the humanities and social sciences, combining cutting-edge scholarship with high editorial and production values to produce academic works of lasting importance. For more information visit our website: edinburghuniversitypress.com

© Drew Paul, 2020, 2021

Edinburgh University Press Ltd
The Tun – Holyrood Road
12 (2f) Jackson's Entry
Edinburgh EH8 8PJ

First published in hardback by Edinburgh University Press 2020

Typeset in 11/15 Adobe Garamond by
IDSUK (DataConnection) Ltd

A CIP record for this book is available from the British Library

ISBN 978 1 4744 5612 8 (hardback)
ISBN 978 1 4744 5613 5 (paperback)
ISBN 978 1 4744 5614 2 (webready PDF)
ISBN 978 1 4744 5615 9 (epub)

The right of Drew Paul to be identified as author of this work has been asserted in accordance with the Copyright, Designs and Patents Act 1988 and the Copyright and Related Rights Regulations 2003 (SI No. 2498).

Contents

List of Figures	vi
Note on Translation and Transliteration	viii
Acknowledgements	ix
1 Introduction: Excess, Illusion and the Border	1

I Expanding Borders

2 Return to the Border: Commitment, Utopia and the Inescapable Green Line	45
3 Sayed Kashua, the Palestinian Hebrew Novel and the Failure of Coexistence	77

II Deceptive Borders

4 Border Crossings and Stray Narratives of Return	107
5 Does the Camera Lie? Or, How to Document the Wall	134
6 The Illusion of the One-way Mirror: Filming the Checkpoint in *Divine Intervention*	158
7 Conclusion: Physical and Fictional Borders	186
Bibliography	192
Filmography	205
Index	206

Figures

5.1	A shot in *Mur* depicting the construction of a concrete segment of the wall	143
5.2	A long shot of the wall is pictured during a conversation with a Palestinian farmer	143
5.3	A Palestinian sneaks through a section of the wall, as an Israeli general touts its impenetrability via voiceover	146
5.4	An injury suffered by Burnat in *5 Broken Cameras* is depicted with a shaky, flickering image	150
5.5	The five cameras used by Burnat to document the Bil'in protests	151
5.6	A soldier shines a flashlight into Burnat's camera to blind it	153
6.1	E. S. enters the checkpoint in *Divine Intervention*	159
6.2	A post-wedding celebration at an Israeli military checkpoint in *Rana's Wedding*	166
6.3	Israeli soldiers move in choreographed unison as detained Palestinians wait at the checkpoint	169
6.4	E. S. and his girlfriend silently watch the checkpoint from the parking lot	170
6.5	The checkpoint watchtower collapses as the woman passes through	172

6.6, 6.7	E. S. and his girlfriend exchange glances in a shot/reverse shot sequence	175
6.8	An Israeli soldier follows the balloon as it approaches the checkpoint	179
6.9	The camera captures both the balloon and the car as they move towards Jerusalem	180

Note on Translation and Transliteration

I have followed the transliteration guidelines of the *International Journal of Middle East Studies* for Arabic, and the Library of Congress guidelines for Hebrew. I omit diacritical marks on names of persons, places and titles, with the exception of the ع and ء in Arabic and the ע and א in Hebrew. For author and place names I have used the most common English spelling. For the instances in which I use my own translations, I have cited the Arabic or Hebrew original. Otherwise, I use and cite the English translations of literary works.

Acknowledgements

Writing is a largely solitary and sometimes lonely affair, but this book would not have come to fruition without the support of many friends and colleagues. This project has gone through several iterations and drafts, and I want to thank the colleagues and friends from the University of Texas who have collaborated with me and supported me in various ways, from informal conversations to reading drafts and giving feedback at various stages in the process, among them Blake Atwood, Zeina Halabi, Michal Raizen, Benjamin Koerber, Johanna Sellman, Anna Ziajka-Stanton and Angela Giordani. My work has been made possible by excellent mentors and colleagues throughout my graduate education. Tarek El-Ariss, who showed me the dynamism that is possible in this field of study, and whose boundless enthusiasm for my project and belief in my potential as a scholar have inspired me to push myself further than I ever knew possible. Karen Grumberg helped me (re)discover my love for literature in the first class I ever attended as a graduate student and has been a vital source of encouragement and knowledge ever since. I would not be here without Kristen Brustad's unfailing support, from the first day of beginning Arabic to the present, and her passion for and knowledge of all things Arabic is an inspiration. Mahmoud al-Batal's infectious enthusiasm and energy, both in the classroom and outside of it, is a model that I aspire to emulate.

After leaving Texas, my new institutional home, the University of Tennessee, has provided me with a solid foundation for building an academic career. The Department of Modern Foreign Languages and Literatures and Department Head Adrian Del Caro have provided consistent and unwavering support for my work and my development as a scholar. I would like to thank the University of Tennessee Graduate School for supporting my research through a Professional Development Award, Alan Rutenburg from the Office of Research and my fellow newly arrived humanities faculty colleagues who helped craft this project into a viable book proposal, and the College of Arts and Sciences for its repeated support of my work.

At MFLL I have found wonderful interlocutors who have given me guidance and feedback throughout this process. My colleague, friend and faculty mentor, Maria Stehle, has been a voice of wisdom and calm when I needed it the most and has guided me through the processes of book publication and adjusting to the demands of being an assistant professor. Douja Mamelouk immediately welcomed me and made me feel like an equal partner in what was then a nascent Arabic programme. Nicole Wallenbrock has become a consistent collaborator and dear friend who constantly pushes me to think in new ways. Chris Holmlund welcomed me to Knoxville before I even arrived, and she has continued to do so with many martinis and dinners at her house. She has been a steadfast advocate for me both at UT and in the larger world of Cinema Studies. I arrived at UT at an auspicious time for Middle East Studies, as an influx of faculty sparked a new energy. My colleagues in Arabic and Middle East Studies have built a dynamic and growing community of scholars here, and I thank them for all of their support: Phillip Stokes, Elodie Dabbagh-Buehler, Amel Djouadi, Erin Darby, Tina Shepardson, Krista Wiegand, Alison Vacca, Manuela Ceballos, Lillie Gordon and Matt Buehler.

The editing team at Edinburgh University Press have been a pleasure to work with at all stages of the publication process, and I would especially like to thank Adela Rauchova for her early and enthusiastic interest in my project, and Kirsty Woods for hers. I would like to thank Jose Duarté and Timothy Corrigan for publishing my chapter, 'The Palestinian Road(block) Movie: Interrupted Journeys in Elia Suleiman's *Divine Intervention*' in their edited volume, *The Global Road Movie* (Bristol: Intellect, 2018, pp. 104–17). A revised version appears as Chapter 6 of this book. I also thank the editors of *Scritture Migranti* for permission to reprint an earlier version of Chapter 4, which appeared as 'One House, Two Shadows: The Rupture of Return in Contemporary Palestinian Literature' (*Scritture Migranti* 6, 2012, pp. 107–30) in 2013.

While I have only realised it after the fact, at some point in the last five years, Knoxville became home. I would like to thank the friends I have made at the University of Tennessee who have provided community, solidarity and friendship of the best kind, through countless coffees and late-night work sessions, spin classes, gym sessions, dinners, happy hours, trips, and more: Patrick Grzanka, Joe Miles, Bernie Issa, Dustin Manning, Sarah Eldridge, Lillie Gordon, Jessi Grieser, Christopher Ojeda, Gerard Cohen-Vrignaud, Jason Stinnett and Harrison Meadows. I am also grateful for many friends who have opened my eyes to Knoxville and helped me build a life here: Drew Sparks, Oren Yarborough, Mark Marlow, Ben Roach, Hana Akimoto, Jeremy Mills, Jonathan Repass, and many others.

I am lucky to have a wonderful, fun, supportive and beautifully large family, and part of the pleasure of being in Tennessee is being closer to them. My parents have steadfastly encouraged me, as I have gone to places and in directions they (and I) never expected. Their wisdom and guidance always helps me maintain perspective, and the curiosity about the world around that they cultivated from a young age led me across the globe, and then here. My two sisters and my niece Ruby, the newest addition to the family, bring light, laughter and joy into my life every day.

As a writer, I am inspired by my Aunt Jenny, whose writing skills are famous in the family. When I was frantically finishing my dissertation in 2013, I skipped town one weekend to attend her wedding, and it provided me with the final boost of energy I needed to make it to the end. Six years later, as I was completing the final round of edits of this book, she lost her long battle with cancer. I hope I have channelled even a fraction of her clarity, concision and persuasiveness in my own writing. I credit my grandfather, who left us a few years ago, with sparking my interest in languages. Soon after he retired, he decided to learn French, and one summer when I was thirteen years old, he enrolled me in a language immersion programme near Nice, France. Although much of the French I learned there is long forgotten, this experience showed me for the first time the excitement of speaking in a tongue that was not my own. Looking back, that is where it all began.

1

Introduction: Excess, Illusion and the Border

Palestinian writer and architect Suad Amiry's book *Nothing to Lose But Your Life: An 18-Hour Journey with Murad* (2010) chronicles the trials and tribulations of a group of Palestinian workers as they attempt to cross from the Palestinian territory of the West Bank into Israel in order to work illegally. Ten hours into their dangerous journey, they finally reach 'the wall', also known as the 'separation barrier' or the 'security fence', which was built by Israel to separate Palestinian-controlled regions of the West Bank from Israeli-administered territories. Upon arrival at the wall, Amiry's narrative, up until this point a largely matter-of-fact journalistic narrative interspersed with some gallows humour, takes an abrupt turn towards the fantastical. Amiry, narrating the story in first person, stands at the wall, looks left and sees London, to the right Zurich, and as she looks up the 'eight-metre-high concrete wall' she says she can see 'the tops of Berlin's buildings'.[1] She writes of a hallucinatory dream, 'Animals' nightmare', in which the animal dolls from her childhood come alive and tell the story of the wall's destruction. She describes goats eating produce that Palestinian farmers are banned from selling, a mole with paws bloodied from trying to dig into the asphalt, a lizard that turns grey to blend in with the concrete, and an uprooted ancient olive tree that speaks to her. An 'activist fox' asks her to sign a petition to Al Gore – to whom he has turned after receiving an unhelpful response from God – that decries the construction of this 'monster' wall and the environmental destruction that it has brought.[2]

The journey does not end here. Amiry then turns to a daydream in which murals on the West Bank wall, famously drawn by the international graffiti artist Banksy, come alive. Many of Banksy's murals depict people climbing over, looking through or tearing down the wall, and in Amiry's story she takes a seat in a mural of a living room. She writes, 'I looked out of the window carved into that wall and saw an alpine landscape. I also saw workers running through two big holes cracked in the Wall.'[3] She describes a horse that helps workers across, smiling whenever one made it safely and concludes that

> had it not been for my imagination and for the cosy living room of Banksy's canvas wall, I wouldn't have been able to gather the energy or the morale required to carry on my trip . . . I looked back at the wall and went: Ctrl-Alt-Delete. And all was fine.[4]

Eventually she comes out of her dream state and finds herself on the other side of the wall, in Israel, running toward her friends, and the book resumes its largely chronological narrative.

I begin with this encounter with the wall because it illustrates the larger focus of this study of border spaces in Israel and Palestine in a number of ways. First, Amiry's narrative places the border, in this case the wall, at the centre of the journey, as it is the moment of tension to which the narrative builds from the beginning of the book. This reflects a tendency towards the increasing centrality of border spaces in Palestinian and Israeli literature and film since the 1990s. Second, Amiry's approach to the wall produces a shift from realism to a surreal dream sequence in which an ostensibly non-fictional narrative of border crossing gives way to fantasy. Likewise, in many of the works I examine here, the more intensively that representations engage with the physicality of the border space, the more experimental and less realist they become. Third, it is precisely the phantasmatic nature of the encounter with the wall that allows Amiry to think beyond the border and consider possibilities of transgression. The wall is the site of both nightmare – the harsh reality reflected in the destruction it has wrought on nature and humanity – and of a fantasy of subversion by way of graffiti art and talking animals. It is both locally focused, in the uprooted olive trees and displaced residents, and transnationally relevant, from Banksy and the invocation of the Berlin Wall, to the more unexpected appeal to Al Gore. By crediting Banksy's art and her own 'imagination' with giving her the strength and endurance to cross over the wall, Amiry makes an argument for the role of artistic engagement and imaginative projection in responding to a proliferation of spaces that constrict and violate one's freedom of movement. The self-consciously fantastic nature of the hallucination places the horrors of the wall in stark relief, and she begins to think about how to crack it open, climb over it, cross it or 'delete' it.

Israel/Palestine: Representations of the Border in Literature and Film explores how literature and film can articulate such imaginative responses to the wall and other such barriers. The relative centrality of border spaces, the modes by which the border is represented, and the moments of critique and transgression that these border narratives trigger, are crucial to the texts and films I analyse in this study. It considers how the proliferation of physical borders – walls, border crossings, checkpoints, partitioned cities – has shaped literature and film in the region. It draws on works of both Palestinian and Israeli writers and filmmakers from a number of different subject positions, though with a greater emphasis on Palestinian works, as befits the more pervasive presence and salience of borders in the daily lives of many Palestinians. While it is a commonplace that the Israeli–Palestinian conflict has revolved around contested territories and borders since its inception nearly 100 years ago, Amiry and her contemporaries respond more specifically to a dramatic expansion of physical borders that has occurred since the Oslo Accords in 1994. Movement has never been free for Palestinians in the West Bank and Gaza, and Palestinians in exile and in Israel have also experienced many restrictions on mobility, but an unprecedented regime of spatial restrictions within the region in recent years has now made borders an unavoidable fact of daily life for many. Rashid Khalidi goes as far as to describe 'those many modern barriers where identities are checked and verified' as the 'quintessential Palestinian experience'.[5] Borders are physical spaces where identities are constantly subject to interrogation, and they are frequently the sites of the most explicit and brutal articulations of state power.[6] Helga Tawil-Souri writes that checkpoints have become 'like Palestinian living rooms, the new downtowns of everyday life'.[7] These ostensibly exceptional and marginal spaces have disrupted and occupied the centre of public and private life. As a result of their ubiquity, they have become, in a sense, quotidian spaces where economic, political, personal and cultural interactions of all types occur.

As Anna Ball notes, there is reason to be wary of overemphasising the centrality of borders, so as to avoid normalising distinctly exceptional spaces such as the checkpoint and thereby losing sight of the physical danger and oppressive control that these sites produce.[8] However, Amiry's work suggests that surrealism and fantasy might serve as a means of countering this normalisation. Borders seem to invite such representations. Inge Boer argues convincingly that borders are self-effacing and naturalising, meaning that they tend to conceal their own constructedness and project both invulnerability and inevitability.[9] In *Israel/Palestine*, I argue that borders are deceptive in multiple senses of the word, and that they are spaces that both produce and rely upon illusion, delusion and fragmentation. Their self-effacing and naturalising tendencies produce an image of permanence and of power. Yet the power projected by borders and walls is often itself illusory and can be, as Wendy Brown argues, a manifestation not of strength but rather of the fragility of the nation state in an era that she terms 'post-Westphalian'.[10] Amiry, by marking the border as a space that is both pervasively present and distinct from other spaces, uses fantasy to de-naturalise the wall and to destabilise its deceptions. She shows that it is out of place, and she reminds the reader of the horrors and destruction that it has wrought. Like Amiry, many of the works I examine in this book emphasise the illusory nature of borders and seek to challenge them by exposing the deceptions and sleights of hand that undergird and naturalise them.

As border spaces have expanded, their effects on cultural production have also intensified. A wave of cultural engagements with border spaces, spanning multiple media, languages and nationalities, has appeared. The effect of the expansion of these borders on cultural production goes far beyond sheer quantity, however, and has proved a catalyst for variation and innovation in form, structure, style and genre. Much as Amiry's narrative suddenly shifts from realism to a fantastical dream sequence at the wall, works inflected by the border reformulate and disrupt narrative tropes and produce particular literary and filmic genres, as if the presence of the border demands distinct artistic responses. The border as a site of fantasy, imaginary and formal experimentation is common in both Israeli and Palestinian works, including – among many others – writings by David Grossman, Raja Shehadeh and Mourid Barghouthi.[11] In many, the more pervasive the border's presence, the less cohesive and more fragmented the narrative. Encounters with checkpoints, walls and other borders frequently produce experimental, fantastical and fragmented aesthetics, as reflected in Amiry's fracturing of a spatially cohesive and temporally linear narrative into a perplexing juxtaposition of spaces, historical and cultural figures, and hallucinations.

Finally, Amiry's references to Berlin, Zurich and Banksy in her depiction of crossing the wall reminds us that while *Israel/Palestine* is rooted in the specific spaces of Israel and Palestine, the implications for its analysis are much broader, particularly within a global context. At the time of writing in 2018, plans and proposals for walls and tightened border controls have become commonplace in Europe. The European Union's regime of open borders threatens to fracture under the weight of the worst refugee crisis since World War II;[12] Hungary has built a wall on its border with Serbia in an attempt to keep out the flood of migrants and police are engaged in blatant racial profiling at train stations;[13] Austria temporarily re-imposed document checks at its borders, severely disrupting the flow of goods and people, and has itself threatened to build a wall with Hungary.[14] In the Middle East, the borderlands of Syria's neighbours have become home to millions of displaced persons who live, hungry and exposed to the elements, in squalid refugee camps with nowhere else to go.[15] Meanwhile, in the United States, Donald Trump made the construction of a massive wall on the Mexican border a centrepiece of his successful 2016 campaign for President, and he has used the Israeli wall to justify his proposal.[16] As states across the world increasingly turn to physical barriers as a response to anxieties produced by globalisation, economic stagnation and mass migration, considering the cultural implications of border spaces is vital. In this light, we can see the proliferation of borders in Palestine and Israel not as an exceptional case, but as a more explicit manifestation of a larger trend that complicates common narratives of globalisation. Israel/Palestine functions as what Eyal Weizman calls a 'laboratory of the extreme' and a 'worst-case scenario' of larger trends.[17] If the spaces and practices I examine in this book appear exceptional, it is within a context in which the exceptional is becoming the norm. The Israeli-built walls and checkpoints are places of experimentation, where techniques of physical control are tested and honed before being deployed elsewhere, but the corollary is that they can also offer spaces in which the possibilities – and limits – of cultural responses to borders can be explored.

Expanding Borders

Before turning to the conceptual and scholarly contexts in which *Israel/Palestine* intervenes, I begin with a brief overview of the history and development of border spaces in Palestine and Israel, in order to situate my analysis in relation to the physical spaces of the region. These borders have remained both ever present and rapidly changing. The borders around and within the area currently made up of Israel, the West Bank, and Gaza have been characterised by an instability that is unusual in a post-World War II, postcolonial world in which borders have been, with certain exceptions, fairly stable. After the establishment of Israel in 1948 and the ensuing war, historic Palestine was divided between Israeli, Jordanian and Egyptian rule. In 1967, Israel conquered land controlled by Egypt, Jordan and Syria, giving it control of all of historic Palestine as well as Syria's Golan Heights and Egypt's Sinai Peninsula, from which it later withdrew as part of the Egyptian–Israeli peace treaty of 1978. Further changes occurred with Israel's occupation and subsequent withdrawal from southern Lebanon, as well as the signing of the Oslo Accords in 1993, which demarcated Israeli- and Palestinian-controlled zones of the West Bank and Gaza.

Within this history of shifting borders, there have been notable moments of border erasure, such as the removal of the seam line dividing Jerusalem and the opening of the border between Israel and the territories it occupied in 1967.[18] However, within Israel and Palestine, particularly within the Israeli-occupied territories of the West Bank and Gaza, the overall trajectory has been towards the imposition of more borders and spatial restrictions, particularly in the last twenty-five years. While the construction of certain barriers such as checkpoints occurred prior to the 1990s,[19] the turning point that accelerated this process of increasing spatial restrictions was the Oslo Accords, the provisional peace accord signed between Israel and the Palestine Liberation Organisation in 1993. These accords established limited Palestinian rule over parts of the West Bank and Gaza, territories that Israel had ruled under military occupation since the Six Day War of 1967.[20] At the time of their signing, the Oslo Accords were heralded by many (but not all) as a triumph for peace that would serve as an interim step to a permanent resolution of the Israeli–Palestinian conflict. It divided the West Bank and Gaza into three 'areas', A, B and C, which are under full, partial or no Palestinian administrative control, respectively.²¹ Most Palestinian population centres fell under Area A, to be administered by the newly established Palestinian Authority, but many others were designated Area B, shared Palestinian and Israeli authority, and 60 per cent of the West Bank, including Israeli settlements and all of Jerusalem, became Area C, under full Israeli control.²² This created a fragmented patchwork of small areas of non-contiguous territory under partial Palestinian control. In essence, these became a whole new network of administrative borders with a double-headed bureaucracy, reflecting a shift toward an Israeli strategy of separation.²³ The temporary divisions of Oslo became the basis for the establishment of movement restrictions, primarily in Area C, often limiting Palestinians to a few square miles of territory, and separating people from their places of employment, schools and even farmlands.²⁴ The Oslo Accords created the conditions necessary, from a legal and bureaucratic perspective, to allow a large expansion of the checkpoint system that restricted Palestinian movement, as well as the network of Jewish settlements and the roads needed to connect them, and the construction of the wall separating the vast majority of Palestinians from Israel and parts of the West Bank. Many of these barriers were justified as a means of preventing terror attacks, but their expansion continued long after the main terror threat had subsided. As is often the case with systems of power and control, the spatial restrictions have become self-perpetuating and self-justifying.²⁵

Though Palestinians in these territories before Oslo certainly faced restrictions on their movement – they were generally allowed to travel to and work in Israel, but were required to return home in the evening, and Israel had begun building Jewish-only settlements on Palestinian land – there were few physical barriers dividing the landscape. This began to change during the first Intifada, or Palestinian uprising, of 1987–91. Israel reacted harshly to this largely nonviolent protest against military rule and established numerous checkpoints and imposed greater restrictions on Palestinian movement.²⁶ Yet even this was not as extensive as what came after the Oslo Accords. In the post-Oslo period, the military checkpoint, because of its ubiquity in the West Bank, has become a powerful symbol of continued Israeli rule. Numbering approximately ninety-eight as of November 2017,²⁷ these checkpoints regulate movement both between the West Bank and Israel and within the West Bank. They range from fairly small, intermittently staffed outposts to permanent border terminals through which thousands of people cross each day.[28] Many of these checkpoints exist to protect Jewish settlements, which have occupied many hilltops of the West Bank, and a network of roads restricted to vehicles with Israeli license plates that link the settlements and connect them to Israel.[29] This settlement/highway network represents yet another form of spatial restriction that acts as a border, cutting off Palestinian towns and villages from other parts of the West Bank.

The other crucial turning point in the development of the network of border spaces is the construction of the West Bank wall. The first sections of barbed wire and concrete that would become the wall appeared near the Palestinian city of Jenin in 2002. Soon, other segments popped up across the West Bank. In some areas, this barrier followed the Green Line, which demarcates the internationally recognised boundary between Israel and the West Bank, while in others it burrowed deep into Palestinian territory, cutting off formerly adjacent villages and towns from each other and separating farmers from their fields. Eight-metre-tall concrete slabs and watchtowers snaked through the dense web of neighbourhoods between Jerusalem and Bethlehem, while in rural areas it took the form of barbed wire and ditches. Gradually, disconnected segments met, and the barrier worked its way towards completion (date unknown), at which time it is expected to reach 710 kilometres in length[30] and leave approximately 9.5 per cent of the West Bank territory on the Israeli 'side' of the barrier.[31] The wall incorporated previously improvised, ramshackle Israeli military checkpoints and replaced them with elaborate, imposing 'terminals' that might be aptly described as a combination of a prison and an airport. The successive Israeli governments – representing a variety of political parties and perspectives – that constructed this wall, officially the West Bank 'separation barrier', argued that it would protect Israelis from the threat of Palestinian terrorism with little effect on their daily lives. They claimed it was impenetrable, but people continued to pass through, legally or not, and the wall became a central feature of Palestinian life.

The wall is also crucial because, more than any other border space, its construction immediately provoked strenuous opposition, both local and international. Palestinians of all political stripes as well as Israeli peace activists and global human rights groups quickly cried foul. They protested the seizures of land, the destruction of Palestinian homes and farms, and the collapsed economies of suburbs cut off from their livelihoods that ensued. In the village of Bilʿin, residents organised a weekly protest that inspired others across the West Bank. Others affected by the wall filed lawsuits in Israeli and international courts, to varying effect. The Israelis largely ignored an International Criminal Court ruling against the barrier, but the Israeli High Court of Justice forced changes to the route in several places.[32] This wall was not the first nor the last border space to appear in this region in recent decades, but it represents a crucial moment in a process of crystallisation and consolidation in which a system of improvised checkpoints and blockades in the Palestinian territories gradually transformed into an increasingly cohesive, comprehensive (if constantly changing) system of restrictions on movement.

My discussion has largely focused on the Occupied Territories and the effects of expanding borders on their Palestinian residents, which reflects the reality that these populations face the most restrictions to freedom of movement. To a lesser degree, such restrictions also affect Palestinians within Israel. They are afforded a greater amount of mobility due to their status as Israeli citizens, but still face more limits than Israeli Jews in the form of geographical segregation in housing, enforced by quasi-governmental entities and ethnicity specific housing pacts, and so-called 'flying' police roadblocks in heavily Arab areas. Policies that encourage the Judaisation of regions such as Galilee, the Negev,[33] and ethnically mixed cities such as Jaffa, Haifa and Akka[34] have constricted the space available to Palestinians. Additionally, Israel has largely refused to build new Palestinian towns or recognise Palestinian villages that have been established since 1948, leaving many residents without basic services.[35] Finally, the experience of leaving and entering Israel is much more difficult, as added scrutiny toward Palestinian citizens at Ben Gurion Airport and other border crossings is quite common. Thus, while spatial restrictions within Israeli territory are not as explicit as the West Bank and Gaza, the tendency towards limiting the space and movement available to Palestinians is clear.

The logic of border construction as securitisation has become almost an article of faith within the Israeli government, and it is reflected in the state's construction of fences along several of its other borders to address various threats. Gaza has been enclosed in 'various and increasing ways since the 1950s', with an intensification after Oslo.[36] The fence along the Israel–Lebanon border has a long history, and was part of the 'Good Fence' policy during the 1980s and 1990s in which goods and people flowed between Israel and Israeli-allied Maronite forces in South Lebanon prior to Israel's withdrawal in 2000.[37] Yet recurring rocket fire by Hamas in Gaza, and to a lesser extent Hezbollah in Lebanon, show the defensive limits of both fences. Recently, Israel has also built portions of fences along the Egyptian border, and between the Israeli-occupied Golan Heights and Syria, in order to stem the flow of migrants from Africa and to insulate Israel from ongoing fighting in the Syrian civil war, respectively. Many of these fences and walls are manifestations of Prime Minister Benjamin Netanyahu's stated desire to surround Israel with walls to defend against 'wild beasts',[38] reflecting a prevailing colonial narrative of Israel as an outpost of civilisation in a dangerous, alien region.

It is also important to note that these spatial configurations are in flux. The wall's path has not been fixed from the beginning but rather has emerged from an improvised process of planning, revision and rerouting.[39] Checkpoints are opened or closed and built or removed depending on the whims of military and political leadership or the time of year.[40] Official settlements expand, and so-called unauthorised outposts of Jewish settlers are either removed or retroactively legalised.[41] The various fences surrounding Israel are frequently changed, expanded or strengthened according to political and military decisions. Eyal Weizman terms the constantly changing nature of borders in the Occupied Territories 'elastic geography'.[42] The checkpoints and the wall are 'dynamic, constantly shifting, ebbing and flowing', creating a situation that is always in flux and therefore is perhaps even more dangerous than a stable and predictable spatial and political configuration.

Finally, while I will delve more into the specifics of the border spaces represented in different works in subsequent chapters, it bears mentioning that the spaces discussed above often differ significantly in their function and purpose. A concrete wall is obviously intended to block all movement between one side and the other, but a military checkpoint has more of a filtering effect, giving the authorities the ability to decide who can cross and when. All checkpoints are not equal, however. Checkpoints situated deep within the West Bank tend to be more ramshackle and improvised in appearance, while a series of elaborate terminals between Palestinian-controlled areas of the West Bank and Israel function on a more permanent and regulated basis so as to nearly resemble international border crossings. Meanwhile, official international border crossings, such as the one at Allenby Bridge between the West Bank and Jordan, or at Ben Gurion Airport, function with different sets of rules and restrictions.[43] Other physical barriers to movement in the West Bank, such as Israeli settlements and Israeli-only roads, further limit and channel Palestinian movement in distinct ways. Spatial restrictions within Israel, such as the de facto limiting of Palestinian residents to certain areas and the Judaisation of regions and neighbourhoods, do not prevent Palestinians from visiting certain areas, since there is general freedom of movement within Israel for residents, but it precludes them from residing in predominantly or prospectively Jewish areas. While the various borders that shape Palestinian and Israeli lives exist as an interconnected network and are manifestations of a larger impulse to contain and control Palestinian movement, they often function quite differently, which is reflected in their representations in literature and film.

From National Borders to Internal Borders

Engagement with borders has a long history in both Palestinian and Israeli literature and film, but the advent of the Oslo Accords has refigured both the types of borders depicted and the ways in which cultural products have engaged with them. In terms of Palestinian cultural production, the period from 1948 to the beginning of the Oslo Accords is marked by an emphasis on national borders, which reflects both the predominance of works by authors in exile, such as Mahmoud Darwish, Ghassan Kanafani and Jabra Ibrahin Jabra, and the orientation of Palestinian culture and politics towards the twin projects of national liberation and resistance. Such orientations are also reflected in film production, which was heavily weighted towards documentaries produced outside of Palestine, often funded by Palestinian resistance movements seeking to document and publicise the struggle for national liberation. Post-Oslo, the cultural preoccupation with national borders is augmented by works of literature and film that grapple with the expansion of internal borders as Israel rapidly built its network of checkpoints, walls and settlements that restrict Palestinian space and movement. As the question of national borders, now confined and postponed to an undefined future phase of negotiations, has faded from the conversation, it is perhaps no surprise that authors and filmmakers have increasingly focused on the immediate border spaces that consume so much of contemporary Palestinian time and space, what Zeina Halabi terms the 'evasive notion of the Palestinian ordinary'.[44] Since one aim of this book is to trace this shift and to identify the distinct representations and genres that emerge from this proliferation of borders, a brief engagement with the longer history of Palestinian border representations will help provide a point of comparison for the chapters that follow.

The borders that preoccupied Palestinian literature for much of the twentieth century were primarily national borders, which reflects both Palestinians' lack of their own national borders, and their status as stateless and exiled figures subjected to the often unwelcoming borders of others. Edward Said writes in *After the Last Sky* (1986) of the Palestinian plight: 'If we are not stopped at borders, or herded into new camps, or denied reentry and residence, or barred from travel from one place to another, more of our land is taken . . .'[45] Here it is notable not only that all of these verbs refer to forms of spatial restriction or displacement, but that they are ongoing (as reflected by the use of present tense). Further, the use of the passive voice ('are stopped . . . herded . . . denied . . . barred') reflects the extent of Palestinians' lack of agency. They are subject to the acts, decisions and violence of others. And borders are where the powerlessness and disenfranchisement of being Palestinian is experienced most viscerally and forcefully. Later in the same work, in which Said brings together a mixture of literature, images, oral histories, conversations and first-person accounts to paint a humanistic portrait of Palestinian lives, he concludes that 'in fact our truest reality is expressed in the way we cross over from one place to another'.[46] Borders and border crossings define the existence of a people whose living history and memory consists of a series of multiple displacements and defeats.

Borders are crucial sites of this trauma of defeat and displacement, and subsequent border encounters reproduce these traumas and the lack of agency that they embody. In many cases the encounter with the border occurs as a pivotal part of a journey to/from/within Palestine.[47] The protagonist of Sahar Khalifeh's *Wild Thorns* (1976) crosses from Jordan into the West Bank, where he encounters the humiliation of being subjected to Israeli inspection and detention, and the shock of a formerly lush Palestinian landscape denuded of its vegetation and natural beauty;[48] the border is ugly, unnatural and painful, and it marks his first encounter with the West Bank under Israeli occupation. In Kanafani's *Returning to Haifa* (1969), crossing the newly opened border between the West Bank and Israel prompts a reckoning with long suppressed memories and a lost son. In Habiby's *The Pessoptimist* (1974), the protagonist Said sneaks across the border from Lebanon and immediately surrenders to the authorities, becomes a collaborator for the Israelis and sets off a chain of farcical and tragic events and misunderstandings.[49] Habiby's interest in the border also manifests itself much earlier in his short story, 'The Mandelbaum Gate' (1954), which is set at the border crossing between Israel and Jordan that existed in Jerusalem until 1967.[50] In all of these works the border marks a narrative turning point, focusing attention on the loss, helplessness and violence that Israeli borders impose upon Palestinians. Additionally, while Palestinian literary production is often analysed in terms of a dichotomy between exiled writers and those who remained within Israel, the West Bank and Gaza, interest in the border is a common thread among all of these groups of writers that reveals the limits of such taxonomies.

Also common are representations of other borders, in Europe, the Arab world and elsewhere, where displaced Palestinians often find themselves subjected to similarly hostile treatment or denied the ability to cross. Darwish's 'Athens Airport' (1987) captures the endless limbo and transit in which Palestinian exiles find themselves and concludes with a question: 'We stayed, chairs on chairs, waiting for the sea. / How many more years, Athens airport?'[51] Liana Badr's 'Airport' (1991) depicts a narrator's hostile treatment as a Palestinian in a 'brotherly' Arab country, where she feels the need to conceal her nationality and is ultimately denied boarding for her flight.[52] The narrator is overcome with a sensation in which earth and sky are reversed, the narrator sees through her ears, and her head changes places with her feet, reminding us that the border crossing produces and reproduces the disorientation of displacement or, as Joseph Farag argues, 'the protagonist's physical instability comes to mirror the instability of the condition of exile itself'.[53] Kanafani's *Men in the Sun* (1963) ends with three Palestinian refugee men in Iraq who, desperate to get to Kuwait to make a living for themselves and their families, suffocate and die locked in a trunk as they are smuggled across the Iraq–Kuwait border.[54] The novel lays bare the vulnerability and physical danger of exile and statelessness and the haunting despair and resignation of endless waiting.[55] The death of the men at the border serves an indictment of the silent complacency of the wider Arab world towards the Palestinians' plight.[56]

The deaths in *Men in the Sun* also reveal an urgent need for action. The driver, upon discovering their deaths, cries out, 'Why didn't you knock on the walls of the trunk? Why didn't you say anything? Why?'[57] Bashir Abu-Manneh describes the men's silence as they asphyxiate as a form of 'unresisting',[58] reflecting (in its absence) the necessity of resistance as means of reinvigorating a depleted and moribund commitment to Palestinian liberation. The desire for Palestinian action becomes even more urgent after 1967, when the *Naksa* exposed the failure of Arab modernity and its cultural and political institutions[59] and provoked a moment of intense self-critique and re-evaluation. In the Palestinian context, a major lesson was the need for Palestinians to take a more active role in their liberation, and thus began the heyday of leftist Palestinian resistance movements. Border representations by many of the authors mentioned above provide opportunities for the characters and/or readers to realise the necessity of resistance. In Kanafani's *Returning to Haifa*, as we will see in Chapter 2, the experience of return prompts a shift from resigned defeat to renewed commitment. Khalifeh's protagonist in *Wild Thorns* finds in the denuded horror of the border a convincing validation of his desire to resist. Border crossings represent a crucial moment in the production and reinforcement of political consciousness for many authors of this period.

While the scope and availability of earlier Palestinian cinema is much more limited than literature, due in no small part to the destruction of archives during the Israeli invasion of Beirut in 1982,[60] the aforementioned emphasis on documentary reflects the politically engaged orientation of Palestinian cinema in the 1960s and 1970s, as the Palestine Liberation Organisation (PLO) and other groups funded film units and countries such as Syria sought to burnish their revolutionary bona fides by supporting filmmaking about Palestine.[61] In this sense, Palestinian cinematic production of the time both reflects a larger trend toward the deployment of film in service of anticolonial and postcolonial revolutions, as seen in places like Algeria and within the Third Cinema movement writ large,[62] and it also mirrors the preoccupation with national borders that appears in the literature. In one sense, as Nadia Yaqub notes, the focus on depicting refugee experiences produces a prevalence in film of images emphasising the extent to which they are trapped and unable to cross borders. Additionally, several of the few prominent feature films made during this time period were adaptations of the most border-focused novels from Palestinian literature, such as Kassem Hawwal's film version of *Return to Haifa* (1982), and Tewfik Saleh's *The Dupes* (1973), which was based on Kanafani's *Men in the Sun*.

The border as the site of (re)commitment to a politics of liberation, common in the films and realist novels of the 1960s and 1970s, fell out of the dominant discourse during and after the Oslo Accords, which Halabi describes as an era 'in which political pragmatism, neoliberalism and growth under occupation overrule national liberation'.[63] Oslo signified the Palestinian leadership's abandonment of the national struggle in favour of the temporary, limbo-like permanence of quasi-statehood that Weizman aptly terms 'prosthetic sovereignty'.[64] In literary terms, the intellectual disillusionment and sense of failure that followed Oslo has sometimes manifested itself as a shift towards a more ambivalent experience of borders. The contrasting tone of border encounters in early and late works by Darwish – whose poetry, according to Jayyusi, has most clearly mirrored the shifts and ruptures in Palestinian politics since the 1960s[65] – is illustrative. His best-known early poem, 'Identity Card' (1964), is a visceral outburst against the discrimination, displacement and confinement of Palestinians by Israel. Beginning with a command to an Israeli policeman ('Write it down! / I am an Arab'),[66] 'Identity Card' forcefully asserts Palestinian subjectivity in the face of Israeli attempts at suppression and erasure. It became a 'battle cry' for renewed Palestinian pride and assertiveness,[67] which helped earn Darwish the moniker of 'resistance poet'. Like many of the works mentioned above, this declaration of pride and commitment comes at a border, as Israeli police check Palestinian IDs. Yet if we turn to border encounters in Darwish's later works, the defiance of 'Identity Card' gives way to more meditative and ethereal depictions. In *Mural* (*Jidariyya*, 2000), the Arabic title of which invokes the wall (*jidār*), Ferial Ghazoul reads as a moment of ambivalence and ambiguous identity in which references to Palestine are 'oblique' and a metaphor for unrequited love.[68] Likewise, 'State of Siege' (2002), written during the Israeli siege of Ramallah in the Second Intifada, eschews the directly political for more universal themes of suffering, endurance, pain and love.[69] All of his works reflect an enduring belief in the 'tragic necessity' of the Palestinian struggle,[70] and he himself rejected the Oslo Accords and resigned from the PLO in protest.[71] Yet the tone, form and language of his writing shifted towards the abstract and away from political engagement as the revolutionary fervour of the Palestinian struggle gave way to an era of compromise and half measures.

Despite the breaks and shifts brought about by Oslo, as reflected in Darwish's *oeuvre*, earlier representations continue to inform contemporary border depictions in a number of ways. I cover this more extensively in subsequent chapters, particularly Chapters 2 and 4, but for now it suffices to mention two ways in which they remain pertinent. First, many of the thematic and generic elements of pre-Oslo depictions – the limbo of waiting at the border, the suspension of time, experiences of torture, interrogation and detention, and narratives of return – which are primarily set at various national borders, continue to recur, often in modified form, in later depictions of the internal borders within the West Bank, Israel and Gaza. The checkpoints, walls and blockades that have proliferated in the present are read through the lens of earlier borders encountered by Palestinians in exile. This reflects the interconnectedness of forms of movement restriction and physical displacement faced by all Palestinians. Second, the faded notion of the border encounter or crossing as a catalyst for political commitment has become a site of nostalgia in some post-Oslo representations, such as Elias Khoury's *Gate of the Sun* (1998). In Khoury's sprawling, epic-like Palestinian refugee narrative, the memory of a dying generation's resistance efforts is embodied in the comatose former freedom fighter Yunis, whose legendary infiltrations from Lebanon into Israel the novel recounts extensively, and the Israeli–Lebanese border becomes a principle site of the Palestinian struggle. In *Gate of the Sun*, moreover, memory becomes a means of preserving, and perhaps someday reactivating, this struggle,[72] and there have been examples of activism and protests inspired by Khoury's work.[73] Thus, even as cultural representations have turned, unsurprisingly, to the urgent and overwhelming spread of local and internal borders in Palestine and Israel, narratives of crossing and encountering national borders retain political resonance.

Protective Borders

While earlier Palestinian representations of borders functioned as a politically galvanising appeal to national liberation, much Israeli literature from the same time period evinces a desire for strong, protective borders, reflecting the national and colonial imperatives of Zionist settlement and early statehood. The notion of borders as protective frontiers is particularly prevalent in Jewish literature, photography and art from the pre- and post-state periods, particularly in depictions of prototypically Zionist spaces such as the kibbutz and Tel Aviv. Karen Grumberg argues that Amos Oz's depictions from the 1960s and 1970s of the kibbutz, which is perhaps the most iconic spatial embodiment of Zionist ideologies,[74] deploys inside/outside dichotomies in which the 'order and security' of being inside exists in opposition to the 'threatening chaos of outside'.[75] Tel Aviv, while often seen as the bourgeois, urban foil to the collectivist, rural kibbutz,[76] has produced a similar discourse regarding borders. Barbara Mann's study of literary, historical and photographical depictions of Tel Aviv, known as 'the first Hebrew city', shows that the city's embrace of the international style and Bauhaus architecture reflects a Zionist desire to 'rationalize and control the Mediterranean landscape',[77] much as the kibbutz seeks to conquer (and separate itself from) the desert or the wilderness, and to build on a blank slate using settlement and architectural patterns that break radically with the region's traditions.[78] The city's borders set it apart from both the Diaspora, where Jewish safety and freedom is always contingent,[79] and from neighbouring Jaffa and its Arab majority, offering a safe and secure refuge from both.[80] For both the city and the kibbutz, the frontier marks a line between order and chaos and between safety and danger, a notion that today still finds political resonance in contemporary Israel, in which wall building has become nearly synonymous with security.[81]

Given the association of the border with Zionism, the desire to challenge or remove such borders can also signify critique or rejection of Zionism. Rachel Feldhay Brenner argues in her study of A. B. Yehoshua's story 'Facing the Forests' (1968) that the protagonist's desire to contest the Zionist narrative of the land as empty space by acknowledging and naming the destroyed Palestinian village leads to his ostracisation from the city as 'the bearer of the unwelcome truth'.[82] In Anna Bernard's reading of Oz's short story 'Nomad and Viper' (1965), a female kibbutznik's desire for an Arab nomad who resides in the desert outside of the kibbutz signifies alienation from the Zionist community.[83] Likewise, Grumberg argues that in Orly Castel-Bloom's *Dolly City* (1992), a future dystopian version of Tel Aviv produces overwhelming alienation and disorientation, destabilising the Israeli Zionist socio-spatial order and rejecting the borders that define and sustain it.[84]

With the rise of post-Zionism as a cultural, academic and political paradigm beginning in the 1980s,[85] in light of the quagmire of Israel's occupation of Lebanon and as threats from neighbouring states faded, more representations began to critique the notion of borders as necessary protections. Take, for instance, the film *Lemon Tree* (2008) by Eran Riklis, which depicts a legal battle over the destruction of a Palestinian woman's lemon grove to build the wall. The wall's construction is portrayed as an unjust and unjustified abrogation of her rights and, perhaps naively, as an obstacle to peaceful coexistence, as it destroys the possibility of cross-border dialogue and encounter. Shani Boianjiu's novel *The People of Forever Are Not Afraid* (2012), which depicts several soldiers who operate checkpoints and patrol the Israeli–Egyptian border fence and offers vivid descriptions of border spaces and crossings, frames the enforcement of borders not as a national imperative but as a traumatic and self-defeating exercise in futility. One character calls her checkpoint, which controls the entry of Palestinian construction workers into Israel, the 'dumbest' kind of roadblock: 'my checkpoint only showed that we wanted our homes to be cheap, and that the Palestinians' anger could be bought, that very same anger that was so deep it sometimes killed us'.[86] The checkpoint is not necessary but rather reflects moral bankruptcy, and it does not protect from violence but instead (re)produces it. In a very different sense, the evolution of Israeli border representations parallels the Palestinian move away from borders as a reflection of national(ist) commitment towards more mundane and nihilistic local borders.

It should be noted that the desire for protective borders is also found in Palestinian representations. However, it is frequently a mournful nostalgia for the lost protection of home, given the hundreds of thousands of Palestinians who were expelled from or fled their homes in 1948.[87] The village and the village home is an inaccessible object of desire signifying a lost homeliness and authenticity,[88] and it is often depicted in a highly idealised form that emphasises the rural, bucolic landscape and the warm, welcoming home and village.[89] For those in the diaspora, suggests Barbara Parmenter, the protective home contrasts with the landscapes of exile, which are often formless, monotonous and borderless. Kanafani's *All That's Left to You* (1966) depicts the desert as an empty void, the 'antithesis of place,' without centre or limits.[90] Likewise, Jabra, Darwish and others depict the exilic city as ugly, featureless, alienating and anonymous.[91]

For those remaining in their villages that fell under Israeli control, the home(land) is not itself lost, but it is voided of its protective power, as the spatial and cultural constriction that accompanies second-class citizenship refigures home as a site of lost and unrecoverable authenticity. Nurith Gertz and George Khleifi, in their study on Palestinian film, read home as a claustrophobic space, cut off from land or community and the symptom of a broader cultural and social constriction faced by Palestinians in Israel.[92] Grumberg argues that the Israeli–Palestinian village and home, subject to simultaneous pressures to prove Israeliness and the impossibility of being fully Israeli as a Palestinian, have become signifiers of inauthenticity[93] and kitsch,[94] thereby losing their protective power and becoming sites vulnerable to penetration and spatial restriction.[95] Along such lines, Michel Khleifi's film *Wedding in Galilee* (1987) depicts a Palestinian community under the rule of the Israeli military, in which the governor refuses to permit a wedding celebration unless he and his subordinates are invited; even the most intimate rites of passage and spaces are subject to intrusion. As Palestinians have been deprived of control over their own national and local borders, encounters with borders have served as markers of the loss of Palestinian agency over home, nation and body.

Borders Without Limits

Part of the challenge as well as the richness of writing about borders is that they are a powerful and malleable metaphor. Borders both divide and connect. They reflect and inscribe difference, and crossing them can signify commonality and transgression. They are spatial signifiers of cultural, economic, political and historical processes. Borders, and adjacent terms such as boundaries, can be used to talk about all of these concepts. In recent decades borders have become a common academic metaphor for challenging essentialist understandings of culture and politics.[96] Inspired in many instances by Gloria Anzaldúa's notion of the borderlands, in which the US–Mexico frontier and the *mestiza* culture it has produced offers a model of cultural resistance and anti-essentialism,[97] scholars have turned to the border as a metaphor for understanding a postcolonial, neoliberal, globalised moment, characterised by the decline of the nation state.[98] In the context of Israel and Palestine, readings of borders as sites of cultural encounter can provide crucial counterweights to narratives of separation and essentialist difference, as Gil Hochberg offers in her readings of Arab–Jewish literary connections in *In Spite of Partition*.[99]

This study considers borders, in conversation with such approaches, as sites of the production of various forms of cultural meaning, while also centring on specific border spaces in order to emphasise the border's role as a physical manifestation of violence and power.[100] As an example of how these two points connect, we can turn to ʿAzmi Bishara, a Palestinian writer and former member of the Israeli Knesset who now lives in exile in Qatar. He writes in his work *Checkpoint: Fragments of a Novel* (2004) that Palestine has become 'a nation of checkpoints', indelibly shaped by the physical presence of these borders. Further, he notes that the Hebrew word for checkpoint, *maḥsom*, is often one of the first words children learn to speak.[101] While it might be tempting to read this as a form of cultural mixing that occurs at the border, and it is one of many examples of the linguistic influence of Hebrew on Arabic in this region, one cannot ignore that this mixing is borne of coercion and violence. It also evinces what Lital Levy calls a hyperawareness of language, a reflection of anxiety that stems from the particularities of the historical relationship between Israelis and Palestinians.[102] In her study of literary engagements between Hebrew and Arabic, Levy describes a linguistic 'no-man's-land', in which Hebrew and Arabic are bound in a 'continuous state of creative tension'.[103] Her use of the term 'no-man's-land' is apt; it suggests a sense of being lost or stuck, as well as coercion, as evinced by Bishara's use of the term *maḥsom*. Yet it is also 'creative'.

These two seemingly contradictory facets of border encounters exist together, simultaneously. Another passage by Bishara conveys this paradoxical quality of living with the pervasive presence of border spaces:

> The checkpoint has become a declaration of the overpowering presence (*al-wujūd al-ṭāghī*) of those who put it there. The checkpoint is the divider and the connector between two worlds. It is the border and the crossing. It is both pain and the hope (*al-ʿalam wa-al-ʿamal*) for an exit.[104]

Here Bishara lays out a number of dualities that interact at the border and toys with the similarity between the words for 'pain' (*al-ʿalam*) and 'hope' (*al-ʿamal*) in Arabic; one need only switch one pair of letters, and one becomes the other. The border, then, is a space where oppositions intermingle and break down. It is a tangible, undeniable manifestation of Israeli control over space and movement in the region. The adjective he uses to describe the presence of the Israeli occupation, *al-ṭāghī*, denotes something that is overwhelming, excessive and oppressive. It draws everything to it, like a magnet. As the 'divider' and the 'border', the checkpoint demarcates discrete zones of control and belonging. It is an undeniably violent space that brings 'pain', which recalls Gloria Anzaldúa's description of the US–Mexico border as a space where the 'Third World grates against the first and bleeds'.[105] Yet it is also a space of encounter and transition; it is the 'connector' between distinct territorial and administrative divisions, and the place where one can (sometimes) 'cross' between different zones of control. Michel de Certeau captures this dual role of divider and connector in what he calls the 'paradox of the frontier: created by contacts, the points of differentiation between two bodies are also their common points'.[106] For Anzaldúa, this contact is generative, as the 'dividing line' of the border creates a 'border culture' and a 'borderland' that is home to 'the prohibited and forbidden' marginal figures who are 'transgressors' and 'trespassers'.[107] Though she writes specifically of the US Southwest, Anzaldúa's conception of the borderland as a space that is inhabited by the disenfranchised resonates with its emerging role as a central space of Palestinian life and culture.

Marginal spaces like borders have long been vessels for hopes of subversive action and contestation. Henri Lefebvre, whose work helped establish 'space' as a vital field of scholarly inquiry, labels marginal spaces that exist on the edge of cities (fairgrounds, campgrounds) 'heterotopies', or spaces of difference that exist outside of the ordered and regulated 'isotopies' inhabited by most. Both heterotopies and utopias (imagined non-places) contain, to varying degrees, potential to bring about radical transformation.[108] Likewise, de Certeau sees the city as a planned utopian space within which acts of movement and practice can be read as a form of transgression. Furtive movements violate the limits of the paths and spaces that are prescribed.[109] Margins, limits and borders, it seems, exist in order to be violated. Yet, the border's role in delineating and enacting the power of the state poses a particular problem for notions of resistance at the border. Without margins, there would be no centre; the latter only acquires meaning from the former. Thus, if we consider territorial borders to mark some kind of limit to sovereignty, if not an absolute end to it, the border becomes a crucial space for the imposition and performance of state power. The coercive nature of borders in general reminds us that they are spaces in which sovereignty is on full display, where it is codified and performed in an 'overpowering' and 'excessive' fashion, to use Bishara's words. It is of great interest and perhaps paradoxical that the border, the site of the imposition of control where power relations appear at their most brutal and absolute, also becomes the space in which 'hope' – possibilities of escape, transgression, contestation, crossing – is possible. This puzzle presented by the border animates much of my analysis in this book.

The border's centrality as a space that controls mobility imbues it with this dual quality as a site of both the exercise of power and potential contestation. Indeed, mobile bodies are precisely the type of body that crosses and violates borders, and they are an important element of theoretical meditations on power. Deleuze and Guattari turn to the figure of the nomad, who exists outside of, contests and violates the modern subjectivity that is produced by the state. While the state and its subjects inhabit the domain of 'striated space' – segmented, divided and regulated territory that recalls the cells of the prison or the individual, atomised distribution of space in Foucault's conception of discipline – the nomad resides in 'smooth space', a desert-like territory free from the constraints of the disciplinary apparatus, from which he stages guerrilla attacks on the state.[110] Resistance is thus enacted by necessity from a place of exteriority, a point that Edward Said, who lived much of his life in exile, was perhaps trying to make when he joined Lebanese citizens in throwing stones at an Israeli border outpost in celebration of the Israeli withdrawal from southern Lebanon in 2000.[111] By defying this UN-sanctioned moment of codifying and legitimising borders, Said shows that the nomad and the exile will always be excluded from the state and its borders.

In the context of Palestine, however, one must also question the notion of the wanderer as a liberated figure.[112] The fierce response to Said's stone-throwing, which included a campaign to force him out of his faculty position at Columbia University,[113] shows the wanderer is always suspect and an object of fear and criticism. The resistant nomad might resemble the *fidā'iyyūn*, Palestinian freedom fighters who staged cross-border raids into Israel during the first few decades of the conflict. Yet the vast majority of Palestinians who are mobile and live on the outside are refugees, many of whom have been stuck for nearly seventy years in camps where their safety and security are often threatened.[114] They are the most vulnerable and disenfranchised Palestinians, with little capacity for resistance or movement of any kind. Indeed, on a larger scale, those who wander, such as refugees, are some of modernity's most victimised subjects. This reality reminds us to be cautious about glorifying mobile bodies and the transgression of borders, for the desire to uncover resistance and contestation risks eliding the tangible effects of these borders. We are, after all, dealing with a type of space that shapes life for the region's inhabitants in a concrete and often painful fashion, regardless of their representation in writing or on screen. In this book I seek not to depict mobility itself as liberating, but rather focus on the means by which contestation can expose and undermine the mechanisms of power projection.

Looking at border spaces in Israel and Palestine – the concrete wall dotted with watchtowers, the checkpoints manned by soldiers, the visual dominance of hilltop settlements overlooking the Palestinian villages and farms below, and even the former seam line that still divides the city of Jerusalem – the border's role as an apparatus of discipline, surveillance and control is clear. Foucault identifies two types of disciplinary authority, a 'discipline-blockade' that is predicated on explicit force, partition and exclusion and emerges as a result of a crisis, and a panoptic 'discipline-mechanism' that is 'lighter, more rapid, more effective, a design of subtle coercion' that operates on an everyday basis.[115] Though he suggests that power operates on a continuum between these two extremes, his larger intellectual project centres primarily on the latter, more diffuse and 'subtle' form of discipline that is crucial to the production of modern subjectivity through various institutions and forms of knowledge and leading to a 'carceral' society.[116] Yet if an entire society becomes 'carceral', the space of the prison should lose its importance and its distinctiveness. This logic also applies to border spaces. If the sovereign power displayed at the border is diffused across many spaces and contexts, the border should become less essential to the articulation of power, yet in Israel and Palestine we see the opposite.

The border, then, is not so much a reflection of this disciplinary mechanism as a symptom of its failure and/or irrelevance to the context of an ongoing military occupation. Indeed, the emergence of the modern forms of discipline described by Foucault with the advent of the nation state made many protective physical borders such as city walls unnecessary.[117] However, this is not the case in the West Bank and Israel. While walls, checkpoints and other borders in Israel and Palestine might share certain characteristics with this conception of discipline – Weizman's 'elastic geography', for instance, or the attempts to disguise or 'beautify' the Israeli side of the wall[118] – they are for the most part an explicit, unmistakable and sometimes brutal declaration of control and occupation. Efforts at disguise or diffusion are few and far between, hence Bishara's description of the presence they represent as 'excessive' (*ṭāghin*). Here again this adjective is instructive, as these are border spaces that are unconstrained and that respect no limit. At the same time that they impose a web of spatial restrictions, they themselves have few bounds.

'Excessive' is a particularly apt descriptor for the borders I examine in this book. By excessive, I mean that borders in Israel and Palestine have exceeded their places as margins and limits, and have instead come to produce modes of living, moving and interacting for which the borders are ever-present and overwhelming. The excessive nature of borders is a subtext that runs through a number of scholarly studies of space and borders in Israel and Palestine. Hochberg, in her study of visuality and representations of the occupation, argues that Israel must make its control visible at all times to the Palestinians who are subject to it. The presence of walls, checkpoints, watchtowers and settlements 'renders Palestinians visible to military eyes while further rendering the power of surveillance itself visible to Palestinians and, whenever possible, invisible to Israelis'.[119] A prime example of this dynamic is Israeli settlements built atop hills in the West Bank, which allows the settlers to survey the Palestinians while also rendering the settlements visible from miles around: 'The settlements – with their iconic roofs and excessive lights – are seen from virtually everywhere throughout the West Bank.'[120] Visibility goes above and beyond that which is necessary to illuminate and protect the settlements in order to project a constant presence that looms over Palestinian cities and villages. A similar dynamic of excess also governs language within border spaces, as I witnessed myself while crossing Qalandia checkpoint late one night in April 2012. That night, no inspection lanes were opening and the crowd waiting to enter Jerusalem was getting restless. One Palestinian man started asking the invisible soldiers behind a partition when they planned to reopen. Quickly, an unseen soldier came onto a loudspeaker and yelled at the man in Hebrew, telling him to be quiet. Likely not a Hebrew speaker, the man did not seem to understand, but the soldier continued to yell back, her voice drowning out his unamplified shouts. When the man finally stopped, silenced by the soldier's excessive yelling of incomprehensible orders, she declared that he would not be allowed through that night, for no other reason than to punish him for talking back. At the border, language becomes not a tool of communication or of interpellation along the lines of Althusser's policeman who hails a passer-by and thereby incorporates him into society,[121] but of excessive, incomprehensible shouting and noise that silences and alienates those subject to the checkpoint. As Hagar Kotef observes, the few 'lessons' given at the checkpoint are in Hebrew, a foreign tongue, thereby ensuring the failure of the disciplinary effort.[122]

The system of borders seems designed to produce this failure of discipline. First, spatial restrictions, as Weizman argues, are in constant flux. Even as physical spaces like the wall would appear to be fixed and permanent, he shows that they frequently change and shift paths as a result of changing strategic interests, interventions by various interest groups, and military and court orders.[123] However, lest we assume that this improvised quality creates a more benign system, Weizman suggests quite the opposite, noting that chaos is itself a strategy

> to obfuscate and naturalize the facts of domination. Across the frontiers of the West Bank it is undertaken by simultaneously unleashing processes that would create conditions too complex and illogical to make any territorial solution in the form of partition possible.[124]

Confusion and complexity are means of perpetuating and deepening the status quo. The result is a dense system of restrictions that divide space in a myriad of fashions, both horizontally and vertically, using methods ranging from the latest drone technology to crude berms, walls and blockages. This process is taken to its extreme as in Gaza under blockade, where militants hiding underground from air bombardments, renders all inhabited territory – 'the thin crust of the earth where civilians struggle to live' – a vulnerable border space, caught between two warring sides and with no possibility of escape.[125] The entirety of lived space becomes, in the end, consumed by the excessive borders that grow and multiply with no apparent end.

Kotef proposes that the unpredictable and unsettled nature of the system of spatial restrictions serves to perpetuate its existence in a different sense. The continuation and expansion of occupation even as peace and withdrawal are touted as the ultimate goal depends upon the depiction of Palestinians as 'unruly' subjects, unworthy of governing themselves.[126] A series of unclear, impossible to fulfil obligations and restrictions ensures that the Palestinians will violate the regulations imposed upon them. Often these restrictions are spatial, consisting of invisible lines that shall not be crossed. Under occupation they become, as Kotef puts it, 'one dimensional subjects: moving subjects' whose mobility requires constant monitoring and control.[127] The regime of borders actually depends on transgression to justify its own existence, and the impossible and excessive system of borders renders Palestinians as failed modern subjects, unworthy of the rights and responsibilities such a designation entails. As Hochberg notes, the relevance of Foucault's notions of the disciplinary gaze that is internalised by the subject of the state is limited here, where Palestinians do not constitute part of the Israeli state but rather are occupied by a foreign power.[128] This point captures the need to move beyond certain notions of modern discipline and power. The disciplinary regime created by Israel does not produce Foucault's model of a modern subjectivity but instead fractures it altogether. Palestinians are reduced to figures that are silenced, yelled at but not spoken to, surveyed, herded and fenced in, who exist only in their transgression of incomprehensible and constantly changing limits.

As we have seen above, the overwhelming and excessive nature of border spaces is reflected in cultural production, as borders have become more and more central to spatial representations in the region. Yet, as Anna Ball notes, this poses a dilemma of normalisation: an emphasis in literary and filmic representations on 'collective and routine experience' could divert attention from the 'enduring *oddity* and *ab*normality of the checkpoint within the Palestinian landscape'.[129] In her reading, works can resist this tendency by de-normalising the checkpoint's performance of its authority by revealing the Kafka-esque nonsensible and idiosyncratic nature of the 'laws' that govern the checkpoint.[130] Instead of performing the script imposed by the checkpoint, works of literature and film emphasise the illogical unpredictability of the checkpoint. They show that the expansive regime of borders and its instability do not produce a new normal but only an illusion of such and instead destroy any possibility of 'normalcy'. Any attempts to locate a routine are fleeting and bound to fail, as Tawil-Souri argues in her study of the transformation of Qalandia checkpoint, in which an economic and cultural ecosystem that had emerged at the checkpoint was soon strangled by new Israeli military and spatial practices.[131] If life is carried out at the border, it is always an opaque, contingent facsimile of a real life.

Borders as Illusion

Performance of power and control has long been a part of how border spaces such as walls function, even as conceptions of borders and their functions have shifted over time. Crucially, one of the primary spatial transformations that marked the advent of European modernity (to which Israel claims to belong) in many contexts was the *removal* of the city wall. Previously necessary to protect the centres of power from attacks from the unruly hinterland, as the projection of power became more and more comprehensive it became unnecessary.[132] In Vienna, the city walls that had protected the city from multiple sieges by the Ottoman Empire came down in the nineteenth century, and in the space they occupied was built the *Ringstraße*, a circular street lined with monuments to the cultural and political dominance of the Habsburg Empire. Architecturally elaborate state institutions – museums, universities, government buildings – replaced walls as markers of power.[133] While walls marked the limits of power, their absence proclaimed the possibility of ever-expanding territories as Europe accelerated its colonial exploits.

At present, however, just thirty years after the fall of the Iron Curtain and the Berlin Wall and the advent of open borders in Europe, which seemed to signify a post-border era, walls are making a comeback. From a micro-level, in gated compounds and subdivisions across the world, to the fortification of borders in the Americas, Europe and the Middle East, walls and fences are back in vogue. Wendy Brown, in *Walled States, Waning Sovereignty*, draws from Israel–Palestine, the US–Mexico border, and other contexts to argue convincingly that this trend reflects weakening state power in an age in which sovereignty has increasingly been separated from the entity of the 'state'.[134] While in some ways the return to walls cleaves to a more pre-modern notion of power, the new walls seek primarily to thwart transnational threats – terrorism, migration, disease – rather than international threats such as invasion by another country.[135] Notably walls are rarely effective tools to fight such threats,[136] and Brown claims that they are 'spectacle' and 'theatricality' and that they 'stage sovereign power' in a way that harkens back to a premodern era but is very much situated in the contemporary neoliberal present.[137] As in the case of the Israeli wall, they are often temporary or improvised but also claim impenetrability. Both external and internal barriers seek to inspire 'awe', to invoke a near-religious form of the sublime.[138] Brown writes that the 'Israeli wall, like the others, both performs and undoes a sovereign boundary function, just as it performs and undoes sovereign stability.'[139] The states that build these walls seek to display a kind of overwhelming hyper-sovereignty through their excess, but this excess also is a symptom of an underlying weakness and in fact contributes to the further erosion of sovereignty.[140] These walls and other similar barriers produce an *illusion* of power, but their actual potency is surprisingly limited. For instance, the German Democratic Republic sought to buttress a political system built on lies and unreality with the Berlin Wall, a symbol of overwhelming physical force. Yet once the illusion was exposed, the wall came tumbling down. The Kafka-esque quality identified by Ball finds expression in the deceptiveness of such borders: they confuse, divert, lie, obscure.

The notions of illusion and projection both suggest a relationship between borders and visuality, perhaps even seen in written forms such as Amiry's description of the wall, which vividly captures the visuality of the border in a written text.[141] Scholars have noted the particularly visual resonance of borders and their representations. For Hochberg, the occupation is characterised by the militarisation of vision and an inequality of visual rights, and film, photography and art offer means of challenging this dominance through moments of queering and altering vision.[142] Ball uses the concept of 'haptic visuality' to consider how visual representations of the wall and other borders can produce a form of touch that forces both viewer and artist to confront the tactile nature of the border, by conveying its grating quality and its weight, for instance.[143] It implicates the viewer critically and ethically in the artist's work without eliding the distinctions between them.[144] Ball and Hochberg's readings demonstrate the potential of cultural production to contest visual control while also acknowledging the limits of this paradigm, something to which I will return, particularly in Chapter 6. Such approaches necessitate a consciousness of power dynamics without naturalising or succumbing to them and illustrate the particular power of the image in relation to the highly visual space of the border.

To push this point further, if we consider not only the vision that the occupation controls, but also the image that it projects, to be a form of illusion, the act of representing this space presents the problem of depicting the illusion without reproducing it. Jacques Rancière hints at the difficulty of this task in his critique of Guy Debord's claim, in *Society of the Spectacle*, that images and their passive consumption displace lived experience.[145] If images are simply an inversion of life, according to Rancière 'it suffices to turn it upside down' in order to unleash active power.[146] Rancière argues that it is necessary to go beyond a simple 'inversion of the image', and it is therefore not sufficient to merely appropriate the tool of suppression as a means of liberation. Instead, Rancière proposes what he calls an 'indeterminate' effect, and gives the example of a photographer who took bird's-eye view photos of small roadblocks in the West Bank in which the perspective and distance seemingly turned the barriers into elements of the landscape. This creates not indignation, but a sense of 'curiosity, the desire to see closer up'.[147] In this reading, an effective critique does not simply invert the image but looks at it askance, in a way that reveals its indeterminence, demands further investigation, and draws the viewer or the reader into the work in a fashion similar to Ball's notion of touch. This could take the form of a bird's-eye view in the case of Rancière's photo, or in Amiry's fantastical description of crossing the wall, in which animals narrate its destructive presence and Europe is visible from its summit. This incongruence beckons the reader to pause and dwell upon this unexpected diversion within the text.

In choosing works to analyse in this study, I have focused on novels and films, particularly in Part II, that use distinct narrative, visual and formal strategies to urge a closer look. Written through multiple layers of narrator and author, filmed with unsteady or unreliable cameras, or depicted through various screens and mirrors, a number of the works I examine evince scepticism towards a full, direct and straightforward depiction of borders and beckon us to look carefully at such spaces. When considering cultural responses to these borders, perhaps it is not only transgression or inversion that we should look for – although these are crucial in many of my readings – but different angles of viewing that expose and denaturalise these spaces and uncover the fragility, rot and fragmentation that produces the impulse to build walls and checkpoints. Through attention to the excessive, hyper and compulsive qualities of building barriers, we can see moments of incongruence and illogic from which political critique can emerge.

Many of the works I examine feature one or more border spaces as a major setting, but this is not the only way in which the border's presence is reflected in cultural production. I focus in particular on instances where a border shapes the narrative or structure. In other words, the border's formative role can extend beyond specific passages and scenes set at the border, though these are important. The form that this takes depends on the specific border(s) and the type of work in question. In order to reflect the diversity of border spaces and the ways in which they are represented, for this monograph I have chosen works that depict different types of borders; some, like checkpoints, channel and selectively filter movement, while others, such as walls, aim at near-complete blockage, and thus crossing them entails not engaging with soldiers and other authorities but rather eluding them. The type of border can shape the range of possible narrative modes, tropes and forms; depictions of a border that has been deliberately obscured, such as the oft-violated Green Line, focuses by necessity less on attempts to cross physical barriers than works that focus on checkpoints and walls that have been fortified and amplified in order to constrict mobility. In general, the order of the chapters in this book follows a progression towards increasingly concrete and excessive borders, in order to trace a shift from borders as reflections of political and ideological constructs, in earlier chapters, to borders as coercive, physically threatening edifices of violence. It is also no coincidence that the chapters on film come later in the monograph, which reflects the greater visual resonance of spaces such as checkpoints and walls. Given that my choice of works is intended to amplify, not obscure, the diversity of forms and media that engage with borders, my aim is not to identify a particular 'border' genre, for this would suggest that the effect of borders on cultural representation can be confined to certain types of texts. Rather, I aim to consider how borders are implicated in a variety of forms and genres. My choice to consider both literature and film, in multiple languages, reflects a similar desire.

While it is tempting to consider Israel and Palestine in isolation, recent scholarship points to rising interest in the cultural and artistic effects of borders across the globe, a reflection of their contemporary relevance and a necessary corrective to the notion, prevalent in the 1990s, that national borders were fading in importance due to globalisation, mass migration and technological change. In recent years, scholars have increasingly examined how various borders, from national borders to checkpoints and partitioned territories, have shaped genre, language, form and image. A 2014 special issue of the *Journal of Postcolonial Writing* on the global checkpoint expands beyond the most obvious contemporary instances of checkpoints – Israel/Palestine and the US and Mexico – to identify a 'checkpoint aesthetic', both in terms of literary representations and as a physical space itself, in places such as Kashmir, Latin American prisons, and the Berlin Wall.[148] In Emily Apter's *Against World Literature*, border spaces produce moments of untranslatability that reveal the limits of world literature as a critical and cultural paradigm.[149] Joe Cleary's explicitly comparative approach demonstrates the formative role of border making and partition to the production of national literatures in Ireland, Israel and Palestine.[150] Such borders offer moments of contestation, as suggested by Anna Bernard, whose study of works from India/Pakistan and Israel/Palestine identifies certain genres and modes of writing, such as romance and fragmented narratives, that are used to challenge 'the logic of partition by lamenting its forgotten alternatives'.[151] Gil Hochberg posits that visual media, through the act of looking back, can contest and queer the military gaze of the checkpoint.[152] Together, these studies among others constitute an emerging scholarship of the global border imaginary, a critical engagement with the proliferation of borders that seeks also to theorise points of resistance to forms of spatial control.[153] Finally, in all of these instances, Israel/Palestine is not merely an example but rather often functions as a test case, reflecting the potential of scholarship on the region to shed light on broader global phenomena. Through my argument that the spatial conditions in post-Oslo Israel/Palestine lend themselves to certain forms of artistic responses, in particular reflexive and self-critical modes of narration and filmmaking, I hope that *Israel/Palestine* will contribute fruitfully to this growing field of inquiry.

Israel/Palestine engages with both Palestinian and Israeli works, but with a weight towards the former, a choice that stems from the unequal power relations that exist between the two. The centrality of borders to contemporary Palestinian experiences means that the border is more tangible for Palestinians – indeed, the same borders that cause Palestinians to wait for hours are sometimes largely invisible for Israelis[154] – and thus I believe it is fitting that an examination of border representations should place a stronger emphasis on Palestinian works. Though my choice of authors and filmmakers includes representatives of a variety of subject positions, it is by no means comprehensive. For instance, this list does not include any Ashkenazi Jewish writers, even though there are many examples of representations of borders in works by such authors.[155] I approach the relationship between Israeli and Palestinian literatures and cinemas not as one that requires some kind of imposed parity, but rather as one that intervenes in, as Anna Bernard describes it, a 'shared arena of geographical, historical, and discursive reference'.[156] This 'shared arena' allows (even requires) the acknowledgement of disparate power relations, violence and conflict between the two as a crucial part of the search for points of commonality, and focusing on authors and filmmakers who occupy some type – or in many case, multiple intersecting types – of non-privileged position in Israel/Palestine allows a clearer focus on this element.

As Levy shows through what she terms the 'poetics of misunderstanding', moments of failure, friction and contestation are crucial to readings of Israeli and Palestinian cultural and linguistic encounters.[157] I have chosen both Palestinian and Israeli authors and filmmakers whose works do this through their choice of subject matter, their own subject position, or a combination thereof. For instance, Chapter 2 examines a literary dialogue between novels by Ghassan Kanafani and Sami Michael, a Palestinian and an Iraqi Jew, for both of whom exile represents a formative experience. Chapters 3 and 6 both centre on works by Palestinians who hold Israeli citizenship but position themselves in different fashions: while Sayed Kashua has found success as a cultural figure in Israel, Elia Suleiman has primarily made a place of prominence for himself in the transnational film festival circuit. Chapter 4 revolves around a novel by Palestinian exile Raba'i al-Madhoun in which a border encounter between a Palestinian man and an Israeli woman structures much of the narrative and refigures the Palestinian literary trope of return. In Chapter 5, I analyse two documentaries, one by Moroccan-French-Israeli director Simone Bitton and one by Palestinian Emad Burnat in cooperation with Israeli director Guy Davidi, in which the filmmakers' individual or combined abilities to negotiate both the Palestinian and Israeli sides of the border make their interventions possible.

Chapter Overview

The chapters of this book are grouped into two parts. Part I, 'Expanding Borders', charts the border's role in disrupting two literary–cultural paradigms of political commitment in Israel and Palestine: resistance and peaceful coexistence. The two chapters in this section elaborate upon the notion of the border as excessive by showing how its continued presence transforms these visions from political platform to failed utopia. As borders are established, solidified and expanded, political engagement gives way to disillusionment and fantasies of escape in literary works by both Palestinian and Israeli authors. It shows how the proliferation of border spaces has played a crucial role in reshaping political and cultural discourses.

Chapter 2, 'Return to the Border: Commitment, Utopia and the Inescapable Green Line', focuses on two novels that imagine utopian alternatives to the border that divided Israel and the West Bank until 1967 and remains the internationally recognised basis for the borders of a future Palestinian state. Israel's 1967 conquest of the West Bank and other territories led to the reopening of this closed border, known as the Green Line. The first, Ghassan Kanafani's seminal novella *Returning to Haifa* (1969), depicts a Palestinian couple living in the West Bank who, following this opening, travel to Haifa and to the home they had fled in 1948, where they encounter their son, who has been adopted by an Israeli couple and is now a soldier in the Israeli military. The shock of this moment of crossing and return galvanises the main character, and he renews his commitment to Palestinian resistance and revolution. The second, *Doves in Trafalgar* (2005) by Sami Michael, an Israeli author of Iraqi-Jewish descent, extends Kanafani's novel into the contemporary era to imagine a reconciliation between the lost son and his Palestinian family many decades later. It refigures Kanafani's commitment to Palestinian liberation into a utopian vision of Israeli–Palestinian coexistence. However, the Green Line's presence forces reunifications to take place in exile (London and Cyprus), revealing the border's role in producing the failure of utopian imaginaries. It also demonstrates the failure of the Israeli left to engage with the problematic posed by expanding borders, which reflects the fact that today it is the so-called 'peace camp' that most stridently advocates for the sanctity of the Green Line as a future Israeli–Palestinian border. Borders, in this reading, are post-utopian spaces that signify the decline of certain political ideologies and commitments in both Palestinian and Israeli culture.

Chapter 3, 'Sayed Kashua, the Palestinian Hebrew Novel and the Failure of Coexistence', builds on the idea of the resilience of the border and its implications for notions of coexistence. It centres on two novels by Sayed Kashua, a prominent Palestinian journalist and writer who publishes primarily in Hebrew. The novels *Second Person Singular* (2010) and *Let It Be Morning* (2004) reveal the failure of coexistence through the persistent re-emergence of the very borders that coexistence seeks to cross or render irrelevant, and the hollowness of strategies of linguistic and cultural assimilation. In his novels, assimilation attempts constantly fail at the border, a space that produces myriad forms of alienation and, taken to its logical conclusion, exile. The analysis focuses on the locales of the Palestinian village, suddenly cut off from its surroundings by a blockade, and on the de facto still-divided city of Jerusalem as the twin sites of this paradigm's failure. Kashua's engagement with borders reveals what he eventually calls the 'lie' of coexistence. It traces Kashua's journey into disillusion and despair, expressed through the silence and alienation imposed by a set of borders that grow ever more constricting with no relief in sight. Kashua and his characters become trapped in these borders and, confronted with the failed myth of coexistence, seek escape.

Part II of this book, entitled 'Deceptive Borders', turns to a set of literary and filmic engagements with the border spaces that have appeared in the region in order to expose and contest their deceptive power. The three chapters in this section are bound primarily by the idea of the border as an illusory space, both in the sense that it produces illusions but also that itself is deceptive, a performance of power that masks its own vulnerability. By reconfiguring existing tropes and creating new genres, the authors and filmmakers I study seek to harness the disillusionment produced by borders to expose and contest their overpowering presence.

Chapter 4, 'Border Crossings and Stray Narratives of Return', considers a literary response to the repeated borders encountered on the Palestinian journey of return from exile in Rabaʻi al-Madhoun's *The Lady from Tel Aviv*

(2009). While many earlier narratives that fall into the common Palestinian literary trope of return, such as Jabra Ibrahim Jabra's *In Search of Walid Masoud* (1978), either stage border crossing as a politically galvanising moment or go silent altogether at the crossing towards Palestine, al-Madhoun's novel reimagines the narrative of the protagonist's return from London to Gaza by way of Tel Aviv as a series of encounters with borders that progressively tug at the lines separating past from present and real from imaginary. At each border, distinct narrative voices appear and disappear, and gradually the lines between the myriad characters, narrators and authors disintegrate, producing a cacophony of voices and a 'stray' narrative of return over which the author loses control. The novel mimics and thereby reveals the disorienting effect of borders and their production of an uncontrollable, careening, 'stray' life. The border in Gaza is not simply a line to be crossed but rather represents a new way of living, a bare and uncontrollable life under the shadow of borders. Finally, if the border crossing in *In Search of Walid Masoud* produces silence, we see in *The Lady from Tel Aviv* that an unruly multitude of voices can offer a response to the silencing effect of the border.

While the previous chapter interrogates the possibility of narrating the border, Chapter 5, 'Does the Camera Lie? Or, How to Document the Wall', considers the problem of depicting it on screen by returning to the vicinity of the Green Line during and after the construction of the West Bank barrier. It examines two films that exemplify an emerging genre of wall documentaries. The first, *Mur* (2004) by Simone Bitton, centres on the construction of the wall and its impact on those who live in its shadow. It juxtaposes rhetoric and image to interrogate official narratives of the wall, and it shows the danger of taking the wall at face value and letting it speak for itself. *Mur* reveals the deceptive nature of the border, namely that it lays claim to an invincibility and a power that is in large part a lie. The second film, *5 Broken Cameras* (2011), directed by Emad Burnat and Guy Davidi, largely draws on Burnat's amateur video footage of weekly protests against the wall in the Palestinian village of Bilʿin. It interrogates the ability of the camera to reveal the border's lies by intertwining its rhetorical power with its physical fragility, as camera after camera is shot, knocked on the ground, or somehow destroyed. Filming the border is constantly fragmented and interrupted. Both films seek a means of using film and documentary to protest the wall but remain wary of attributing the genre with too much power.

If filming the wall produces a fragmented aesthetic that can only partially convey the experience of the border, Chapter 6, 'The Illusion of the One-Way Mirror: Filming the Checkpoint', turns to the genre of the checkpoint film, and in particular its most surrealist iteration, in Elia Suleiman's feature film *Divine Intervention* (2002). Suleiman's film, which features little dialogue or plot, repeatedly stages scenes at a checkpoint where the silent protagonist spends hours waiting to meet his lover. Here, the pair watch the goings on at the checkpoint, play tricks on the soldiers manning it, and stage fantastical acts of subterfuge. Through these surreal acts and staged set pieces, *Divine Intervention* frequently calls attention to its status as a filmic representation, and I argue that by doing so, Suleiman's film exposes the checkpoint itself as a staged charade of sovereignty and power. Suleiman's use of the camera shows the power of the checkpoint, a site that stakes a claim to visual control, to be built on an illusion. By calling attention to its own status as a film through techniques of framing and staging, as well as jarring interjections of fantastical sequences, *Divine Intervention* also reveals the instability of the checkpoint and raises the possibility of contesting it to produce forms of political engagement distinct from those examined in Part I of this book.

In Chapter 7, I conclude with a return to the question of border as spaces of deception and illusion, and I consider how this question intersects with both the tangible physicality of border spaces and the representational (and even fantastical) engagements with borders seen repeatedly throughout the chapters. I end by positing that the illusion of the border has begun to fray in the late Oslo period, and that intensive cultural engagements with borders could play a role in this fraying. Finally, while other historical instances such as the fall of the Berlin Wall suggest that the exposure of a border's deceptions can hasten its collapse, this is far from inevitable, and they also warn against underestimating the durability of the system of borders in Israel and Palestine.

Notes

1. Amiry, *Nothing to Lose But Your Life*, p. 108.
2. Ibid. p. 114.
3. Ibid. p. 117.
4. Ibid. p. 118.
5. Khalidi, *Palestinian Identity*, p. 1.

6. See Hochberg, *Visual Occupations*.
7. Tawil-Souri, 'Qalandia Checkpoint as Space and Nonplace', p. 16.
8. Ball, 'Kafka at the West Bank Checkpoint', pp. 75–6.
9. Boer, *Uncertain Territories*, p. 4.
10. Brown, *Walled States, Waning Sovereignty*, p. 21.
11. See Grossman, *Isha Borahat Mi-Bsora*; Shehadeh, *Palestinian Walks*; and Barghouti, *Ra'aytu Ramallah*.
12. UNHCR, *Global Trends*.
13. Nolan, 'One Year On'.
14. Lowe, 'Austria "Ready" to Build Hungary Border Fence'.
15. UNHCR, *Global Trends*.
16. Wilkinson, 'Trump Says Walls Work: "Just Ask Israel"'.
17. Weizman, *Hollow Land*, pp. 9–10.
18. Shehadeh talks about the effects of this border erasure in creating a greater sense of the region as 'one country'. Shehadeh, *Palestinian Walks*, pp. 103–4.
19. Yael Berda notes that, before 1987, movement restrictions and closures were individualised and local. Berda, *Living Emergency*, p. 37.
20. Weizman, *Hollow Land*, p. 11.
21. Many elements of 'sovereignty', such as air and water rights, remain under Israeli control. Weizman, *Hollow Land*, p. 11.
22. Brown, 'The Immobile Mass', p. 504.
23. Berda, *Living Emergency*, p. 28. See Berda for a more in-depth look at how the interaction of spatial barriers, Byzantine bureaucratic structures, and rule through legal exceptions and states of emergency combine to produce and perpetuate extreme restrictions on Palestinian movement.
24. Brown, 'The Immobile Mass', pp. 507–8.
25. Ibid. p. 506.
26. Ibid. p. 504.
27. B'Tselem, *Restriction on Movement*.
28. For example, elaborate terminals have been constructed between Jerusalem and Ramallah and between Jerusalem and Bethlehem. These more closely resemble permanent border crossings than temporary roadblocks.
29. Weizman, *Hollow Land*, p. 81.
30. B'Tselem, *The Separation Barrier*.
31. B'Tselem, *The Separation Barrier*.
32. Kershner, 'Israeli Court Orders Barrier Rerouted'.
33. Ghanem, 'The Expanding Ethnocracy', pp. 21–7.

34. LeVine, 'Modernity and Its Mirror', p. 295.
35. For an in-depth anthropological study of an example of an unrecognised village, see Slyomovics, *The Object of Memory*.
36. Tawil-Souri, 'Digital Occupation', p. 40.
37. Shlaim, *The Iron Wall*, pp. 341–7.
38. Moore, 'Netanyahu: We Will Surround Israel with Walls'.
39. Weizman, *Hollow Land*, p. 175.
40. 'Closures' of the West Bank became much more frequent after the Oslo Accords. Weizman, *Hollow Land*, p. 142.
41. Ibid. pp. 3–4.
42. Ibid. pp. 6–7.
43. For instance, holders of Palestinian authority ID cards cannot use Ben Gurion airport at all.
44. Halabi, *The Unmaking of the Arab Intellectual*, p. 23.
45. Said, *After the Last Sky*, p. 19.
46. Ibid. p. 164.
47. The border as theme and space appears in a wide range of Palestinian works, from both exile and from within Israel and the Occupied Territories. See Abdel-Malek, *The Rhetoric of Violence*, p. 35.
48. Sahar Khalifeh, *al-Sabbar*, p. 20.
49. Levy, 'Exchanging Words', p. 110.
50. Abdel-Malek, *The Rhetoric of Violence*, p. 30.
51. Darwish, 'Matar Athina', p. 23.
52. Badr, 'Matar'.
53. Farag, *Politics and Palestinian Literature in Exile*, p. 186.
54. Kanafani, *Rijal fi al-Shams*.
55. Abu-Manneh, *The Palestinian Novel*, p. 80.
56. Jayyusi, 'Introduction', p. 29.
57. Kanafani, *Rijal fi al-Shams*, p. 109.
58. Abu-Manneh, *The Palestinian Novel*, p. 78.
59. El-Ariss, *Trials of Arab Modernity*, p. 155.
60. Yaqub, *Palestinian Cinema in the Days of Revolution*, p. 8.
61. A prominent example of this trend in Syrian cinema would be Borhane Alaouié's 1975 film *Kafr Qasim*, a dramatisation of the massacre perpetrated by Israeli forces in 1956 in the Palestinian village of the same name.
62. Shafik, *Arab Cinema: History and Cultural Identity*, p. 144.
63. Halabi, *The Unmaking of the Arab Intellectual*, p. 23.
64. Weizman, *Hollow Land*, pp. 139–41.

65. Jayyusi, 'Introduction', p. 61.
66. Darwish, 'Bitaqat Huwiyya'.
67. Ghazoul, 'Darwish's Mural', p. 38.
68. Ibid. p. 51.
69. For instance, Darwish invokes Job and the necessity of enduring pain and waiting for hope. Darwish, 'State of Siege', p. 6.
70. Jayyusi, 'Introduction', p. 62.
71. Sazzad, 'The Voice of a Country Called "Forgetfulness"', p. 115.
72. Abu-Manneh, *The Palestinian Novel*, p. 168.
73. Paul, 'The Grandchildren of Yūnis', pp. 178–9.
74. Grumberg, *Place and Ideology*, pp. 26–7.
75. Ibid. p. 46.
76. Mann, *A Place in History*, p. 18.
77. Ibid. p. 161.
78. Ibid. pp. 74–5.
79. Ibid. p. 89.
80. Ibid. p. 196.
81. Moore, 'Netanyahu: We Will Surround Israel with Walls'.
82. Brenner, *Inextricably Bonded*, p. 192.
83. Bernard, *Rhetorics of Belonging*, pp. 106–7.
84. Grumberg, *Place and Ideology*, pp. 107, 121–2.
85. Silberstein, *The Postzionism Debates*, pp. 1–2.
86. Boianjiu, *The People of Forever are Not Afraid*, p. 61.
87. Walid Khalidi's *All That Remains* provides a detailed and comprehensive account of the Palestinian villages destroyed or depopulated in 1948, reconstructed through documents, photos and recollections. This is part of a larger Palestinian cultural and academic effort to preserve the memories of what has been lost.
88. Slyomovics, *The Object of Memory*, p.176.
89. Parmenter, *Giving Voice to Stones*, p. 43. Slyomovics also examines how these lost spaces have been remembered and preserved through literature, photography, maps, return narratives and 'memorial books' that describe and document lost villages. Slyomovics, *The Object of Memory*, p. 28.
90. Parmenter, *Giving Voice to Stones*, pp. 56–7.
91. These urban spaces are often unnamed, as opposed to representations of lost villages which tend to be very specific. Parmenter, *Giving Voice to Stones*, p. 60. As Hana Wirth-Nesher observes, the notion of an urban wasteland echoes the alienation and displacement has characterised many literary depictions of modern urban life. Wirth-Nesher, *City Codes*, p. 17.

92. Gertz and Khleifi, *Palestinian Cinema*, p. 173.
93. Ibid. p. 152.
94. Ibid. p. 141.
95. Ibid. p. 144.
96. Parker and Vaughan-Williams, 'Introduction', pp. 1–3.
97. Anzaldúa, *Borderlands/La Frontera*.
98. The notion of hybridity, articulated by Homi Bhabha, is a prominent example of how this type of approach has been deployed in cultural studies, but one could also look to Arjun Appadurai's anthropological notion of transnational flows, among many others. See Appadurai, *Modernity at Large*, and Bhabha, *The Location of Culture*.
99. Hochberg, *In Spite of Partition*, p. 19.
100. I seek to avoid what Emily Apter critiques as the 'soft, hospitable border' that is often discussed in humanities scholarship, in which an emphasis on fluid, open borders obscures the border's violence. Apter, 'Translation at the Checkpoint', p. 60.
101. Bishara, *al-Hajiz*.
102. Levy, *Poetic Trespass*, p. 12.
103. Ibid. p. 12.
104. Bishara, *al-Hajiz*, p. 11.
105. Anzaldúa, *Borderlands/La Frontera*, p. 26.
106. De Certeau, *The Practice of Everyday Life*, p. 127.
107. Anzaldúa, *Borderlands/La Frontera*, p. 25.
108. Lefebvre, *The Urban Revolution*, p. 9.
109. De Certeau, *The Practice of Everyday Life*, pp. 94–6.
110. Deleuze and Guattari, *Nomadology*, pp. 30, 34.
111. Marrouchi, *Edward Said at the Limits*, p. 257.
112. There are other critiques of Deleuze and Guattari that are worth considering, including the vaguely orientalist, de-racialised and de-gendered idea of the nomad. See Cresswell, *On the Move*, p. 54.
113. Marrouchi, *Edward Said at the Limits*, p. 257.
114. Some examples of the continued displacement and trauma that refugees have been subject to include: the massacres of Sabra and Shatila in Beirut (1982), the destruction of Tel al-Zaatar camp in Beirut (1976), fighting in Nahr al-Bared camp in Lebanon, the bombardment of Yarmouk camp in Damascus during the Syrian Civil War (2012) and the Kuwaiti expulsion of Palestinians following the first Gulf War (1991).

115. Foucault, *Discipline and Punish*, p. 209.
116. Ibid. p. 304.
117. Brown, *Walled States, Waning Sovereignty*, p. 47.
118. Gil Hochberg points to and photographs attempts to beautify sections of the wall in areas and roads primarily used by Jewish Israelis. See Hochberg, *Visual Occupations*, pp. 18–20. Another example is travelling, as I did in 2012, on Israel's Highway 6, a relatively new state-of-the-art tolled freeway that sits just inside the Green Line and passes within a few hundred metres of the West Bank cities of Qalqilya and Tulkaram, separated by a section of the West Bank barrier. However, the wall is disguised by greenery, so that both it and the cities on the other side are barely visible.
119. Hochberg, *Visual Occupations*, p. 27.
120. Ibid. p. 27.
121. See Althusser, *Lenin and Philosophy*, p. 118.
122. Kotef, *Movement and the Ordering of Freedom*, p. 38.
123. Weizman, *Hollow Land*, p. 163.
124. Ibid. p. 8.
125. Ibid. p. 258.
126. Kotef, *Movement and the Ordering of Freedom*, p. 29.
127. Ibid. p. 38.
128. Hochberg, *Visual Occupations*, p. 27.
129. Ball, 'Kafka at the West Bank Checkpoint', pp. 75–6. Emphasis in the original.
130. Ibid. p. 80.
131. Tawil-Souri, 'Qalandia: An Autopsy', pp. 75–6.
132. Brown, *Walled States, Waning Sovereignty*, pp. 39–40.
133. Schorske, *Fin-De-Siecle Vienna*, pp. 27–30.
134. Brown, *Walled States, Waning Sovereignty*, pp. 66–7. She emphasises the rise of transnational, neoliberal actors that react to capital, part of a larger critique of neoliberalism that she elaborates in other works such as *Undoing the Demos*.
135. Brown, *Walled States, Waning Sovereignty*, p. 21.
136. Ibid. p. 112.
137. Ibid. pp. 70, 84 and 104.
138. Ibid. p. 26.
139. Ibid. p. 90.
140. Ibid. p. 114.
141. Rancière, for instance, argues against the 'irreducible opposition of speech and image'. Rancière, *The Emancipated Spectator*, p. 93.

142. Hochberg, *Visual Occupations*, pp. 8–9.
143. Ball, 'Impossible Intimacies', pp. 181–2.
144. Ibid. pp. 179–80.
145. Debord, *Society of the Spectacle*, pp. 12–13.
146. Rancière, *The Emancipated Spectator*, p. 87.
147. Ibid. p. 104.
148. Fieni and Mattar, 'Introduction: Mapping the Global Checkpoint', pp. 2–3.
149. Apter, *Against World Literature*.
150. Cleary, *Literature, Partition and the Nation-State*.
151. Bernard, 'Forms of Memory', p. 28.
152. Hochberg, *Visual Occupations*, pp. 79–80.
153. Fieni and Mattar, 'Mapping the Global Checkpoint', p. 2.
154. An example of this is the checkpoint on the so-called 'tunnel road' near Bethlehem, where Israeli vehicles are waved through with little or no hassle, while Palestinian vehicles (even, for instance the buses with Israeli license plates) are subject to additional scrutiny.
155. Examples include David Grossman, Amos Oz, S. Yizhar and Etgar Keret.
156. Bernard, *Rhetorics of Belonging*, p. 13.
157. Levy, *Poetic Trespass*, p. 105. Also, see Hochberg, *In Spite of Partition*.

EXPANDING BORDERS

2

Return to the Border: Commitment, Utopia and the Inescapable Green Line

I begin my study of recent proliferation of border spaces in Palestine and Israel, perhaps counterintuitively, with the opening of a border nearly fifty years ago. In 1967, Israel's conquest of the West Bank and Gaza Strip gave it control of the entirety of historic Palestine, which had previously been divided among Israeli, Jordanian and Egyptian control. The pre-1967 border that divided Israel and West Jerusalem from the West Bank and East Jerusalem, known as the 'Green Line', went from a closed national border to a porous internal border. It largely ceased to have an on-the-ground physical manifestation, although the construction of the wall partially followed the Green Line, albeit with significant diversions into Palestinian territory. After 1967, Israeli authorities, particularly in the formerly divided city of Jerusalem, moved quickly to erase the walls and fortifications that marked its location and to assert Israeli control over the entire territory. East Jerusalem was annexed into Israel, and Israeli settlement construction began to occur beyond the Green Line.[1] It exists on international maps, but is often unmarked on both Israeli and Palestinian maps.[2]

Yet the Green Line did not disappear completely, for it continued to manifest in some realms and for some people, but not others. In particular, it still remained as a legal limit to the movements of Palestinians in the West Bank and Gaza, who became subject to a military occupation and were at first allowed to enter Israel but not remain there.[3] The causative relationship between the opening of this border and the emergence of the complex system of spatial constrictions (checkpoints, walls, settlements, roads) that are the subject of this book is fairly straightforward. The Israeli effort to maintain this dual status – an open border for Israelis that allows access to and settlement of the West Bank, and a closed border for West Bank Palestinians – led to both the Oslo Accords and the expanded network of internal borders that followed. It also continues to exist as a kind of phantom political border; it remains the internationally recognised border between Israel and the West Bank, and efforts to negotiate a 'two-state solution' to the conflict almost always take the Green Line as the starting point for a potential national border between Israel and Palestine. Many Israeli and Palestinian political actors accept in principle the idea of a return to the pre-1967 border, even as it becomes increasingly unlikely.[4] The Green Line also has become, particularly among Israeli supporters of peace, a signifier of the lost simplicity and normalcy of clearly defined national borders.[5]

One consequence of this border opening was that Palestinian refugees who had fled to the West Bank and Gaza were able, after 1967, to visit the people and places from which they had been cut off for nearly twenty years.[6] This produced many emotional stories of people who had returned to their homes and was the impetus for Palestinian author Ghassan Kanafani's novella *Returning to Haifa* (*'A'id Ila Hayfa*, 1969), one of the most widely read and enduring Palestinian works of literature. Kanafani's narrative chronicles a Palestinian couple that return to their lost home in Haifa, to find that their home was inhabited by Israelis and that the son they left behind had become an Israeli. *Returning to Haifa* has inspired a number of adaptations in Arabic, Hebrew and English, including films and plays.[7] One of the more interesting responses to Kanafani's novella is the novel *Doves in Trafalgar* (*Yonim be-Trafalgar*, 2005) written in Hebrew by Sami Michael, an Israeli author of Iraqi descent. *Doves in Trafalgar*, which is heavily indebted to Kanafani's work but is neither an adaptation nor a sequel, returns to the characters from *Returning to Haifa* many years later, albeit with new names; the Palestinian couple's lost son is now a successful businessman in Israel, and he seeks to reconnect with his biological Palestinian mother and extended family. Interestingly, and in contrast to Kanafani, *Doves in Trafalgar* has been one of Michael's more obscure works, a point to which I will return later.[8] Taken together, these two novels create a revealing if uneven literary dialogue that remains largely unexplored.

This chapter considers how Kanafani's work and its literary afterlife – in particular Michael's novel – engage with the Green Line, its erasure and reconstitution, and its simultaneous presence and absence. I locate engagement with the border in direct depictions of crossing the Green Line, but I also consider how this border's relative presence and absence permits and produces encounters of confrontation and reconciliation between Palestinian and Israeli characters in both texts, while precluding other types of encounter. Its temporary disappearance in 1967 provides the impetus for both Kanafani and later Michael to offer vastly different visions of the future and the role of the Green Line in it. Kanafani's novel is a revolutionary call to resistance, for all of the borders of Palestine to open through a victorious return,[9] while Michael considers the possibility of peaceful reconciliation and coexistence.

I begin by considering the utopian nature of both of these visions and the relationship of the concept of utopia to borders – in particular the notion of utopia as a space that is antithetical to borders – before turning to Kanafani and then Michael. For Kanafani, writing in a post-1967 moment in which Palestinian resistance movements were reinvigorated,[10] the utopian vision of national liberation imagined what Bashir Abu-Manneh terms a 'universal Palestine of the future' in which justice and equality for all would prevail.[11] In Michael's novel, set in a period marked by the intense violence of the Second Intifada, the dream of coexistence already seems out of reach. In reading between the two novels, we can see a transition from a declaration of a coming revolution to mourning a form of coexistence that has no place within Israel/Palestine. I trace this shift through the differing relationship to the border in the two novels. In the progression from Kanafani to Michael, the Green Line reasserts and imbeds itself into the text, functioning as an anti-utopian space as it shifts from a newly opened proto-national border to the anchor of a larger network of internal borders. In this shift, furthermore, we can see cultural-literary-political paradigms of both resistance and coexistence begin to falter.

Starting with the disappearance of a border might seem like an odd choice for a book about such spaces, but it is only a partial disappearance, and this choice is intended to act as a counterweight to the sometimes overbearing discourse of globalisation and opening borders that has dominated many debates until very recently.[12] The progression towards fewer borders, enabled by global movement of people and goods, technological progress and cultural exchange, is often taken as teleological and a sign of progress. However, in Israel and Palestine the opening of the Green Line in 1967 is not a moment of liberation or progress, but rather it set the stage for the border regime that we see today. After this moment of disappearance, a much more complex series of borders began slowly but surely to reconstitute themselves, expand, shift, multiply and proliferate until they have become nearly ubiquitous in the present. By starting with the Green Line's opening, and the (unrealised) imagined futures in which its disappearance is permanent, we can trace the gradual recession of utopian dreams that parallels the entrenchment and spread of border spaces.

Two Novels in Dialogue and Conflict

Ghassan Kanafani is well known for deploying his writing skills in service of the Palestinian cause. Both his activities while living in Beirut and the manner of his untimely assassination in 1972 by a car bomb planted by Mossad affirm his credentials as a resistance writer, and much critical discourse around his work has focused on his political activities.[13] He was active in the leadership of the Popular Front for the Liberation of Palestine and was the founder and editor-in-chief of *al-Hadaf*, the PFLP's weekly newspaper; he played a principle role in bringing popular and critical attention to authors like Mahmoud Darwish and Emile Habiby through his study *Adab al-Muqawama fi Filistin al-Muhtalla 1948–1966* (*Resistance Literature in Occupied Palestine 1948–1966*);[14] and he published many novels and short stories of his own that offer a model of literary commitment to the Palestinian cause, even if they did not shy away from critiquing the Palestinian leadership. *Al-Hadaf* under Kanafani's editorship was filled with articles on Palestinian and global anti-colonial movements, with an interest in global resistance literature and cinema, from South America to Vietnam.[15] It also kept tabs on political developments in Israel, and published articles on communists and other leftist movements in Israel as well as occasional translations of works originally published in Hebrew. This suggests that Kanafani and his cohorts nurtured an interest in certain aspects of Israeli society and politics that sometimes, based on the tone of the articles published, went beyond a simple desire to know the enemy.

Glimpses of this curiosity also appear in Kanafani's novel *Returning to Haifa*, in which a complex and nuanced encounter between intertwined Palestinian and Israeli families spawned a critical debate over the form and extent of 'resistance' found in this novel.[16] The novel begins with the arrival of the Palestinian couple (Said and Safiyya) in Haifa in 1967, where they find a cityscape transformed by twenty years of Israeli rule. Their encounter with their city and eventually their home and its new inhabitants reflects a tension between curiosity and horror. While the novel sympathetically recounts the Jewish family's plight as Holocaust survivors and refugees, the encounter between Said and his lost son Khaldun, who has been adopted by the Jewish family, produces anger and revulsion. The son, now named Dov and a soldier in the Israeli military, disavows any connection to his Palestinian past. This discovery hardens Said's resolve to support his other son Khalid's desire to join the Palestinian resistance. He pledges that the brothers will meet on the battlefield. The stark reality of loss that Said confronts through his encounter with Dov reminds him and the reader of the necessity of struggle and sacrifice for the Palestinian cause. While he ends with a call for resistance, Kanafani's sympathetic portrayal of the plight of the Jewish Holocaust survivors reminds us that his vision is not narrowly nationalist but of a revolutionary Palestine that 'can provide a universalist future for all'.[17]

Of the many adaptations and reworkings of *Returning to Haifa*, Michael's *Doves in Trafalgar* is perhaps the most substantive and fully articulated transformation of Kanafani's narrative. Michael, who was born in Baghdad in 1926 and migrated to Israel in 1949, has long been considered one of the most important Mizrahi[18] writers in Israel and is part of cadre of Iraqi-Jewish writers in Israel that also includes Shimon Ballas, Eli Amir and Samir Naqqash.[19] He began his career writing in Arabic before eventually mastering Hebrew.[20] He wrote for *al-Ittihad*, the Arabic-language newspaper of the Israeli Communist Party, under the editorship of Emile Habiby, and he settled in the primarily Palestinian neighbourhood of Wadi Nisnas in Haifa. Michael's writings reflect not only his own background as an Iraqi-Israeli – his novel *Victoria* (*Viktorya*, 1993) for instance takes place in the Jewish community in Baghdad – but also a particularly strong interest in exploring the connections between Arabs and Jews in Israel. In addition to *Doves in Trafalgar*, his novel *A Trumpet in the Wadi* (*Hatsotsira ba-Vadi*, 1987) revolves around a love affair between a Jewish immigrant and an Arab Christian living in Wadi Nisnas in Haifa. His interest in these intersections extends beyond literature, as Michael serves as President of the Association for Civil Rights in Israel, an organisation that works for equality between Jews and Arabs. Both his writings and his non-literary work reflect an abiding interest in Jewish–Arab exchange and coexistence.

Crucial to understanding Michael's interest in Palestinian–Israeli relations is his self-proclaimed subject position as an Arab Jew.[21] Orit Bashkin identifies a number of Mizrahi authors who have written of the Palestinian *Nakba*[22] as a way both to contest Israeli deployment of the Mizrahi narratives to justify the denial of Palestinian rights and to explore shared yet distinct experiences of displacement and exile experience by Palestinians and Mizrahim.[23] Identifying as an Arab Jew is a political act, one that Lital Levy describes as a 'a statement of *dis*association or *un*affiliation with a national project – a rejection of the Eurocentric terms of Israeli national identity'.[24] It opposes an ethno-nationalist separatism that is so pervasive that it problematises the very existence of the category of Arab Jew, rendering the claiming of that identity an 'impossibility' in Levy's words,[25] or the connection between Arab and Jew 'a link that is erased at the very moment it is staged', as Hochberg puts it.[26] The crucial point here is that in Israel, which espouses an essentialist diametric opposition between Arab and Jew, the Arab Jew always exists within and on the margins of Israeli culture and society,[27] to the extent that Michael refers to himself as a 'stranger in my own land'.[28] This uneasy position is reflected in Michael's novels, which often centre on characters who defy easy categorisation.[29] Perhaps it is then unsurprising that he would use Kanafani's character, who is Palestinian by birth and Jewish by adoption, to problematise the current borders of Israel, as in their present form they offer no place for this type of hyphenated subjectivity.

Doves in Trafalgar, published thirty-five years after Kanafani's text, depicts the son as a grown man in Israel with a successful business career who reconnects with Nabila (a renamed Safiyya), his biological mother, who lives in the West Bank. He seeks to reconnect with his lost Palestinian family, as he and his mother navigate restrictions on movement, a hostile political system, sceptical family members, and his own conflicted relationship with his Palestinian heritage. Critics have offered different interpretations of Michael's political message in the novel; Ariel Sheetrit argues that the novel's complex narrative and cacophony of represented voices, both Arab and Jew, obscures any 'clear-cut' political message,[30] while Doli Benhabib sees the main characters as an embodiment of the 'possibility of coexistence' (*efshariyut ha-du-kiyum*).[31] Given Michael's dedication to ideals of coexistence and their presence in the novel, Kanafani's novel of resistance might seem an odd choice of work with which to engage. While there is evidence that Kanafani's widow, Anni, has expressed interest in a joint Israeli–Palestinian follow-up to *Returning to Haifa*, and this was in part Michael's inspiration for his novel,[32] Michael himself acknowledges this tension when he notes that Kanafani was part of the leadership of the Popular Front for the Liberation of Palestine, 'whose members thought there was no possible solution with Israel except for its elimination'.[33] Given this perception, extracting a vision of coexistence from Kanafani's original narrative in *Returning to Haifa* required substantial revision, elaboration and a bit of erasure.

The reshaping of Kanafani's story manifests itself in the characters' changed names;[34] however, it also appears through parallels and contrasts in narrative structure, the spaces and motifs used, and the dramatic expansion of the cast of characters and spaces when compared to Kanafani's minimalist story. *Doves in Trafalgar* exists in a tense conversation with *Returning to Haifa*, oscillating between a clear indebtedness to the characters and frame narrative of Kanafani's novel and major differences that emerge in the lessons and implications it draws from the events of the original. To a certain extent, Michael's approach can be described as filling in the blank spots in Kanafani's story by producing a detailed exploration of the characters, their motivations and their complications. Kanafani's slender volume, less than seventy-five pages and with only four characters who appear in the text aside from flashbacks and indirect reference, largely eschews minute detail in favour of broad strokes and big ideas. This choice, which is typical for Kanafani's concise writing style, allows it to 'speak' to many different audiences and undoubtedly plays a role in its ability to resonate strongly in Palestine and beyond. However, this also leaves space for Michael to elaborate further on many elements of *Returning to Haifa* that remain open ended.

Comparing the two works reveals the ways in which Michael's novel envisions a future Israel and Palestine that broadly parallels Kanafani's own attempts to imagine a new way forward for Palestinians, but it also articulates a commitment to coexistence that arises from a very different set of assumptions than Kanafani's paradigm of resistance. While Kanafani envisions a secular, democratic state that would emerge as a *result* of Palestinian resistance and the defeat of Israeli power,[35] Michael might be said to imagine both Israeli militarism and Palestinian armed resistance as obstacles to achieving a form of secular, democratic coexistence. Michael's novel exudes a tension between a desire to re-read Kanafani's Palestinian/Israeli character Khaldun/Dov as a catalyst for peace, and contemporary conditions in Israel and Palestine that render this utopian vision untenable. Despite vast ideological and temporal gaps between *Returning to Haifa* and *Doves in Trafalgar*, both reflect forms of commitment – to particular idealised visions of victory, peace, a better future – that become more difficult to discern in the works of later generations of writers and filmmakers, as the overwhelming presence of borders makes imagining their erasure increasingly difficult.

Opening Utopian Borders

In an interview with *Haaretz* soon after *Doves in Trafalgar* was published, Sami Michael offers a vision of peace and coexistence for Israel and Palestine: 'If (*im yehiyeh*) the two sides are sane, a joint federation of the two nations will be established here, like that utopian (*utopi*) project that Zeev dreams up in the book "Doves in Trafalgar".'[36] Michael articulates a hopeful vision of coexistence, in which he professes belief, yet it is tempered by the conditional 'if' (*im*), which in Hebrew is followed by the future tense 'will be' (*yehiyeh*), as if to emphasise its unrealised and perhaps unrealisable status. Michael's utopia, depicted in the language of what might have been, is explicitly tied to a removal of borders, to a 'joint federation' in which the Green Line would, presumably, no longer be operative. In *Returning to Haifa*, the utopian imaginary is likewise predicated upon open borders. Said, ruminating on the newly opened border between the West Bank and Israel, says to his wife Safiyya: 'You know, for twenty years I always imagined that the Mandelbaum Gate[37] would be opened some day, but I never, never imagined that it would be opened from the other side.'[38] For Said, Palestine's imagined future includes the opening of the border that separated his family from their former home, in this case the Mandelbaum Gate, which was the pre-1967 checkpoint on the border between Israeli-controlled West Jerusalem and Jordanian-controlled East

Jerusalem. Like Michael, Said's usage of a conditional future tense indicates that his vision remains unfulfilled. Yet he has also witnessed the opening of the border, creating the sense that it is within reach. This interplay of tantalising possibility and frustrating impossibility animates my understanding of utopia and its relationship to the Green Line as a border that was erased but still exists and is both present and absent.

My use of utopia here warrants further discussion, as the precise usage of the concept in both popular discourse and critical theory remains highly varied.[39] Utopia in the present has become a byword for failed ideologies and dreams that reside in the realm of the impossible. For instance, Marx and Engels themselves rejected utopian socialism even as their writings inspired myriad utopian projects.[40] In this view, utopia suggests at best a naive fantasy or disconnect from reality; at its worst it represents a dangerous form of idealism that, when attempted in practice, leads to the totalitarian excesses of ideologies like Stalinism.[41] Indeed, even attempts to rescue utopia from its bad reputation can remain tentative at best, as seen in Frederic Jameson's advocacy of what he ambivalently terms 'anti-anti-Utopianism'.[42] Ruth Levitas on the other hand argues for a more open definition of utopia as 'the expression of desire for a better way of living and of being'.[43] It can be fleeting, temporary and incomplete. It is not absolute (perfection) but relative (improvement). It can exist beyond the realm of pure imagination and outside of the binary of wishful thinking or destructive ideology. Levitas describes it as a crucial form of human knowledge that is not simply 'a dream to be enjoyed, but a vision to be pursued'.[44] If we understand utopia in its broader sense – an image of a future that is better and more complete than the present – Said's imagined opening of Mandelbaum Gate, if not a fully articulated utopia, certainly contains elements of such a vision.

The region of Israel and Palestine has long been the subject of many political, cultural or religious utopian visions. The most consequential of these is Zionism, which itself includes many different iterations that range from a secular, pluralist Jewish state[45] to a territorial expansionist Jewish theocracy.[46] The loss of Palestine and the desire both to preserve the connection with the land and to kindle a desire to return has produced utopian visions of Palestine among Palestinians and Arabs, from idyllic images of an idealised pre-1948 Palestine[47] to the free, just Palestine that will follow a Palestinian victory over

Israel.[48] One could even view the proposed solutions, from a two-state solution to a confederation or a binational state – the vision expressed at the end of *Doves in Trafalgar*, to which I will return later – as existing to various extents within a utopian discourse of peace and prosperity. Jerusalem as utopia pervades religious thought, including travel narratives of Western religious pilgrims to the Holy Land,[49] Jerusalem's designation as the third holiest city in Islam, and the Passover refrain of 'Next year in Jerusalem'. Jerusalem has also inspired utopian efforts elsewhere, most notably the idea of the 'city on the hill' imagined by Puritan settlers of Massachusetts and later deployed in support of American Exceptionalism writ large, and perhaps we could even include the Crusades as motivated in part by utopian visions of the Holy Land. As this far from exhaustive list suggests, Israel/Palestine is a space in which utopia is overdetermined; it is the site of multiple overlapping, incompatible and often violent utopian visions that range from religious imaginary to political visions that potentially lie within reach.

The passage from *Returning to Haifa* in which Said and Safiyya cross the Green Line toward Haifa also reveals a crucial connection between utopian imagination and borders; it is no coincidence that the opening of Mandelbaum Gate is a necessary (albeit not sufficient) precondition to the realisation of this particular vision. Utopia is a concept that both depends upon and resists the limits of borders, and borders exist in a complex relationship with utopian images. On the one hand, the border as we understand it today – a line that demarcates sovereignty, access and power – is indelibly intertwined with the modern nation state, itself a project that tends towards the utopian. The idea that each national group should be unified under a single flag, language, culture and territory is a concept that has always claimed to reflect a 'natural' order but in reality sought to produce a new form of society.[50] The production of the nation state necessitates the creation of the ideal citizen through education, discipline and interpellation, the construction of monumental spaces like capital cities, and other methods of shaping modern subjectivity.[51] The sacrosanct nature of borders, both physical and otherwise, is an integral part of the utopian sovereignty and power of the nation state, delineating inside and outside, belonging and otherness.

However, at the same time that utopias rely on borders they also resist them. This tension, as Louis Marin suggests, extends to the origin of the concept itself with More's *Utopia*. More, in his attempt to imagine a land ruled by rationality rather than custom and tradition, describes in great detail the physical, social and political features of his island Utopia. Marin, writing nearly 500 years after More in *Utopics: Spatial Play*, attempts to map the spaces of the island described in *Utopia*, as well as the political and economic systems outlined, and finds numerous incongruencies and incompatibilities. All of the pieces do not fit together – certain spaces and figures (the marketplace, the governor, money) are erased or occupy 'blank spots'. Utopia, it seems, can never be fully mapped.[52] These blank spots, what Marin calls 'white spaces' and '*terrae incognitae*' are 'the places for unthinkable theoretical concepts' to be considered and articulated.[53] In the case of More, this 'unthinkable' concept is a capitalist modernity that has yet to come into being. Utopia makes space for this new order that has not been fully articulated and thus cannot be fully represented in the spatial and discursive terms of the present. Utopia's relationship to borders and limits is an important element of this gap, for Utopia's limits cannot be defined in conventional ways, and utopia in a sense lacks borders ('Utopia, in fact, never admits anything exterior to itself; Utopia is for itself its own reality'),[54] even as its very existence is only made possible by a very clear distinction that divides here from there and interior from exterior.[55] We can see this tendency to eschew borders in the thought of many contemporary theorists whose concepts tend toward the utopian. Deleuze and Guattari's rhizomes and nomads resist linearity and borders of any kind as a form of liberation from the control of the nation state,[56] and much of the discourse of globalisation heralds a far-fetched utopian world of few borders in which the nation state has been superseded by global movements of goods, information and people.[57]

The border, then, is a barrier to utopian imagination by limiting that which by definition seeks to transgress limits. We can begin to see Kanafani and Michael's respective commitments to resistance and coexistence as utopian ideas that resist the concrete finality of the border. By examining these two texts together we can trace the shift in utopian imagination that occurs alongside the perpetuation and entrenchment of borders that took place in the thirty-six years between the publication of *Returning to Haifa* and *Doves in Trafalgar*. Kanafani's disappearing border signifies despair at defeat but also hope for opening the border once again in victory. However, decades later,

Michael's utopian project of coexistence as embodied in the figure of the Palestinian/Israeli son from Kanafani's novel reveals its own futility, as the very idea of opening borders appears either endlessly distant or hopelessly naive in the face of inexorably expanding checkpoints and walls. In the remainder of this chapter I trace this shift in order to consider how the decline of utopian hopes and desires as forms of commitment (to victory and/or peace) gives way to an era of borders.

Open Border, Defeat and Resistance

At the end of *Returning to Haifa*, Said tells the Israeli occupants of his house, Miriam and Khaldun/Dov, the son that he left behind who now sees himself as Israeli: 'You two may remain in our house temporarily. It will take a war to settle that.'[58] With this statement, particularly in his use of the modifier 'temporarily' (*muʾaqqatan*), Said affirms his belief in a coming liberation of Palestine. He asserts his claim to ownership of the home. It is an act of recommitment to a vision of struggle and resistance that he mourns at the beginning of the novel. Through the course of the novel it becomes clear that as Said and Safiyya travel back to Haifa to confront their past, they also rekindle their dream of victory that Said earlier mourns as he ponders the re-opening of the Green Line. The novel's structure – a largely chronological and realist narrative of a round trip to and from Haifa, interspersed with occasional flashbacks – serves to emphasise the marked contrast between the journey there and the journey back, during the course of which the couple reconceptualises their relationship to both of their sons, their traumatic past, and the Palestinian cause.

Early in the novel we learn that the couple's second son Khalid had, in the immediate aftermath of the defeat, declared his desire to join the *fidāʾiyyūn*, the armed Palestinian resistance. Said's response is to refuse his son's request and even to threaten to disown him (*tabarruʾ*) if he defies his father's wishes.[59] Said's rejection of the resistance movement reflects the disenchantment that followed the 1967 war. He describes the period since then as a 'nightmare that ended in terror' and a 'strange world'.[60] There is no hope, only terror and despair. Yet, later, after his encounter with his firstborn son who has disavowed Said (using the same term Said used against Khalid, *tabarruʾ*),[61] Said wonders in retrospect how he could have refused Khalid's request to join the *fidāʾiyyūn*. After departing Haifa, he declares, 'I pray Khalid will have gone – while we were away!'[62] The narrative arc stages the breakdown and subsequent reconstitution of a utopian vision of resistance and victory that is also, as I will show, marked by a transformed engagement with the opened Green Line and the act of crossing it.

Said and Safiyya's journey of return begins as a journey to the past in defeat, and it is preoccupied with borders. Defeat and loss permeate what they had imagined would be a triumphant return. During their drive to Haifa they talk endlessly of the defeat: the bulldozing of Mandelbaum Gate, the fighting in the streets of Jerusalem, the enemy 'who reached the river, then the canal, then the edge of Damascus in a matter of hours'.[63] Kanafani here traces the physical contours of Israel's victory, mapping the borders that fell and the vast expanses of land that were lost. As they drive through the scorched landscape onto which the sun of that 'terrible June'[64] 'spilled the tar of its anger', Said's forehead burns and the asphalt 'ignites' beneath them.[65] They experience their trip as a journey through a post-war apocalypse, a hellscape in which the fires of war still burn even as it has ended. This imagery, some of the most vivid in the novel, conveys an intense, embodied pain produced by the act of return and specifically of crossing the no man's land of the Green Line, invoking the border as a site of physical pain even in its temporary opening.

As the couple cross to return to Haifa, the fact of the Green Line's opening serves as a reminder of the loss. Said says of the Israeli decision to open it:

> They opened (*fataḥū*) the border as soon as they completed the occupation, suddenly and immediately. This has never happened in any war in history . . . This is part of the war. They're saying to us, 'Help yourselves, look and see how much better we are than you, how much more developed.'[66]

The opening of the border here is an act of war and conquest,[67] illuminated by the dual meaning of the Arabic verb *fataḥa* as both 'to open' and 'to conquer'. We see the latter meaning in terms such as *al-futūḥāt al-Islāmiyya* (the Islamic conquests, which refers to the rapid spread of Muslim armies out of the Arabian Peninsula across the Middle East into South Asia and North Africa in the seventh century CE), though such usage typically denotes a favourable victory. This notion of *fatḥ* as victory finds expression in Palestinian politics through the name of the 'Fatah' movement, the Palestinian political faction to which long-time Palestine Liberation Organisation leader Yasser Arafat belonged, and which remains dominant in the West Bank today. In *Returning to Haifa*, however, the use of *fataḥa* provides a reminder of the setback. The meaning of opening is inverted and here signifies not liberation but political failure. It is not Palestinians but Israelis who opened the border and now seek to use this opening as a psychological tool to reinforce the military defeat by demonstrating a form of cultural and economic defeat.

Yet Said recovers at least a hint of a moral victory in noting the failure of the Israelis' aim of showing 'how much better' they are than the Arabs. He notes that many of the people who have travelled back find that the 'miracle' (*al-muʿijaza*) of Israel was 'nothing but an illusion (*wahm*)'.[68] If Said's commitment to Palestine's future falters in the face of defeat, here we see another failed vision – the Zionist dream of Israel[69] – exposed in its moment of victory. It is the *opening* of the border that reveals its failure in the eyes of the Palestinians voices in the novel. The fall of the border exposes and calls into question this and other illusions. The border is deceptive in the sense that its presence produces fantasies and illusions – the mystery of what lies on the other side – that are deflated by the act of opening.

The border has produce an image of a transformed Israel that is not really there, at least from Said's perspective, which allows the couple to return to Haifa and feel as if 'nothing has changed', as Said declares repeatedly.[70] The sense of stasis and familiarity permits Kanafani to blur the lines between the present (1967) and the past (1948) in revealing ways. Said perceives Haifa as an amalgam of his memories and the present. He drives through the city as if he has never left these streets, recounting their pre-1948 names (Wadi Nisnas, King Faisal Street, Hanatir Square). The narrator does not note that some of the names were changed after the Israeli conquest, leaving the line between past and present ambiguous.[71] Indeed the memories and emotions of return overwhelm the narrative of their present-day arrival in Haifa. Said's flashbacks disrupt the largely chronological progression of the narrative. As Said drives he sees a young boy, which triggers a flashback to the traumatic events of 1948: 'With that scene the terrible past came back to him in all its tumultuousness. For the first time in twenty years he remembered what happened in minute detail, as though he were reliving it again.'[72] A key phrase here is 'for the first time', for it reveals the extent to which these memories have been suppressed, unspoken and forgotten. The open border unleashes a wave of memories that Said has long resisted, and we see that the presence of this border for nearly twenty years has, perhaps unconsciously, served as a shield for Said, protecting him from confronting his loss. If crossing the Green Line disrupts illusions and fantasies, it also forces an encounter with a suppressed past.

The flashbacks and recollections of Said and his wife that pepper this section of the narrative repeatedly invoke images of borders and walls. Said hears the sound of the sea and memories resurface, not gradually, but he says, 'it rained down inside his head the way a stone wall collapses (*kamā yatasāqaṭ jadārun*), the stones piling up, one upon another'.[73] The separation of places and times, a wall Said so carefully constructed in order to protect himself, falls down. The Arabic word used for collapse here, *yatasāqaṭ*, is reflexive and suggests two entities falling in upon each other, as if Said's two selves – past and present – are no longer distinguishable in this moment of encounter with the sea, which was an integral part of his previous life.[74] The sea floods through the fallen wall and he later says that it was as if 'twenty years of absence had dwindled away'.[75] Though the return of suppressed memories can be cleansing and necessary, it is also painful for Said: 'Suddenly the past came, sharp (*ḥāddan*) like a knife.'[76] The word *ḥāddan* is an adjectival form of *ḥadd*, border, recalling Gloria Anzaldúa's characterisation of the border as a space that wounds, bleeds and scrapes.[77] Yet here the pain comes not from the border itself but crossing the open border in defeat, as the opening of the Green Line produces this encounter between past and present in an embodied, painful fashion.

If the opening of the Green Line forces a confrontation with dormant fears and memories, this confrontation also engenders possibilities for reimagining the meanings of commitment and victory. The narrative climax of the novel revolves around precisely this type of clash, as Said and Safiyya come face to face with their former home, its inhabitants and their lost son. The novel dramatically changes tone as it shifts from a relatively subdued recounting of the specificity of the tragedies experienced by the novel's characters – not only Said and Safiyya but also the Israeli inhabitants of the home, Holocaust survivors Iphrat and Mariam – to an emotionally charged debate about concepts of humanity, commitment and blame. The catalyst for this shift is the arrival of the son, formerly Khaldun, now Dov, who Said learns now proudly wears an Israeli military uniform as a reservist.[78] At this moment dialogue gives way to nonverbal outbursts of emotion as Safiyya sobs, Mariam remains silent, and Said laughs uncontrollably. Said's laughter is a moment in which his delusions and false hopes are exposed. He realises this moment was inevitable – he feels like 'he was watching a play prepared ahead of time in detail. It reminded him of cheap melodramas in trivial movies with artificial plots'[79] – but the shattering of his illusions about Palestine, his lost home and his son finally allows him to see the reality that he and the Palestinian people face in the aftermath of 1967.

This moment of realisation produces in Said a reordering of hopes, expectations and beliefs about the state of the conflict and the meanings of kinship and nation. As he argues with Dov/Khaldun, Said's mournful fatalism about his loss and Palestine's defeat is replaced by a desire to reimagine the future, a shift that mirrors many of the political and intellectual debates that emerged in the Arab world in the moment of mourning, reflection and self-criticism that followed the defeat of 1967.[80] Said asks, 'What is a homeland (*al-waṭan*)? . . . The picture of Jerusalem on the wall? The copper lock? The oak tree? The balcony? What is a homeland? Khaldun? Our illusions (*Awhām*) about him?'[81] Said lists a plethora of different meanings, symbols and metaphors that have signified *al-waṭan* in Palestine at various times and places – land and the sustenance it provides, commemorative objects like keys and pictures, and people. By seeking to shatter 'illusions' about their son, about their home and about Palestine, Said calls into question the terms by which *al-waṭan* has been conceived for Palestinians, in particular the desire to return to a past that, as he learns through confronting his son, no longer exists. He and Safiyya have searched for Palestine in the 'dust of memories', but they were wrong and Khalid understands that *al-waṭan* is actually the future.[82] Dov utters perhaps the best-known sentence in the novel here, his enigmatic statement that 'Man is a cause' (*al-Insān huwa qaḍiyya*).[83] Said responds by agreeing, but asks what cause he means. He tells Dov that Khalid is also a cause, that man 'has nothing to do with flesh and blood and identity cards and passports'.[84] Said now rejects the elements that had consumed him – the desire to find his own lost flesh and blood, and his concern with borders of nation and kinship as defined by ID cards and passports – in favour of commitment to a cause and a future-focused vision that, like utopia, remains unembodied and unrealised but appears achievable.

This transformation further reveals itself in the contrast between the journey to Haifa and the drive back to Ramallah. At the beginning, on the way to Haifa, Safiyya asks why Said keeps talking about 'philosophy', 'gates' and 'everything else'.[85] He cannot stop talking, overburdened as he is with loss, uncertainty and anxiety. The return to Ramallah, by contrast, is silent. The novel states that the concerns that preoccupied Said a few hours before now seemed 'less important'.[86] The silence, then, reflects the resolution and certainty that has displaced the doubts and fears that drove the couple to Haifa. They are no longer consumed by the past and the border but are contemplating what comes next. Likewise, notably absent is the crossing of the border, the source of much discussion and consternation before. If the border loomed large on the journey to Haifa because it dictated their ability to visit Haifa, the renewed commitment to resistance has rendered it irrelevant on the return journey. The signifiers of borders – passports and IDs – have lost their power as the border disappears from their conversation. The current situation of the border is temporary, and their imaginations of the future are no longer bound by its presence or absence. Said's embrace of the *fidāʾiyyūn*, the resistance fighters whom Khalid wishes to join, who were well known for their cross-border raids into Israel, signifies a new relationship with the border that is staged primarily through its violation and irrelevance. If the utopian imaginary is incompatible with defined borders, Said's refusal to be bound by the border and its signifiers marks a renewed commitment to a utopian vision of Palestine.

At the beginning of the novel, the opening of the border is traumatic; its existence has safely contained the couple's terrible memories and loss for twenty years, and its fall allows this past to return and overwhelm the Palestinian couple. By reliving and confronting these experiences for the first time, Said transforms his conception of the homeland (*al-waṭan*) and the cause (*al-qaḍiyya*) in a manner that goes beyond particular borders and spaces and allows him to imagine new forms of commitment to Palestine, to the resistance, and to the future of his now only son Khalid. He is able to view the current borders as temporary – after all, they had only changed very recently, and the border that Said and Safiyya pass through had not yet achieved the sacred status that the Green Line possesses today. If *Returning to Haifa*'s renewed commitment to a utopian vision is enacted through a repudiation of the border, later entrenchment of the border and of border spaces in general would render such a task all the more difficult thirty-five years later, when Michael wrote *Doves in Trafalgar*.

Faltering Visions of Coexistence

While *Returning to Haifa* concludes with a recommitment to the dream of Palestinian resistance that is enacted through the erasure of the Green Line, the expanded presence of this and other borders in *Doves in Trafalgar* casts doubt on the vision of coexistence articulated and embodied by the novel's main character, Ze'ev (the renamed Dov/Khaldun from *Returning to Haifa*). Now a successful adult with a wife and daughter, Ze'ev has established contact with his Palestinian biological mother Nabila (Safiyya in *Returning to Haifa*), who resides in the West Bank, and much of the novel centres on his efforts to facilitate a detente between the two sides of his family. Michael effects this change in tone by reinterpreting the crucial confrontation scene between the Palestinian father and his now Israeli son in *Returning to Haifa* in order to make space for a different, more conciliatory interpretation of Kanafani's narrative. It enacts this revision primarily by refocusing onto the mothers in the story – particularly the Palestinian mother – who remain largely silent in Kanafani's original. In *Returning to Haifa*, Safiyya and Mariam do not intervene: Mariam says nothing and Safiyya, rendered mute by a language barrier, sobs as her husband and son fight and angrily confront each other.[87] Safiyya does not speak after these events, and her silence is easily interpreted as quiet acquiescence or agreement to Said. However, in *Doves in Trafalgar*, Nabila's silence is re-read as a form of quiet disagreement. She follows her husband's wishes reluctantly at best, while also learning English in order to communicate with her son and then reaching out to him after her husband's death. While the father–son relationship produces loud confrontation, the mother–son connection offers a quieter, more conciliatory mode of engagement, repositioning the narrative from one centred on conflict to one seeking coexistence.

An early passage in which Ze'ev's Jewish and Palestinian families cross paths in a park establishes both Ze'ev's (and Nabila's) desire to effect a reconciliation and the difficulties of doing so. While in the park, Nabila's daughter Sana (Ze'ev's biological sister) notices Ze'ev, whom she does not recognise, with his wife and daughter. Sana, unsettled by this near encounter, finds herself torn by an unusual interest in the man and a suspicion of Jewish Israelis produced by a tragic history in which 'the family's contact with Jews has produced only death'.[88] She notices Ze'ev, whom she calls 'the stranger' (*ha-zar*),[89] a word in Hebrew that means both 'stranger' and 'foreigner', surreptitiously staring at her and her family ('It's like he's stalking us'[90]). Sana's immediate response to this Israeli and his interest in her family foregrounds the suspicion and fear that enforces the separation of Palestinians and Israeli Jews, reflecting what Gil Hochberg calls the 'separatist imagination'[91] that problematises Arab–Jewish encounters at this particular historical moment.

However, this passage also complicates this separation, as Sana notes that this ostensibly Ashkenazi Jewish man is 'brown' (*shaḥum*) and bears a strong resemblance to her brother Karim (Khalid from *Returning to Haifa*). There is an unsettling moment of recognition that casts doubt upon the distinction between Sana and the 'stranger', and Nabila sows further doubt by asking Sana if she is 'certain that he and his son are Jewish?'[92] Even as it establishes a separation of Israeli and Palestinian – the two families never speak, and the Israeli man is viewed as a stranger/foreigner – the novel also calls into question the assumptions that underlie the fixity of Jewish–Palestinian difference. An initial reaction of suspicion and fear that establishes such a distinction begins to unravel under further scrutiny, as the absolute categories of 'stranger' and 'Jewish' gives way to an uncanny familiarity and a middle ground of indeterminacy that beckons a closer look. If Kanafani's novel presents Dov/Khaldun's self-identity as an either/or proposition – he must choose between his Palestinian and Jewish parents – *Doves in Trafalgar* situates Ze'ev in a more ambiguous position. It hints at the potential for a connection between Ze'ev and his Palestinian family, but a prevalent logic of fear, separation and mutual suspicion presents a formidable obstacle.

At the same time that the novel teases the possibility of a different type of relationship between Israelis and Palestinians, it repeatedly emphasises the physical barriers that make this nearly impossible. The Palestinian family's journey from the park to Jenin, in the West Bank, following this encounter, emphasises the ways in which the Green Line and other border spaces such as checkpoints have implicated themselves in daily life by this period. The text notes that they cross the Green Line (*ha-Kav ha-Yarok*), but there would have been no physical marking to signify the crossing, for the separation barrier was only in its early stages of construction at the time of writing.[93] However, the use of the proper name 'the Green Line' signifies the extent to which its importance as a once and future border has been codified, in contrast to *Returning to Haifa* in which it remains unnamed. Despite the absence of a physical barrier, their crossing is marked in other ways. Karim makes note of the contrast between the roads and driving behaviour once they cross into the West Bank. The order of Israel and 'the Western world' fades away.[94] As they approach an intersection, the novel notes that Karim prefers to 'pass through this place as quickly as possible because of the Israeli soldiers who stayed there most of the day'.[95] The occupation, a new reality in Kanafani, is now a routine ordeal that simultaneously produces familiarity (knowledge of the soldiers' routines) and alienation (desire to avoid the area). The discussion among the passengers repeatedly touches on the Green Line between the West Bank and Israel – what kind of cars can cross, whether to cross or not – an illustration of the outsized role this space plays in the daily lives of this Palestinian family.

The novel establishes a contrast between the Palestinian family's journey home and that of Ze'ev and his family, for whom the border is a non-issue, in the following chapter. For them, the trip home involves not soldiers and borders but pizza.[96] Even as the Green Line has grown in importance and border spaces around the West Bank have proliferated, it remains unnoticed and often invisible to many Israelis, even if they pass in close proximity.[97] If the encounter in the park raises the possibility of moving beyond the absolute separation of Israeli and Palestinian, the spectre of borders and spatial control that hangs over this journey immediately casts doubt upon this vision and amplifies the different realities inhabited by the two families. They share the same space here but they experience it in radically unequal ways, much as the two families experience the home in *Returning to Haifa*. The house is at once a refuge from death and horror for the Israeli couple and the site of unspeakable loss for the Palestinian couple. Though far less significant a space, the park for Ze'ev and his Israeli family signifies normalcy, an outing to enjoy nature and pizza, while for the Palestinian family it reveals the abnormality of Palestinian life and the near constant anxiety this produces. Even as they occupy the same spaces, the different ways in which the spaces are experienced re-inscribes separatism, as they exist together but do not coexist.

The novel thus questions the possibility of coexistence spatially, through the resilience of the border, even as it advocates for such a vision. Ze'ev's attempts to bring his own family together reflects this impossibility; Ze'ev's unusual position as both Israeli and Palestinian allows him to act as an embodiment of the spirit of cooperation and reconciliation, and he seeks to overcome mutual suspicion by getting to know his Palestinian relatives and bringing together the two sides of his family. These efforts culminate in a climactic encounter between Ze'ev and his Palestinian family in London, from which the novel takes its title. If the near encounter in the Israeli park and the respective journeys home mimic the simultaneous proximity and inaccessibility produced by the Green Line, the later meeting of the two families in London reveals the resilience of this separation. The novel traces the journey of the various family members to London and makes note of the difficulties presented to Palestinians who wish to travel abroad. One of the Palestinian characters tells Ze'ev that many Palestinians never even attempt to travel because of the 'obstacles raised (*me'erimim*)' in the form of searches and interrogations for those flying out of the Israeli airport in Lod.[98] The Hebrew word *me'erimim* means 'to pile up' or 'to heap', emphasising the connection to some type of border or wall. While Kanafani also makes reference to stones that 'pile up', he uses it to describe a collapsing wall; here it signifies the opposite, the construction of barriers. The reference to borders in London reminds us of the oddity that this meeting takes place intentionally on neutral ground, far from the contested spaces of Israel and Palestine. Even if the meeting logistically could have taken place in Israel or the West Bank, the choice of London signifies the necessity of going elsewhere and reflects the utopian quality of the vision of coexistence offered here, which is antithetical to the regime of borders that pervades contemporary Israel and Palestine. Substantive coexistence cannot happen under the shadow of the borders, restrictions and checkpoints that dominate Palestinian lives and movement. Yet, unlike *Returning to Haifa*, the potential for opening or erasing these borders appears so distant as to verge on impossible, leaving escape to neutral ground as the only option.

An encounter between Ze'ev and Karim within Israel/Palestine – in the West Bank – affirms this impossibility. In this passage, both are killed by a Palestinian militant; the militant targets Ze'ev because he is an Israeli, and Karim dies while trying to rescue his brother. The killing reflects the endemic violence at the time Michael wrote *Doves in Trafalgar*, during the height of the Second Intifada when death was a daily occurrence.[99] Even as Ze'ev himself is a bridge between Israeli and Palestinian, at once both and neither, militant ideologies make no space for such middle ground. If Sana, by looking more closely in the park, can see beyond Ze'ev as a 'stranger', the killer of Ze'ev and Karim maintains this separation by not looking closely, by refusing to see. Nabila later declares that her husband was wrong when he predicted that the two brothers would meet on the battlefield: 'Karim and his brother did meet, but they did not kill each other. Just the opposite, actually.'[100] Sana responds, 'but what difference does it make? They both still died.'[101] Nabila's desire to find meaning and significance from the death of her sons and Sana's refusal to do so reflects a larger conflict in the novel between a desire to extract meaning from tragedy and loss, as Said does at the end of *Returning to Haifa*, and the ways in which nihilistic violence subverts this desire and precludes the possibility of utopian imaginaries that require some form of hope to function.

While Ze'ev's desire to merge his families certainly contains utopian elements, utopia as a spatial concept finds a more explicit expression in a coexistence project he conceives but is also unable to implement. Inspired by his desire to bring his two mothers together, Ze'ev seeks to establish an elderly home in Cyprus for both Israelis and Palestinians, a type of microcosm for a shared future of coexistence and cooperation. He imagines it as a 'refuge' (*miklaṭ*) from 'fire' and 'hate', in case of 'emergencies'.[102] The use of the word *miklaṭ*, the same term used for bomb shelters, suggests that it is a temporary space, only necessary because violence is out of control, and that it would do nothing to address the causes of the conflict but merely treat the symptoms. Moreover, the reaction of the Palestinian family reveals the extent to which this utopian vision depends upon a level of privilege accorded to Ze'ev as an Israeli (by identity, if not by blood) that is unavailable to Palestinians. Nabila, normally supportive of Ze'ev, rejects it as a 'dream', to which Ze'ev responds that 'even a temporary utopia cannot cause harm'. Even if a shelter is only possible in his dreams, he will cling to it because 'woe is me if all hope (*tikva*) is lost'.[103] The word for hope, *tikva*, perhaps captures at once the most meaningful and most painful effect of utopian thought. Utopia both relies upon and keeps hope alive, but it is always slightly out of reach. The concept of hope pervades both Israeli and Palestinian nationalist thought,[104] yet here Ze'ev pleads for hope, as if the very concept is on its deathbed, an intangible ideal that withers under the assault of constant violence, proliferating borders and the diverging realities inhabited by Israelis and Palestinians.

This utopian project reveals a vast chasm between Ze'ev's lived reality and that of his Palestinian family that verges on mutual incomprehensibility, as the novel reveals the blind spots in his vision and tangible harm that his utopia could produce. His notion of a temporary utopia assumes an ease of travel, that one can move back and forth between Israel, Palestine and Cyprus at will, that the proximity of Cyprus means his dream is not simply an escape from the violence of home but that it is a space from which change can be effected. But his Palestinian relatives attempt to disabuse him of that notion, noting the phenomenon of present-absentees in Israel[105] and the very real possibility that they could become stuck in Cyprus with no way to return in the event that Israel closes its borders; for the Palestinians, departure has brought nothing but tragedy (the *Nakba*, for instance), and the notion of *ṣumūd* (perseverance) has construed the act of staying on the land and persisting in whatever way possible as a moral imperative. Nabila asks him, 'Do you know why they call it "utopia"? There's no danger in the take-off and flight, my son, the danger only arises when you want to return to the land of reality.'[106] Part of the appeal of utopia is that it is always elsewhere, but for Palestinians living under occupation, the language of elsewhere offers little appeal when even 'here' is largely inaccessible. The brutal Palestinian reality reveals the limits of the utopian imaginary, as tangible threats to safety and liberty, physical barriers to movement, and the economic, cultural and political realities of occupation push dreams of coexistence and victory far into the realm of the impossible.

The deaths of Karim and Ze'ev prompt Nabila and Sana to consider Ze'ev's dream a second time, as they travel to Cyprus to meet Ze'ev's Israeli wife and daughter, a meeting that again takes place at a neutral, external site. This reconciliatory meeting is meant to continue the work of Ze'ev to establish a joint Israeli–Palestinian home for the elderly in Cyprus. As they stand on the beach, 'Nabila straightened her chin, pointing to Israel and Palestine that are across the sea. They were silent, the silence of survivors looking out over the traces of their world that has been consumed by fire.'[107] The imagery of this passage – sea, fire, silence – at the end of *Doves in Trafalgar* brings us back to the beginning of *Returning to Haifa*. Upon arrival in Haifa, Said suddenly hears 'the sound of the sea', and the journey to Haifa takes them across earth that has been scorched by fire.[108] The fire and sea function as metaphors for the overwhelming emotional and sensory experience of both passages, which produces an inability to speak. Despite Said's chatter along the journey, as they arrive in Haifa, Said and Saffiyya 'were silent together' and they realise they have not said one word about 'the matter for which they came'.[109] Said breaks their silence by asking 'where do we begin?' but Safiyya says nothing.[110] Their silence contains an unspoken hope – that their son will welcome them, that they can find meaning in their loss – for the moment they have anticipated for twenty years. At the end they do find meaning in their recommitment to resistance. Nabila and Sana also break their silence to mourn and process their loss, to find meaning in it. Sana, the most sceptical toward Ze'ev in the family, in the end admits that she never hated him and that she struggled with herself to love him.[111] Breaking the silence of mourning here is likewise a transformative moment, found not in anger but in Sana's new openness to a connection with her brother, a will to coexist.

Yet this acceptance also requires distance to blur the lines between Israeli and Palestinian. Standing on the shores of Cyprus, Nabila refers to Israel and Palestine as a single entity, but one that is 'across the sea'.[112] This casual acceptance of a land and future that encompasses both Israeli and Palestinian comes from a vantage point of exteriority. To imagine this land undivided by myriad borders is to engage in a form of wishful thinking that necessitates the ambiguity of distance, of blurred borders and distinctions. In this case, however, the choice of neutral ground also reveals the impossibility of escaping borders and of achieving this exteriority, for Cyprus is itself a land that is partitioned by conflict and occupied. While Kanafani begins his novel with a border crossing, a spatial enactment of erasure, here circumventing the border comes in the form of an escape to a different partitioned land. The border is inescapable, and it cannot be erased but is only rendered invisible or indistinct by distance. If Ze'ev's utopia does, in the end, come into being, it can only exist elsewhere, outside of the system of borders that governs everyday interactions in Israel and Palestine, and it can only be temporary.

Doves in Trafalgar, while it offers visions of coexistence where borders are rendered irrelevant, calls the possibility of such visions into question and leaves the borders indistinguishable but still intact. However temporary or incomplete, the opening in Kanafani's work codifies the possibility of undoing the border in a way that is absent in Michael's. Both novels intervene in the same fundamental question: What alternatives exist to the status quo, and what kind of commitment and vision is possible? Both make clear that erasing the border is key, but *Returning to Haifa* declines to offer a detailed articulation of what this would look like in favour of broad strokes and open-ended conclusions. *Doves in Trafalgar* attempts to fill in the blanks but is left stymied, able to imagine life outside of these borders but unable to reimagine the borders themselves. The persistence of the border then forecloses the realisation of the novel's visions for coexistence. If both utopia and commitment necessitate the tearing down or remaking of borders, then perhaps the inverse is also true: the entrenchment of borders in Israel and Palestine tears at and corrodes the commitment to utopian visions and precludes the act of imagining this space as one that might someday be radically different. The border is a space that is post-utopian and post-commitment, and it offers little room for hope, the abode of dreamers, idealists and ideologues everywhere.

Conclusion: The Border as Object of Desire

The inability to imagine a possible alternative to present borders – escape, after all, would simply leave borders in place – or to see beyond them signals a failed commitment to visions of coexistence in Israel and Palestine. *Doves in Trafalgar* attempts to offer such a vision, but the regime of borders has become so entrenched that it forecloses a multitude of imaginative possibilities. While the resonance of Kanafani's widely read and translated work might in part be attributed to its arrival at the zenith of postcolonial liberation movements, the much more limited reception of *Doves in Trafalgar* (which, unlike many of Michael's novels, has not been widely translated) could reflect the fading resonance of such visions in a post-Second Intifada Israel and Palestine. By the time Michael's book appeared in 2005, scepticism towards such visions had grown – and has continued to grow – in the intervening decade. If the concept of utopia resides in tension between the ideal and the possible, a utopian vision that appears unachievable risks incurring the all too common critique of utopia as a naive form of wish fulfilment. It was not only the Second Intifada but also the Oslo Accords (an outcome of the 'peace process') of the 1990s that contributed to this development. Both of these developments inscribed additional borders onto the landscape, as the temporary borders of Oslo, the division of the West Bank into 'areas' of Palestinian and Israeli control, further subdivided the land and provided the legal basis and political justification for more checkpoints and walls.[113] The Green Line was no longer *the* border but it became one of many.

As its distinctiveness faded from the physical map, the Green Line became an object of political desire, particularly on the part of leftist activists and members of the peace camp who sought to solve the conflict by drawing the 'right' border. Paradoxically, this desire to enforce the border came in response to repeated Israeli violations of it. Israeli occupation, settlement and wall construction on the Palestinian side of the Green Line were met with calls to respect the border, the only one recognised by international law. The Green Line acquired a quasi-sacred status at the moments in which it was rendered irrelevant to military and political action. To return to the novels, while an ending that ignores the border is sufficient to sow commitment to a utopian future in *Returning to Haifa*, when the meaning of the Green Line was in flux as a recently opened border with an uncertain and contested future, a similar utopian desire in *Doves in Trafalgar* falters against the accumulation of borders – and a desire for settled borders – that has accelerated in the thirty-five years between the two works. Reading these two works together tells us that the border can no longer be ignored.

Notes

1. The annexation of East Jerusalem is unrecognised by the international community, and settlement construction is considered illegal under international law regarding military occupation of territories.
2. Yair Wallach refers to the tendency of both Israeli and Palestinian national maps to claim the entirety of the disputed territory as their own as 'mirror-maps'. Wallach, 'Trapped in mirror-images', pp. 258–9.
3. Palestinians from the West Bank and Gaza were not allowed to reside in Israel, but in the early years most Palestinians could travel into Israel on the condition that they returned home at night. See Chapter 1 for a more detailed discussion of this history.
4. It must be noted that faith in the two-state solution has waned considerably in recent years as lack of progress towards a peace agreement, expanding Israeli settlement and the continued blockade of Gaza make such a solution feel increasingly out of reach.
5. Israeli writer and journalist Yuval Ben-Ami's series of blog entries in which he chronicles a journey to trace the borders of Israel begins with a wistful nostalgia for simple, clear borders: 'My country once had internationally accepted borders, but that ended with the Six Day War of 1967.' Ben-Ami, 'The Round Trip, Part 1'.
6. It is worth noting the changing mobility restrictions for Palestinians since 1967. Though movement was never completely free for Palestinians under Israeli occupation, the notorious permit regime that severely restricts movement today did not begin to materialise until the first Intifada (1987–91); prior to that most Palestinians were able to come and go into Israel at will on the condition that they returned home in the evening, and Palestinian workers became a crucial source of cheap labour for Israel. However, in the early 1990s Israel began a policy of general closure that has continued until today and was entrenched by the implementation of the Oslo Accords. See Brown, 'The Immobile Mass', pp. 504–6.
7. Kassem Hawal made a film version of the novel in 1982, and there have been various stage versions of the story, including recently a bilingual version adapted by the Israeli playwright Boaz Gaon that was performed in Israel and the US. For more on Gaon's adaptation, see Sheetrit, 'Call Me Dov/Khaldūn/Ze'ev/Badīr', p. 92.
8. Michael's novel has only been translated into Turkish, in contrast to other novels like *Victoria* and *Trumpet in the Wadi*, which have found a larger global audience.
9. Harlow, 'Return to Haifa', p. 16.

10. The 1967 defeat served as a catalyst for invigorating Palestinian liberation movements, the most prominent of which was Yasser Arafat's *fataḥ* movement, by discrediting the Arab regimes as a potentially liberating force. Baumgarten, 'The Three Faces/Phases of Palestinian Nationalism', p. 32.
11. Abu-Manneh, *The Palestinian Novel*, p. 88.
12. See chapter 1 for a more detailed discussion of this idea.
13. See Harlow, *Resistance Literature*, and Khoury, 'Lil-Dhikra al-Arbaʿin li-Ghiyab Ghassan Kanafani', p. 157.
14. Harlow, 'Return to Haifa', p. 6.
15. For example, see Sufyan, 'Mulahizat hawl Tabiʿat Adab al-Muqawama'.
16. See, for instance, Siddiq, *Man is a Cause*, and Campbell, 'Blindness to Blindness', p. 53.
17. Abu-Manneh, *The Palestinian Novel*, p. 89.
18. The term Mizrahim refers to Jews of Arab descent, many of whom migrated to Israel from countries like Iraq, Morocco and Yemen willingly or unwillingly in the 1940s and 1950s.
19. The documentary *Forget Baghdad: Jews and Arabs – The Iraqi Connection* by the director Samir is structured around lengthy interviews with Michael, Ballas, Naqqash and other Jewish writers of Iraqi origin.
20. Most of the authors in this group chose to write in Hebrew, but Naqqash notably insisted on writing in Arabic his entire career, which severely limited the audience of his work.
21. In a 2015 interview, Michael stated that he has always considered himself an 'Arab Jew', which at least in part appears to be a political statement against the diametric opposition of Arab and Jew in Israeli state discourse. Ehling, 'Monday Interview: Sami Michael (Israel)'.
22. Orit Bashkin argues that this interest is more common among later generations of Mizrahi writers, but Michael seems to be an exception. Bashkin, 'When the Safras Met the Dajānīs', p. 141.
23. Bashkin, 'When the Safras Met the Dajānīs', p. 142.
24. Levy, 'Historicizing the concept of Arab Jews in the Mashriq', p. 464. Emphasis in the original.
25. Ibid. p. 464.
26. Hochberg, *In Spite of Partition*, p. 39.
27. Grumberg, *Place and Ideology*, p. 242.
28. Goldman, 'Sami Michael: "Israel – Most racist state in the industrialized world"'.
29. Ehling, 'Monday Interview: Sami Michael (Israel)'.

30. Sheetrit, 'Call Me Dov/Khaldūn/Ze'ev/Badīr', p. 104.
31. Benhabib, 'Mi She-Einenu Karish', pp. 223–4.
32. Karpel, 'With Thanks to Ghassan Kanafani'.
33. Ibid.
34. Sheetrit goes into significant detail about the plays on words Michael performs through his choice of names, which shed light on the relationship between the two novels. Sheetrit, 'Call Me Dov/Khaldūn/Ze'ev/Badīr', pp. 108–9.
35. Harlow, 'Return to Haifa', p. 16.
36. Karpel, 'With Thanks to Ghassan Kanafani'.
37. The Mandelbaum Gate was the checkpoint by which one crossed between Jordanian-controlled East Jerusalem and Israeli-controlled West Jerusalem prior to the 1967 war.
38. Kanafani, *Palestine's Children*, p. 150.
39. Jameson, *Archaeologies of the Future*, p. xv.
40. Ibid. p. xv.
41. Ibid. p. xi.
42. Ibid. p. xvi.
43. Levitas, *Utopia as Method*, p. 4.
44. Levitas, *The Concept of Utopia*, p. 1.
45. See for instance, Theodor Herzl's *Altneuland: Old-New Land*. In this tome, Herzl, the founding father of Zionism, lays out his vision of a democratic, pluralistic Jewish state in Palestine, nothing less than a 'new and happy form of human society', as the novel declares at the end. Herzl, *Altneuland*, p. 227. However, it also propagates the idea of Palestine as an empty land, a blank slate upon which to build a Jewish nation.
46. This is seen clearly in the Greater Israel movement and settler movement ideologies.
47. Bardenstein, 'Trees, Forests, and the Shaping of Palestinian and Israeli Collective Memory', pp. 149–50.
48. Khalidi, 'Observations on the Right of Return', pp. 29–30.
49. Mark Twain's account of his trip to Palestine provides a fascinating account of the contrast between the utopian, religiously inspired expectations of the 'Holy Land' and his perceptions of the reality he finds during his visit. He remarks upon the desire of pilgrims to find beauty in the region, but that their descriptions are 'well calculated to deceive' and that 'no ingenuity could make such a picture beautiful – to one's actual vision'. Twain, *The Innocents Abroad*, p. 509.

50. The nation is of course frequently understood through the lens of various types of imagination, most notably in Benedict Anderson's *Imagined Communities*.
51. This ground has been well covered in theoretical literature. For instance, see Foucault, *Discipline and Punish*, and Althusser, *Lenin and Philosophy and Other Essays*.
52. Marin, *Utopics*, p. 137.
53. Ibid. p. 140.
54. Ibid. p. 102.
55. Ibid. pp. 135–6.
56. Deleuze and Guattari, *Nomadology*.
57. As argued by Appadurai, *Modernity At Large*.
58. Kanafani, *Palestine's Children*, p. 187. In Arabic, Kanafani, *'A'id Ila Hayfa*, p. 79.
59. Kanafani, *'A'id Ila Hayfa*, pp. 68–9.
60. Kanafani, *Palestine's Children*, p. 182.
61. Kanafani, *'A'id Ila Hayfa*, pp. 68–9.
62. Kanafani, *Palestine's Children*, p. 188.
63. Ibid. p. 150.
64. *Ḥuzayrān al-rahīb*, which refers to June of 1967, the month of the Arab defeat in the Six-day War.
65. Kanafani, *Palestine's Children*, p. 149. In Arabic, Kanafani, *'A'id Ila Hayfa*, p. 6.
66. Kanafani, *Palestine's Children*, p. 151.
67. Thomas Abowd wrote of the opening of the border in Jerusalem and the Palestinians who crossed over to visit their former homes, often hopeful that they would be able to reclaim their property. Instead, their hopes were dashed and they became exiles within their own city. Abowd, 'Present and Absent', p. 250.
68. Kanafani, *Palestine's Children*, p. 160.
69. This discourse of Israel as a utopia of democracy and economic advancement in a sea of backwards authoritarianism continues to this day. The contemporary twist is the perception of Israel as a seductive high-tech paradise (the 'Silicon Wadi') of prosperity and tolerance (for LGBT rights, and so on). As an example of this narrative, see Senor and Singer, *Start-Up Nation*.
70. Kanafani, *'A'id Ila Hayfa*, p. 9.
71. Kanafani, *Palestine's Children*, p. 152. For instance, Wadi Nisnas remains a largely Palestinian area of Haifa, while Sāhat al-Ḥanātīr (Carriages Square) is now Paris Square.
72. Kanafani, *Palestine's Children*, pp. 152–3.
73. Kanafani, *Palestine's Children*, p. 149. In Arabic, Kanafani, *'A'id Ila Hayfa*, p. 6.

74. The sea in Palestinian literature and culture is a rich topic that warrants extended exploration in its own right.
75. Kanafani, *Palestine's Children*, p. 158.
76. Kanafani, *'A'id Ila Hayfa*, p. 12.
77. Anzaldúa, *Borderlands*/La Frontera, p. 26.
78. Kanafani, *Palestine's Children*, p. 180.
79. Ibid. p. 179.
80. See, for instance, al-'Azm, *al-Naqd al-Dhatt ba'd al-Hazima*.
81. Kanafani, *Palestine's Children*, p. 184; in Arabic, Kanafani, *'A'id Ila Hayfa*, p. 72.
82. Kanafani, *Palestine's Children*, p. 187.
83. Ibid. p. 181.
84. Ibid. p. 182.
85. Ibid. p. 151.
86. Ibid. p. 187.
87. Ibid. p. 180.
88. Michael, *Yonim be-Trafalgar*, p. 11.
89. Ibid. pp. 7–8.
90. Ibid. p. 8.
91. Hochberg, *In Spite of Partition*, p. 19.
92. Michael, *Yonim be-Trafalgar*, p. 14.
93. Ibid. p. 15.
94. Ibid. p. 15. This turn of phrase: 'in Israel, like in the entire Western World' reflects Israel's self-perception as a modern, western, even European, country. In this way it recalls *Returning to Haifa*'s critique of Israeli efforts to show the Palestinians that it is an enlightened, developed nation.
95. Ibid. p. 15.
96. Ibid. p. 30.
97. For instance, Israel's Highway 6 hugs the Green Line but one must make an effort to realise that there is a border (and the West Bank city of Tulkaram) within plain sight.
98. Michael, *Yonim be-Trafalgar*, p. 185.
99. The Second Intifada, or Palestinian uprising against Israeli rule, took place from 2000–05.
100. Michael, *Yonim be-Trafalgar*, p. 261.
101. Ibid. p. 261.
102. Ibid. p. 195.
103. Ibid. p. 194.

104. As a small example, the Israeli national anthem is called 'Ha-Tikva' ('The Hope').
105. The term 'present-absentee' refers to Palestinian refugees who remained inside Israel but were stripped of their property following 1948. See Schechla, 'The Invisible People Come to Light', p. 22.
106. Michael, *Yonim be-Trafalgar*, p. 196.
107. Ibid. p. 260.
108. Kanafani, *'A'id Ila Hayfa*, p. 6.
109. Ibid. p. 7.
110. Ibid. p. 10.
111. Michael, *Yonim be-Trafalgar*, p. 262.
112. Ibid. p. 196.
113. Brown, 'The Immobile Mass'.

3

Sayed Kashua, the Palestinian Hebrew Novel and the Failure of Coexistence

In the summer of 2014, a seven-week conflict broke out between Israel and Hamas. The immediate catalyst of the fighting was the kidnapping and killing of three Israeli teenagers in June, which was followed by the revenge killing of a Palestinian teenager in Jerusalem. Israel retaliated with military operations against Hamas, Hamas fired rockets into Israel, and heavy Israeli bombardment of the Gaza Strip caused many civilian deaths. In the context of a larger breakdown of the peace process in recent years, these events produced a narrative of deteriorating conditions and out of control intercommunal tension and incitement. That July, Palestinian-Israeli author Sayed Kashua published a column in *Haaretz* called simply 'Ze Nigmar', 'It is finished.' In this column, Kashua, who writes solely in Hebrew, dramatically declared that he has lost all hope in the idea of coexistence between Arabs and Jews. 'It is finished,' he tells his wife over and over, and when she asks him to explain, he writes, 'I stayed silent, and I knew that my attempt to live a shared life was over. That the lie that I told my children about Arabs and Jews sharing the same land equally is over.' With these statements Kashua abandons the hope that has animated much of his work as a writer and journalist, and he declares his intention to leave Israel, perhaps forever. He writes, 'I need to escape' (*laʿuf mi-po*, literally 'to fly away from here'). In this statement, he disavows the project for which he has advocated through much of his career. Kashua wrote these words as he was preparing to leave Israel for a teaching position in Illinois. He originally planned to remain abroad for a year, but the 2014 conflict caused him to reconsider, and as of 2018 he has not returned to

Israel. This itself was a surprising shift, for Kashua had long emphasised his desire to stay, stating frequently, even with the difficulties of life as a member of the Palestinian minority in Israel, it was his home.[1] Kashua, it seems, had lost hope.

Kashua, who has published three novels, written television shows and a screenplay, and maintained a weekly column in the Israeli newspaper *Haaretz* until November 2017,[2] is the most prominent Palestinian voice in the Israeli media and cultural scene. He has often used the megaphone afforded him to make a case for greater mutual understanding and coexistence. If Michael imagines coexistence as a grand utopian scheme, Kashua's conception of coexistence is much more quotidian. In his literary and journalistic writings, Kashua often concerns himself with the mundane realities of what a 'shared life' of equality between Arabs and Jews might look like, and how far short of this ideal Israeli society falls. Incremental more than revolutionary, Kashua and his protagonists largely accept the current political system in Israel as reality (if not ideal), but they seek to reform it into a fairer, more equitable version of itself. Moreover, he has framed his use of Hebrew as an effort to build a bridge between the Arab minority and Jewish majority.[3] Yet in this column, he disavows all of these long-held positions and dismisses this hopefulness as a facade of lies that suppress and silence the true impossibility of his dream.

In this chapter I contextualise this turning point in Kashua's political engagement within the broader trajectory of his work, in which his stated hope for a shared life has long been tinged with an undercurrent of doubt and failure. This undercurrent, moreover, has grown stronger with each novel he has published. The seeds of Kashua's despair are all too apparent in two of the novels that preceded his 2014 crisis, *Let It Be Morning* (*Ve-Yehi Boker*, 2004) and *Second Person Singular* (*Guf Sheni Yehid*, 2010). In this sense, we can view Kashua's writing as an elaboration on the failure of coexistence seen in the previous chapter. However, while Sami Michael's novel represents an attempt to finesse a literary dialogue with Kanafani's novel of resistance, Kashua stages clear breaks with the idea of coexistence after repeated failed attempts to make it possible. In both of Kashua's novels, the prospect of cross-cultural dialogue falls apart at the checkpoints and other borders that are repeatedly erected to disrupt his Palestinian characters' aspirations and efforts to forge some kind of equality. The border as a space in Kashua's work delineates the death of the coexistence project, buried under the burden of myriad forms of estrangement that, like Kashua's outburst in his 2014 column, emerge at moments of extreme tension and are embodied at various points in instances of silence and bursts of yelling. While integration into Jewish society might offer a tantalising opportunity for a 'shared life', Kashua's novels reveal the impossibility of true integration long before Kashua explicitly admitted so in 2014.

In *Let It Be Morning*, the unannounced and unexplained Israeli blockade of a Palestinian village within Israel – with water, electricity and communication cut off and the town entrance blocked by a closed checkpoint – physically marks the cultural and political exclusion of Palestinians from Israeli life. It shows how borders are constantly drawn and redrawn to ensure the exteriority of Palestinians, even those living on the 'inside'. When it is finally revealed that the blockade is part of a larger 'peace' deal to redraw the borders of Israel and Palestine to exclude Palestinian villages from the Jewish state, this new border marks and enforces an absolute separation and reveals the impossibility of 'crossing over' or bridging the divide. Moreover, the social breakdown produced by the blockade reveals the corrosive effect of borders within Palestinian society, as they produce a form of double alienation of Palestinian citizens of Israel from the state and from one another. *Second Person Singular*, in turn, stages a failure of the type of cultural integration and equality for which Kashua has advocated through two figures who seek to gain access to Jewish Israeli spaces and society in Jerusalem, only to fail and to turn against each other and lose their own senses of self in the process. As borders are drawn (and redrawn) to ensure Palestinians' cultural and physical exclusion, these efforts to integrate end in failure and produce forms of estrangement manifested through moments of silence, linguistic breakdown, narrative time shifts and emotional outbursts, eventually ending in the physical and metaphorical burial of the possibility of a shared life in Israel. Before turning to these novels, however, I begin by reconsidering Kashua's place within both Palestinian and Israeli literature in light of the understandings of estrangement, exile and borders that are central concerns of this chapter.

Silence, Estrangement and Checkpoints

Over the past decade Kashua has become a literary and cultural phenomenon in Israel. He has published three well-received bestselling novels: *Dancing*

Arabs ('*Aravim Rokdim*, 2002), in addition to *Let It Be Morning* and *Second Person Singular*. *Arab Labor* ('*Avoda 'Aravit*), which Kashua writes, is the first bilingual Hebrew–Arabic television show in Israel and has completed four seasons.[4] It was the top-rated sitcom in Israel, and swept the Israeli equivalent of the Emmys in 2013.[5] In 2015 Kashua wrote and produced a television drama, *The Screenwriter* (*Ha-Tasrita'i*), that centres on a writer who (like Kashua) creates a successful sitcom and becomes more and more alienated by the alter ego he created as the sitcom's protagonist. Finally, Kashua wrote a screenplay for a film based on his work, which was directed by the Israeli filmmaker Eran Riklis and released in 2013. The film, entitled *Dancing Arabs* ('*Aravim Rokdim*, though given the title *A Borrowed Identity* in the English language release), combines the narrative of two of his novels, *Dancing Arabs* and *Second Person Singular*. As a result of these successes, Kashua has come to occupy a cultural position unprecedented for Palestinians in Israel, who constitute more than 20 per cent of the population but are often ignored, silenced, and both marginalised in Israeli society and isolated from the larger Arab world.

Kashua is not, of course, the first Palestinian to write in Hebrew, and he belongs to a small but significant cadre of authors who have done so. The first Palestinian novel published in Hebrew, 'Atallah Mansour's *In a New Light* (*Be-Or Hadash*, 1966), tells the story of a Palestinian who is adopted and raised by a Jewish Israeli couple and only finds acceptance within his kibbutz by negating his Arab roots,[6] a narrative that the author later claimed was intended to attack the idealised Zionist space of the kibbutz.[7] Kashua's most notable predecessor is Anton Shammas, whose 1987 Hebrew novel *Arabesques* ('*Arabeskot*) created a firestorm of critical interest, both due to the 'virtuosity' of his writing[8] and because it appeared at a time in which historians and cultural critics in Israel were interrogating the ideological and historical underpinnings of Zionist ideology. When *Arabesques* appeared, a number of scholars, fellow authors and literary critics weighed in on the implications of Hebrew literature written by a Palestinian for both the state of the Hebrew language and of Israeli literature and culture more broadly.[9] In the intervening decades, scholars have expanded the scope of these analyses, looking at questions of translation, space and passing within works by Shammas and Kashua, and others.[10] These analyses most often position these writers in relation to Hebrew literature, which reflects not only the language of their works but the Israeli audience and institutions that have provided the impetus for their success.

To a greater extent than his predecessors, Kashua's works have resonated beyond the Israeli context in which they were produced and published, in the US and Europe and in the Arab world. Kashua's works and activities garner attention from the Arabic-language Palestinian press.[11] Unusually for a Palestinian writing in Hebrew, Kashua's first two novels have appeared in Arabic translations commissioned by publishing houses in Cairo and Beirut.[12] In this way, Kashua has become not only a source of insight for Israelis into the experiences of the country's large and oft-ignored Palestinian minority, but also a means for other Palestinians and Arabs to peer into the lives of Palestinians living in Israel, on the 'inside' (*al-dākhil*).[13] Kashua is one of the few Palestinian authors who has achieved reasonable recognition in both Israel and the Arab world. In this way he follows in the footsteps of Emile Habiby, whose Arabic novel *The Pessoptimist* (*al-Mutasha'il*, 1978) is one of the most recognisable depictions of the absurdities of Palestinian life in Israel.

While much critical attention has focused on Kashua's deployment of language, I begin my analysis of modes of estrangement and their relationship to borders in Kashua's work by focusing on his use of the lack of language, or silence. As Elias Khoury points out, the silent or mute Palestinian is a figure that has a long history in both Israeli and Palestinian literature, from A. B. Yehoshua's Arab whose tongue is cut off in 'Facing the Forests' to deaf mute twins in Anton Shammas' *Arabesques*.[14] Silence in the Palestinian literary context reflects a larger position of dispossession, expulsion and exile, which Khoury describes as 'part of the muteness of history, or, in other words, part of the inability of the victim to write the story'.[15] Borders offer a particularly visceral venue for the articulation of this muteness and its consequences in Ghassan Kanafani's novella *Men in the Sun*, which ends with the death of three Palestinians who die silently in the trunk of a car while waiting to cross the Iraq–Kuwait border. Upon discovering their deaths, the distraught driver yells repeatedly, 'Why didn't you knock on the walls of the tank?'[16] The answer, of course, is that they feared discovery by the border guards. The border as a space that enforces and reproduces various forms of silence is a point to which I will return in Chapter 4 in my discussion of Jabra Ibrahim Jabra's

In Search of Walid Masoud, in which an exiled Palestinian writer disappears and falls silent at the Iraqi–Syrian border, and in Chapter 6, in which Elia Suleiman's film *Divine Intervention* uses a mute protagonist and long periods of silence to reveal the absurd and deceptive theatricality of the checkpoint.

The necessity of silence, or learning when to be silent, appears repeatedly in Kashua's works. His first novel, *Dancing Arabs*, tells the story of a young Palestinian boy who receives a scholarship to study at a prestigious, mostly Jewish boarding school in Jerusalem. After his first week at the new school, the protagonist travels by bus to his hometown of Tira for the Rosh Hashanah holiday break. The bus comes to a checkpoint (*maḥsom*) near Ben Gurion Airport. While checkpoints are most commonly found within Palestinian territories and between those territories and Israel, they also exist inside of Israel proper. Police frequently set up temporary or permanent roadblocks near sensitive areas, as seen in this passage at the airport. They also appear often in heavily Palestinian areas of Israel, such as near entrances to Arab villages, and Palestinians, like the protagonist, are often singled out for extra scrutiny despite their status as Israeli citizens. At the checkpoint, a soldier forces the protagonist and his classmate Adel to disembark. Their appearance marks them as Palestinian, and therefore too much of a security threat to enter the airport grounds, so they must wait until the bus leaves the airport to re-board.[17] Adel remains unfazed, but the protagonist is traumatised and refuses to get back on the bus. He says, 'I screamed, I cried like a little child.'[18] The checkpoint produces this outburst, this breakdown into tears and screams that renders the protagonist a 'little child'. He calls his father but is so upset that he can barely talk, and later on when his father arrives, he remains silent.[19] The blockage of the *maḥsom* mutes him, renders him unable to speak. Yet the encounter with the checkpoint also produces what Grumberg describes as a moment of identification or recognition, in which he attains a hyperawareness of his own identity and his desire to control how he is seen and heard.[20] The protagonist ascribes his traumatic experience to his own linguistic imperfections and declares his determination to perfect his Hebrew so he can pass as Jewish and avoid these situations in the future.

The linguistic breakdown that the protagonist of *Dancing Arabs* experiences at the checkpoint recalls what Julia Kristeva terms the 'silence of polyglots'.[21] This silence emerges from one's imperfect grasp of the foreign language, and specifically the knowledge of this imperfection that creates a reluctance or hesitation to speak. In the novel, the knowledge of imperfection produces both silence and a desire to overcome that silence, as the protagonist seeks to rectify his linguistic imperfections. Kristeva writes that exile, alienation and estrangement do not by necessity require physical distance but can exist in much closer proximity. The stranger, she writes, 'is the hidden face of our identity, the space that wrecks our abode'.[22] The stranger is not defined *a priori* but rather is a category that individuals and societies produce and reproduce in many ways, including through language and space.

However, silence is not the only form of estrangement that emerges at borders, as we see in Jacques Derrida's description of his linguistic response to migrating from Algeria to France in *Monolingualism of the Other*. Derrida, a French-Algerian Jew, is haunted by the deprival of access to a mother tongue (a native language).[23] While aware that, many generations before, his ancestors spoke Arabic, and that the traces of this difference remain and distinguish him from other French speakers, he also knows he cannot access this lost linguistic heritage. The community of Algerian Jews, he writes, was subject to a 'triple dissociation' from Arabic and Berber language and culture, from French language and culture, and from Jewish memory and history.[24] Derrida is left with the French of his education, but it is a language that belongs to others, not to him. He is not born into this language but rather crosses into it, as he journeys across the Mediterranean from Algeria to France.[25] The act of crossing thus produces an awareness that he speaks and writes in a language not his own and produces a 'neurotic' obsession with 'pure' French, a desire to be 'more French than the French themselves'.[26] For Derrida, this knowledge produces not a general silence like Kristeva, but rather a desire to adhere to and enforce a new form of language, a pure French, that compulsively compensates for the gaping silence left by the lost and inaccessible mother tongue.

This adherence to purity recalls the attempts by the protagonist of *Dancing Arabs* to perfect his Hebrew, and seems to offer a 'solution' to the problem presented by the checkpoint, a notion reflected in Kashua's own career. In a 2012 *Haaretz* column, Kashua describes an incident on the set of *Arab Labor*, his television show, in which a Jewish Israeli production assistant walked into his office and exclaimed in Arabic with a 'terrible accent', '*Kiif*

Halak ya Zalameh?'[27] Kashua jokes that this is probably the only non-profane Arabic phrase that the man had learned during his mandatory military service. Kashua reacts angrily and yells at the man to get out of his office. He explains that he resents that after having learned Hebrew, he is still subject to a former soldier's 'garbled and slow' Arabic, as if he were a janitor or 'standing at one of the checkpoints'. Bad Arabic evokes 'standing' at the checkpoint, recalling the interminable and helpless waiting for permission to cross that many Palestinians experience in this space,[28] as well as the complex linguistic landscape of Arabic, Hebrew, and even sometimes English, that many Palestinians use as a means of 'getting through' the checkpoint.[29] The production assistant's Arabic is thus a means of reminding Kashua of 'his place', that is to say, at a border rather than in an office in Jerusalem. This echoes Abdelfattah Kilito's description of the experience of being forced to speak one's own language by a foreigner as a form of humiliation, silencing and even castrating.[30] Kashua responds to this moment of humiliation by turning to Hebrew. He deploys his own (superior) Hebrew skills to return the favour in the production assistant's language, which he uses 'to shout eloquently at a worker who tried to slight me'.[31] While the soldier's Arabic is 'garbled and slow', Kashua's Hebrew is 'eloquent', it flows smoothly, distinguishing Kashua's grasp of Hebrew from the choppy language of the checkpoint, yet another way in which the checkpoint silences, disrupts and corrupts language.

The checkpoint's linguistic distortions reveal one way in which this space marks Palestinians as other and produces exteriority. In the case of the Palestinian exiles in Kanafani's *Men in the Sun*, the border checkpoint produces silent death; in Sahar Khalifeh's *Wild Thorns*, her protagonist's encounter with soldiers' barking commands and buzzing surveillance equipment at the border checkpoint in the West Bank is the beginning of his progressive alienation from a Palestinian society transformed by occupation;[32] in *Dancing Arabs*, the early recognition of one's own outsider status[33] produces silence and later linguistic transformation. Grumberg suggests that the *maḥsom*, even as it marks a distinction between inside and outside, reveals the ease with which these divisions can be shifted and blurred.[34] Yet it seems that regardless of the particular type of border or particular subject position (whether in exile, under occupation or citizen of Israel), the Palestinian is an irrevocably estranged figure. Moreover, Palestinian attempts to change this, to move to the other side, nearly always fail, as we see in Said, the hapless protagonist of Habiby's novel *The Pessoptimist*, whose constant acts of submission and surrender to Israeli authorities only produce more failure and estrangement.[35] Thus we can begin to see the connections of estrangement to the border that neither silence nor language can overcome. In both of Kashua's later novels, *Second Person Singular* and *Let it Be Morning*, these multiple forms of estrangement are produced and enforced at and by the border, presaging Kashua's eventual declaration of the end of the coexistence project.

Blockaded: A Revealing Silence

In *Let It Be Morning*, Kashua's second novel, which is a largely chronological story narrated by an unnamed protagonist, the residents of a Palestinian village in the Triangle region of central Israel find themselves blocked in by a checkpoint that Israeli police have established at the town's entrance. The initial reaction is nonchalance, for temporary roadblocks are not unusual. However, as small oddities add up – there is no newspaper delivery, and the novel's protagonist cannot get in touch with the editor at the newspaper for which he writes – the severity of the situation comes into focus. Residents find that the entire village has been surrounded by barbed wire, and electricity, phone and water are cut off. Soon it becomes clear that this is a different kind of checkpoint, as no one is allowed through. It is not the mere inconvenience of an ID check, but rather a complete closure, and security forces open fire on people who try to approach the checkpoint with no explanation.[36] The town has been completely cut off from the outside world, and from the conveniences, escapes, distractions and deceptions of modern life. Finally, the siege is lifted, but the village residents find that, as part of an Israeli–Palestinian peace deal, borders have been redrawn and all Arab areas have been ceded to a new Palestinian state. Kashua's depiction of the blockade and excision of this village from the borders of Israel exposes and marks as failure both the fiction of equality between Israelis and Palestinians, and the notion of a redrawn Green Line and the establishment of a Palestinian state (the 'two state' solution) as an appealing option.

The village blockade produces and is enacted by forms of silence and communication breakdown. Phone lines are cut, and entry and exit from the village are forbidden, leading to a complete severing of the flow of information. In the absence of communication, misinformation and wild rumours of nuclear war and an Egyptian invasion of Israel run rampant and produce panic.[37] The Israeli soldiers manning the checkpoint refuse to explain or respond to the increasingly urgent demands of the villagers for an explanation. Some workers try to cross the checkpoint but are shot, with no warning or fanfare, and the pleas, screams and demonstrations of increasingly desperate villagers are met with silence.[38] At this checkpoint, the silence that allows one to be shot without warning is deadly, a form of violence that reflects the checkpoint's function as what Apter describes as a 'threshold of untranslatability'.[39] It is not simply the blockage but the increasingly desperate attempts to make sense of the blockage that engender panic, as the border's effectiveness relies on the production of fear and misinformation.

Yet even as it is deceptive, the blockade in *Let It Be Morning* exposes other deceptions and tensions as it reveals existing and festering forms of estrangement. Shortly before the blockade, the novel's protagonist, a journalist who has lived and worked at a Hebrew-language newspaper in Jerusalem for many years, has returned to his home village after life in the city became untenable due to anti-Arab hostility during the Second Intifada.[40] He faces self-righteous declarations by Israeli Jews that Palestinian citizens of Israel should 'say thank you' for Israeli tolerance of their presence.[41] Despite his successful work as one of the few journalists who could access Palestinian areas of the Occupied Territories, this rhetoric of isolation seeped into his workplace, which he had considered a safe space.[42] His colleagues casually joke that he was 'throwing stones at the entrance' to the building, or sarcastically instruct the guards to 'search him carefully, he's suspicious'.[43] Although expressed in jest, these statements reveal an anxiety toward and fear of Arabs that is palpable to the narrator. The words used – 'search', 'suspicious' – mimic the terminology of ID checks and roadblocks and mark a militarisation of communication between Jewish and Palestinian Israelis. The terminology and practices of checkpoints expand to touch all aspects of life for the protagonist in ways that are not only linguistic but spatial – his family finds graffiti sprayed on the wall of their apartment building declaring that 'No Arabs = peace and security',[44] recalling the checkpoint's delineation of zones of inclusion and exclusion even in ostensibly shared spaces. Kashua's utilisation of the hostile language of the checkpoint presages the protagonist's impending physical separation from Jewish society.

While the blockade obviously presents a new physical barrier to the residents of the village, it also reflects and formalises the estrangement and separation that already existed in other forms. It does not sever the protagonist's connection to the city, for that has already occurred as a result of the increasingly hostile atmosphere that he and his family faced. It does not prevent him from going to work, as circumstances had already rendered him practically jobless. However, it makes certain deceptions impossible. Before the border appears, the protagonist leaves the village every day and goes to the city so that he can pretend for his family that he remains fully employed. He describes this farce as predictable and routine, saying that he will drop his wife off at the school where she works, at which point 'she will ask me when I'll come home, and I will say I'm not sure . . . Sometimes, when there are attacks or major military operations, I stay to circle around the streets of the city until late, since it's only logical' that work would be busy those days.[45] The imposition of the blockade disrupts the protagonist's attempt to structure his days according to some kind of logic and to maintain a fiction of normalcy, but he greets this with a sarcastic exclamation of relief, saying that it 'saves' him from his 'useless' wandering.[46] The blockade in *Let It Be Morning* thus functions as a truth-telling device or a mirror, imposing a physical demarcation of an extant situation and making it explicit and undeniable.[47]

The imposition of this border, and the 'peace' agreement that it entails, reconfigures existing divisions among Palestinians and groups Palestinian citizens of Israel with Palestinians in the West Bank and Gaza, who previously lived under separate legal and spatial regimes. Undergirding such a hypothetical plan, which finds echoes in Israeli political rhetoric around 'territory exchange' and transfer, is an essentialising politics of national identity that assumes a singular Palestinian subjectivity and identity implicit in the logic of a two-state solution. However, Kashua uses the hypothetical border imposition and closure as a catalyst to interrogate these simplistic understandings of national identity by using them as a device to stage conflicts on both an individual and communal level.[48] Indeed, we see not commonality but multiplying forms of estrangement, both that of the protagonist's alienation from his village and his village's alienation from any larger notion of a Palestinian collective.

The protagonist's descriptions of his home village suggest a sense of being out of place, a sense shared by many village residents that perhaps reflects what Grumberg describes as 'spatial flimsiness' of a place that fails to provide access to either Israeli modernity or Palestinian authenticity.[49] The protagonist notices small differences, like the types of cars people drive, or the shift among female students at his former school toward religious clothing, a relatively new trend.[50] While seemingly insignificant, these changes cumulatively produce a feeling of unfamiliarity on the narrator's part and lead him to declare that 'I no longer recognise this place, I recognise a different place that answers to the same name'.[51] Others make similar comments about the changing character of the village as they try to comprehend the narrator's decision to return to a place that most hope to escape.[52] On the first page of the novel, as the protagonist awakens in his childhood bedroom, his mother tells him reassuringly, 'Do you see? Nothing has changed.'[53] Yet his immediate response is to notice that she looks 'so different, so tired and old'. This narrative is not simply one of change but of decay and decline, which the narrator sees everywhere he looks in the people and places of his village.

The blockade reveals and accelerates this process of social and physical decay, as the village cracks under the pressure of isolation. The narrator notes the speed with which filth and dirt consume the town's spaces.[54] The border also exposes (sometimes barely) concealed tensions within the village, which in turn reflect larger conflicts within the Palestinian community in Israel. For instance, given the proximity of the village to the West Bank, one of the issues that appears repeatedly in the novel is that of the relationship between Palestinians who hold Israeli citizenship, and non-citizens from the West Bank who have come to Israel for work, often illegally. Early in the novel, the protagonist and his brother-in-law, Ashraf, are waiting in a truck to cross a roadblock in the village and they encounter West Bank Palestinians begging for work. Their apparent desperation bothers the narrator, but Ashraf tells him 'not to pity them' (*al tirḥam ʿalayhem*, which can also mean 'do not have mercy on them') because their begging disguises their true feelings, which are that all Arabs in Israel are 'traitors and collaborators'.[55] Relations between Palestinians with Israeli citizenship and those in the West Bank indicates mutual suspicion and distrust, and very little if any solidarity or common cause. Ashraf goes on to describe West Bank Palestinians as '*ha-ʿam hakhi dafuk ba-ʿolam*', 'the craziest people in the world'.⁵⁶ The word used for 'crazy', *dafuk*, is a slang term that can also mean 'terrible', 'stupid' or 'unsuccessful' and connotes a mix of disdain and amusement.⁵⁷ Notably, he also uses the term *ʿam*, which means 'people' as in a national or ethnic group, to refer to the West Bank Palestinians as a people or a nation distinct from his own, producing a form of othering that mimics and compounds Israeli exclusionary practices.

The villagers and their leaders, desperate to discern the cause for the blockade and to end it, scapegoat the West Bank Palestinians, particularly undocumented workers, and decide to turn over all migrants to the security forces.⁵⁸ At night, hundreds of youth, many of whom just that morning were 'waving green and red flags, and the flag of Palestine',⁵⁹ are 'drafted' to round up the workers using cars, trucks and buses, and gather them in a school. The villagers turn them over to the authorities, who in turn respond with bullets, making clear that the Israelis make no distinction between the different groups of Palestinians.⁶⁰ The villagers' actions, along with the use of military terminology like *meguyas* ('drafted' or 'conscripted') reproduce the language of Israeli police and military raids against Palestinians in the Occupied Territories. Just as the protagonist's Jewish colleagues and neighbours in Jerusalem project the rhetoric of checkpoint security onto him, so the village's residents turn this same language against the Palestinian workers from the West Bank. It also vacates nationalist rhetoric and symbols of their meaning, as slogans of unity quickly give way to internecine violence. The imposition of a new border here not only delineates an Israeli inside and a Palestinian outside, but it also produces multiple forms of Palestinian division and exclusion and it belies the notion of the border as a space that can produce peace or stability.

Much as the outbreak of fighting in 2014 triggered Kashua's declared abandonment of his hope for a 'shared life', the similarly extreme moment of blockade in *Let It Be Morning* unleashes latent conflicts and tensions. For Kashua, the border is a truth telling device, and as such it challenges illusions and narratives that have continued to self-perpetuate. The appearance of the border – the *maḥsom*, the blockade, the complete severing of any connection to the outside world, and the eventual redrawing of the Israeli border to exclude the residents of the village – contests the illusion that a comfortable life is possible for Arabs in a state that is hostile to them, the illusion of

Palestinian unity, and ultimately the illusion that coexistence is even possible. The final solution, the 'peace' agreement that comes at the end of the novel, decisively rejects the possibility of a shared life in favour of division by drawing a new border that permanently separates Israelis and Palestinians. The hybrid terms Arab–Israeli and Palestinian–Israeli are no longer operable, as any possibility of some kind of dual identity is stripped away. Stunned, Kashua's characters watch as they become citizens of a Palestinian state, highly sceptical that they will be better off there. As they stand watching the Palestinian flag fly over their village, the tone is not celebratory but mournful. They mourn not their severed connection with an Israeli state that offered them little respect, but rather the possibility of a life not defined along ethno-national lines. The result of the border's incursion and the conflicts – between Palestinians and Israelis and among Palestinians themselves – is that it exposes and perpetuates new forms of estrangement and exile. Both of these states of being for Kashua are symptoms of the failure of coexistence that is marked by the new border.

Crossing Strangers

In *Let It Be Morning*, the imposition of the blockade forces a reckoning with illusions of coexistence. But if the border is a truth-telling device, how can it also be deceptive, which is one of the claims of this monograph? In order to address this apparent tension, I turn to *Second Person Singular*, in which a different set of borders function as sites for moments of misinterpretation and misreading staged by two Palestinian–Israeli protagonists living in Jerusalem, a young social worker named Amir and a middle-aged unnamed lawyer. These characters attempt to rectify their estrangement from both Israeli and Palestinian society by negotiating and straddling a socio-spatial divide through moments of silence, language play and deception at checkpoints and along the border between East and West Jerusalem. Yet their efforts cast coexistence not as a liberating paradigm but rather as a compulsory, hollow artifice that produces further forms of estrangement. Moreover, *Second Person Singular* shows us that even as borders reveal important truth claims for Kashua, they do so through moments of deception. These borders reinforce the estrangement entailed in 'coexistence' as currently conceived, even as they conceal it from view.

Structurally, the novel alternates between third-person sections about the lawyer, all set in the present day, with a first-person narration of Amir's story, which begins six years previously and extends to the present, where the two characters meet at the novel's climax. Amir lives a lonely life and works an unrewarding job as a social worker. Out of boredom, he begins a night job caring for a Jewish man named Yonatan who was severely injured in a car accident years before and remains alive but brain dead.[61] Slowly Amir begins to use Yonatan's ID and clothes to disguise himself as Jewish, and eventually he adopts Yonatan's identity, family and aspirations as his own. The lawyer styles himself a member of the city's elite who eats at all of the trendiest restaurants and leases swanky office space in the centre of (largely Jewish) West Jerusalem. He attempts to straddle the divide through an ostentatious form of conspicuous consumption, but the careful balance he has constructed collapses when he finds a letter from his wife to Amir, written many years before, in a second-hand book he purchased. Mistakenly believing that his wife has been unfaithful, he embarks on a manic quest to find Amir/Yonatan and confront him and his wife. The unexpected encounter between the stories of Amir and the lawyer destabilises the various artifices and performed selves that both have carefully constructed in order to negotiate spatial-social divides faced by Palestinians in Israel.

As in *Doves in Trafalgar* and the passage at the airport checkpoint in *Dancing Arabs*, in *Second Person Singular* the relative presence and absence of borders is determined in large part by ethnicity. This is particularly true of border spaces such as the checkpoint that act as filters, allowing some people through, stopping others, and delaying yet others.[62] Yet the novel emphasises the ambiguity that such judgments entail, and its engagement with the question of ethnic difference emphasises moments of (mis)reading and (mis)interpretation through characters who evince a hyperawareness of the modes by which ethnicity is signalled (names, language, clothing) and by which it can be unsettled or subverted. The novel is replete with moments of deceptive performances of ethnicity, particularly by Amir, who (as both himself and as Yonatan) develops and uses this ability to deceive those attempting to 'read' his ethnicity to negotiate and cross borders of various sorts. The first, and most prevalent, is the divide between East and West Jerusalem, about which a few words are necessary. *Second Person Singular* engages repeatedly with the divide between largely Jewish West Jerusalem and predominantly Palestinian East Jerusalem, which was controlled by Jordan from 1948 until the Israeli conquest of the West Bank in 1967. Despite official attempts at unification, including the establishment of a single municipality, which focus not on true integration but rather on facilitating Jewish settlement in the largely Palestinian East Jerusalem, the city remains starkly divided both physically and culturally. Large gaps in standards of living exist, and government policy makes it very difficult to build new housing in Palestinian areas, while encouraging Jewish settlements in East Jerusalem.[63] This divide is inscribed into the cityscape as well. Public transportation is largely separated,[64] which necessitates a less than seamless transfer to travel from one part of the city to the other. Moreover, as one crosses from West to East on foot, manicured sidewalks and well-paved boulevards quickly give way to narrow, rutted roads, reflecting the vastly inferior services provided to the city's Palestinian areas. Though there is no longer a physical barrier, and the distinction has been blurred in some spots, the border between East and West remains tangible and visible in many ways, much like the rest of the Green Line seen in Chapter 2.

Amir learns to use language in particular to negotiate this divide. As he begins to work for Yonatan, the previous caretaker, a man from the West Bank named Ayub, meets Amir and takes him to Yonatan's home in the wealthy West Jerusalem neighbourhood of Bet Ha-Kerem. They meet at the Damascus Gate bus station in East Jerusalem, and travel to the western part of the city, crossing the former seam line that divided the city in two parts (the novel makes note of Ayub darting across the street that marks this border). Once on the western side, they board a bus that will transport them to Yonatan's home. As they board a crowded Jewish bus, Ayub abruptly switches from Arabic to Hebrew. The bus is a space in which, as the passage above from *Dancing Arabs* shows, identifying oneself as Arab subjects one to suspicion and security checks. Ayub's use of Hebrew then, is an attempt to avoid and deflect attention. Amir is surprised by the unexpected switch to Hebrew. He marvels that Ayub did it as if it were the 'most obvious thing in the world',[65] and soon learns to emulate this strategy as he travels from East to West Jerusalem each evening to work; even though the border has ostensibly been open for decades, this linguistic switch reveals the extent to which the divide remains palpable and is marked by language.

As the novel progresses and Amir engrosses himself in Yonatan's world, he eventually begins to use Yonatan's ID to disguise himself as Jewish in a much more extensive manner than linguistic code-switching. A trip to his childhood village reveals how not only passing as Yonatan but strategic switching of identities allows him to traverse borders with greater ease. En route from Jerusalem, he transfers from an Egged (mostly Jewish) bus to an Arab shared taxi at the Sirkin Junction near Petach Tikva. This crossroads functions as a transfer point on multiple levels, a space in which Amir not only changes modes of transport but also names and languages. Entry and exit into this crossroads are controlled by checkpoints and ID inspections. Amir shows one ID to a security guard as he disembarks the Egged bus, identifying himself as Yonatan.[66] Then, as the shared taxi departs for Jaljulia, it stops at a police checkpoint, where Amir shows a Druze policeman his own ID card, making sure to pull out the 'right set of papers'.[67] As Amir boards the taxi to Jaljulia, he says, 'I nodded at the drivers and mumbled against my will (*be' al koreḥi*), "*Salām 'alaykum*".'[68] He wants to suppress his Arabic, and he only utters this greeting at all out of compulsion (*koreḥ*). He does not enunciate the Arabic greeting clearly but 'mumbles' it, producing a suppressed, fractured language. The return to Arabic and to the village proves unbearable for Amir and conjures up 'bad and irrepressible memories'.[69] The transition between Amir and Yonatan and between Arabic and Hebrew is traumatic, and like the production assistant who subjects Kashua to 'checkpoint Arabic', the Arabic produced at this roadblock reveals the fracturing effect of these spaces on language. Switching is not done with ease but is a fraught process that reveals the uneven cultural, linguistic and political terrain that such borders create and enforce.

Amir's anxiety at his return to the village and to Arabic traces his use of multiple languages and identities as a symptom of formative experiences of estrangement. Amir's childhood, which the novel recounts in a series of flashbacks, is marked by distinct forms of alienation from both Jaljulia and the Jewish majority culture. Much like Tira in *Let It Be Morning*, the novel depicts this village as a closed off and claustrophobic space marked by an intense suspicion of strangers (*zarim*). The suspicion of outsiders in Jaljulia stems at least in part from Israeli police practices of resettling so-called collaborators, Palestinians who act as informants or in other ways aid Israeli intelligence gathering efforts, to other Palestinian villages in order to protect them from retaliation. Amir and his mother, who were resettled in Jaljulia following a domestic dispute, find integration into the village impossible, as they are immediately marked as possible collaborators. As a result, Amir faces endemic bullying, including beatings, threatening notes and insults against his mother.[70] Amir says, 'I was a stranger (*zar*) in school, a stranger in the village, with a strange name (*shem muzar*) like all of the other strangers in Jaljulia.'[71] Amir's status as stranger is not a temporary condition that can be rectified through an integration effort or the passage of time; it is carried in his name and cannot be altered. This irreconcilable childhood alienation in effect orphans him, creating an unbridgeable distance between himself and his mother, whose attempts to shield him from bullying only push him away: 'I started to keep my distance from her and today I regret that I can't so much as imagine a hug from her.'[72] Her desire to protect him from bullying leads her to remove him from his Jaljulia school and 'smuggle' (*hivriha*) him into a school in the nearby Jewish city of Petach Tikva.[73] The escape (*briha*) from the local school emphasises the depiction of the village as a claustrophobic trap and the Jewish school as a refuge. In Petach Tikva he is merely ignored, and he revels in his anonymity after the bullying of his previous school: 'The kids simply did not speak to me and I did not speak to them.'[74] Yet he devotes himself to mastering Hebrew, eventually learning to 'speak like them' and to write better Hebrew than his Jewish classmates.[75] Like French for Derrida in *Monolingualism of the Other*, Amir's mastery of Hebrew is a compulsive attempt to compensate for a form of cultural orphanhood. Yet his mastery does not produce a bridge between cultures, as Kashua himself hopes for, which implies a form of shared experience and conversation, but rather escape through silence and isolation.

Amir's formative experience of seeking refuge in Hebrew and a Jewish environment replicates itself in adulthood, as his position working for Yonatan leads him to quit his job and leave his apartment in East Jerusalem, leaving him semi-homeless, staying at Yonatan's at night and roaming the city during the day.[76] He establishes an itinerary of wanderings, like Benjamin's *flâneur*, who is at once carefree and lost; his gaze is 'alienated' and not at home in the city, he seeks 'refuge in the crowd'.[77] Yet for Amir, in a manner that mimics his adolescent embrace of anonymity in the Jewish school he attended, his wanderings bring not anxiety but a feeling of 'calm' (*rigiʻa*).[78] As he assumes more and more aspects of Yonatan's identity, he begins to find a sense of belonging; he uses Yonatan's identity to apply for and matriculate into an art academy to study photography, where he finds the acceptance by his peers that was denied to him as a child. Yonatan's mother, Ruchaleh, gradually takes on the role of surrogate parent, rectifying his estranged orphanhood from his birth mother. Amir begins to entertain a wholesale transformation into a Jewish Israeli man, which might allow him to attain the acceptance that was denied to him both by Palestinian and Jewish societies as his previous self.

Yet Kashua casts this tantalising possibility into doubt in the very moment that it is elucidated, demonstrating the elusiveness of the stable identity that Amir/Yonatan seeks. Yonatan's health has begun to decline, so Amir and Yonatan's mother collude to end Yonatan's life and bury him as Amir, allowing Amir to adopt Yonatan's identity permanently without fear of discovery. This burial requires one final border crossing, as Amir arranges to transfer the body by ambulance from the morgue at Shaare Zadek, a Jewish neighbourhood in West Jerusalem, to the cemetery in the Palestinian area of Beit Safafa, during which he must also switch Yonatan's ID with his own so that the dead body is buried under Amir's name.[79] Speaking in Arabic, he explains that there is no need for an elaborate ceremony because the deceased is a 'stranger' (*gharīb*).[80] This is an interesting moment for language choice in Kashua's text, because while it repeatedly describes Amir as *zar*, using the Hebrew word for 'stranger', here Kashua does not use the Hebrew word but instead transliterates the Arabic word for 'stranger', *gharīb*, into Hebrew letters. This linguistic switch is a marked choice; it reminds us of his Palestinian identity at the very moment when he buries his Palestinian self. Gil Hochberg describes a similar textual switch to Arabic in a story by Orly Castel-Bloom, invoked by a character's mother, as an 'unexpected threat: a fleeting memory that might flash up at any moment and "bite"'.[81] Through this outburst of Arabic, the novel, at the very moment in which Amir tries to excise his Arab self, invokes it linguistically and signals the impossibility of such an excision.

By referring to himself as a stranger, Amir also claims as his own an epithet (stranger) that has dogged him, hurled at him as an insult, all of his life. The derogatory nature of this term is evident even in the moment of

Yonatan/Amir's burial, as the cemetery's gravediggers and onlookers curse the unknown dead man. One elderly man yells, 'Who is going to pray for a dog like that?' as Yonatan's body passes through the neighbourhood. The undertaker encourages Amir to tip the young men who bury Yonatan, and one of the young men yells, 'Yeah, let the little fucker pay.' Amir pretends not to understand the insult and pulls out 100 shekels to give to the men.[82] To preserve his disguise as Yonatan, Amir remains silent, and listens to the curses that rain down upon him and Yonatan's body with no reaction. The silence this moment produces, however, is distinct from the uncertain silence of Ayub's unexpected switch from Arabic to Hebrew, or the quiet relief Amir finds in his escape to the silence of the Jewish school in Petach Tikva. Instead, Amir's silence at the grave is mournful; he mutely watches the young men bury him, as one of them 'spat into the grave and laughed'.[83] He enters the car, preparing to leave, but he keeps returning his gaze to the men as they bury Yonatan. He cannot keep his eyes off of them but he cannot speak either. This experience unsettles him and the reader, as he watches the final indignities faced by the stranger, the ones he himself has born all of his life, but is unable or unwilling to say a word. Silence no longer functions as a respite from estrangement for Amir, but a perpetuation of it. His silent acceptance of his own status as stranger is the price he must pay to become Yonatan. Yet it also shows that for a Palestinian to gain access to the comfort and privileges accessible to Israeli Jews, he must suffer concealment, deception and silent acquiescence to multiple forms of estrangement. A far cry from the 'shared life' for which Kashua advocated, Amir's transformation reveals the impossibility of true coexistence in contemporary Israel.

(Mis)Reading Borders

If Amir's failed attempts to rectify his estrangement by crossing the Arab–Jewish divide reveals the impossibility of coexistence and leads to a severing of the self, the lawyer traces his own less traumatic alienation back to the policing of the Arab–Jewish divide, which he experiences through constant ID checks on buses while a student in Jerusalem. He describes these experiences not as threatening but as 'annoying, grating, constraining'.[84] He does not rebel but ingratiates himself to authority figures, smiling and cooperating enthusiastically as they check his ID; his humiliation prompts him to seek to become a model minority citizen of Israel who emulates the customs and practices of the Jewish majority. In this respect, the lawyer recalls a line of earlier literary figures, from Habiby's Said in the *Pessoptimist* to Atallah Mansour's titular character in *Wa-Baqiyat Samira* (*Samira Remained*, 1962),[85] who seem to internalise common Jewish Israeli prejudices towards Palestinians. As the attorney becomes wealthier, he buys the nice clothes worn by his Jewish peers, and he finds that he faces much less harassment. Rather than resorting to language and impersonation, the lawyer discovers that money, and in particular the image of wealth that intimidates border guards and police (who in Israel often hail from the lower classes) has freed him from the discriminatory treatment he faced as a young Palestinian.[86] As an adult he moves comfortably in East and West Jerusalem. He rents an office on King George Street in the heart of West Jerusalem, and he lives in a neighbourhood that is the best in East Jerusalem and is considered 'friendly' by the Jewish population.[87] His children attend a bilingual Arab–Jewish school, and he perceives himself as enlightened and cultured. Unlike Amir, he does not attempt to fully immerse himself in West Jerusalem, nor does he seek to challenge the divide, just become comfortable with inhabiting it.

For both Amir and the lawyer, the ability to straddle the Arab–Jewish divide and cross borders in Jerusalem and elsewhere does not contest but rather relies upon assumptions of ethnic difference. Amir has learned to play with the differences, and to use them to his advantage, while the lawyer inhabits the Arab–Jewish divide, and he does so by policing other forms of fissure within Palestinian and Israeli society. One of these is socio-economic, hence his obsession with signifiers of status, such as eating at the best sushi restaurant in town.[88] Another is based on citizenship, as he refuses to socialise with local Palestinian residents of Jerusalem, who unlike him do not hold Israeli identity cards. This represents a kind of internalisation of Israeli state discourses that cast Israeli Palestinians as 'good Arabs'[89] in opposition to the violent Palestinians of the West Bank and Gaza. The lawyer uses his social and economic access to redraw cultural divides not between Arab and Jew, but between rich and poor and citizen and non-citizen so as to reposition himself on the side of privilege. He projects the appearance of successful coexistence, but his compulsive desire to maintain and project status reflects a profound insecurity about his place both within Palestinian society and within the larger web of Jewish–Palestinian relations in Israel. Coexistence, for the lawyer, is a superficial artifice that reproduces rather than subverts social and economic power relations.

The lawyer's concern with status and appearance is reflected in a strong interest in reading and interpretation. His weekly stops at a bookstore, in which he purchases books recommended in the *Haaretz* book review section, and his nightly reading sessions are, like many of his actions, a means of maintaining his status and avoiding the 'embarrassment' of appearing uneducated.[90] He enjoys the appearance of reading highbrow literature, so he purchases books by Calvino and Tolstoy out of a desire to read all of the great works that 'his Jewish peers had read'.[91] He basks in the bookseller's praise of his literary taste but sheepishly neglects to tell her that he could not read past thirty pages.

The lawyer's obsession with reading – and his failure to read – is also reflected in his constant attempts to discern and interpret ethnic difference. In the novel's epilogue, the lawyer visits a photography exhibit that features works by Amir (who at this point has adopted the identity of Yonatan). At first the lawyer finds the works unremarkable, but as he looks closer he is impressed by the juxtaposition of detail and ethnic ambiguity: 'The lawyer, who was always proud of his ability to discern between Arab and Jew at a glance, had a hard time determining the ethnicity of these people.'[92] In a manner parallel to the novels he admires but does not read, his inability to read ethnic ambiguity both unsettles and intrigues him. As someone who has ostensibly mastered a specific form of coexistence, ethnic difference provides a code through which he reads the world and makes it legible. The lawyer's experience of 'coexistence' makes sense only when there are clearly delineated categories of ethnic difference, and the blurring of such lines leaves him disoriented.

Through the course of the novel, the lawyer gradually becomes entangled in Amir's deceptions, and the latter's acts of crossing and identity switching produce moments of misreading and misinterpretation that collapse the lawyer's superficial artifice of coexistence. Moments of misreading and misunderstanding have appeared repeatedly in representations of Palestinians in Israel. The lawyer's attempts to ingratiate himself to sceptical authority figures recall Emile Habiby's memorable character Said, a foolish figure who curries favour with authorities through acts of surrender and collaboration. Said constantly misunderstands signals and words, and Lital Levy argues that his mistranslations between Hebrew and Arabic in particular expose and subvert colonial state discourses.[93] A Palestinian who finds himself in the new state of Israel after 1948, Said often makes a fool of himself, as his clueless naivety leads to constant mishaps and misunderstandings.[94] Jeffrey Sacks argues Said's name, 'Pessoptimist' (*al-Mutasha'il*), a portmanteau of the Arabic words for optimist and pessimist, signifies a fissure that is embodied within the character of Said, a contradiction that he must navigate.[95] In an analogous but not identical fashion, the lawyer, a 'model Arab citizen' of Israel who affirms and is a stakeholder in the hierarchies of ethnicity, class and citizenship, misreads and misunderstands information as he seeks to decipher the movements and deceptions of Amir/Yonatan. These misreadings reveal the farce of a complicit form of coexistence to which he aspires.

The lawyer's misreading begins with his discovery of a note his wife Leila had written to Amir many years before, in a second-hand copy of the *Kreutzer Sonata* that once belonged to Yonatan. Though the letter was written many years prior to their wedding, when Amir and Leila were colleagues and potential love interests, the lawyer mistakenly believes his wife is cheating on him. He starts scrutinising her actions and surreptitiously checking on her whereabouts to 'test' her truthfulness. An easily explainable delay in her return home becomes incontrovertible evidence that she is cheating on him, and he reads her genuine fear at his anger as 'pretending to be scared'.[96] His misreading of the note from his wife to Amir causes him to spin into a rage; first he imagines killing his wife, and then he decides to file for divorce using the Sharia courts in East Jerusalem in order to receive more favourable terms than under civil Israeli law. He declares that he has abandoned his formerly 'enlightened' beliefs and now is proud to be a 'conservative' Arab who concerns himself with concepts like 'honour'.[97] Though he has tried strenuously to escape anti-Arab stereotypes imposed upon him, he now retreats to and claims these stereotypes as his own, embodied in a fit of male jealousy, as the only way he knows of acting authentically Arab. He becomes a parody of a stereotype and shows that, far from overcoming or transcending discrimination and difference, his efforts to make his place in Jerusalem has caused him to internalise them.

The lawyer's crisis is also a pedagogical moment that pushes him to recognise his own complicity, as he acknowledges his failure to see the role of the occupation and discrimination in producing the ills in Palestinian society[98] that he so readily critiqued and rejected in order to ingratiate himself with the Jewish majority. He comes to see the coexistence to which he aspired as predicated on a blindness to systemic factors and built on a neoliberal fiction of individual choice and personal responsibility. It is only when he acknowledges and comprehends his complicity that he is able to decipher Amir's mysteries, culminating in his confrontation of Amir/Yonatan and the latter's confessional. He appears at Ruchaleh's home and demands to speak to Amir, then confronts him with all of the evidence he has gathered of Amir's deception. Amir feigns innocence but only briefly, quickly surrendering and finding relief in the unburdening of his secret. For both, this moment allows a rare moment of authentic engagement with another, as they are bonded by their shared estrangements. In this moment of mutual recognition, moreover, they are able to transcend the various forms of deception imposed upon them by the divisions of ethnicity and physical borders.

Conclusion

The impossibility of coexistence, when revealed, is a shock that produces a re-evaluation of assumptions and priorities. The lawyer's confrontation with Amir provides the novel's narrative climax, and in the epilogue that follows, he displays a new sense of humility and self-doubt in his ability to place and categorise others. Kashua's own acknowledgement of this impossibility in his column during the 2014 war produces a profound and angry confrontation with his assumptions about his place in Israeli society. In both instances, these revelations bring to light certain deceptions, namely that one can cross borders with ease by assuming, either through socioeconomic status or linguistic-ethnic disguise, the dress, language and mannerisms of others. It is also at borders, whether checkpoints, a blockaded village or a divided city, where ethnic difference is enacted, enforced and made explicit. At these sites, ethnic distinction is the idiom by which they function – even and perhaps especially to those such as the lawyer who are harmed by the policing of this difference. It also makes the world incomprehensible outside of its framework. In *Second Person Singular*, both the lawyer and Amir abide by the logic of the border and its encoding of ethnic difference, even as they seek to cross it, to avoid its effects, or to circumvent it in search of an elusive coexistence. Yet following this border logic requires certain deceptions and a form of self-estrangement. And even as the border makes estrangement inevitable, it conceals its inevitability from view by naturalising difference. Both characters seek not to undo the divisions that separate them from various sectors of society, they simply seek to cross them. And once the impossibility of coexistence is revealed, the idea of the border as deceptive begins to come into focus. The border is not merely a symptom of the failure of coexistence, but it produces and enforces it. It follows, then, that to attend to the failure not only of coexistence but of any potential for imagining an alternative to the status quo, the border is a crucial site of engagement. The remaining chapters of this book look at works that do just that. They do not try to bury or obscure borders, but rather engage with their disruptions and deceptions intensively, head on.

Notes

1. Kashua, 'Ze Nigmar'.
2. After a few years abroad, Kashua wrote in November 2017 that he had to take a break from his column in *Haaretz*, due to the 'uncertainty and the physical and mental distance I feel'. Kashua, 'Sayed Kashua Bids Adieu'.
3. Kashua, ''Aravi, Daber 'Ivrit'.
4. Hochberg, 'To Be or Not to Be an Israeli Arab', p. 69.
5. Izikovitch, 'New Talent Unseats Old Favorites at Israeli TV Awards'.
6. Mansour, *In a New Light*.
7. Elad-Bouskila, *Modern Palestinian Literature and Culture*, p. 41.
8. Hever, 'Hebrew in an Israeli Arab Hand', p. 73.
9. See, for example, Hever, 'Hebrew in an Israeli Arab Hand'.
10. For instance, Karen Grumberg has studied Kashua in *Place and Ideology in Contemporary Hebrew Literature*. Hochberg has also written about Shammas in *In Spite of Partition*, and Kashua in 'To Be or Not to Be an Israeli Arab'. Ami Elad-Bouskila provides a survey and periodisation of Palestinian Hebrew writings in *Modern Palestinian Literature and Culture*.
11. For instance, see Sha'alan, 'Kayfa Yuhajim Sayyid Qashu' al-Hujum 'ala Ghazza b-il-'Ibriyya?'
12. *Dancing Arabs* was published as '*Arab Raqisun* in Cairo, and *Let it Be Morning* was published as *Li-yakun Sabahan* in Beirut by Dar al-Saqi.

13. The term '*al-dākhil*', meaning 'the inside', is used by many Palestinians to refer to the areas of historic Palestine that became the State of Israel, and to Palestinians who became citizens of Israel, and is distinct from both the diaspora and the occupied West Bank and Gaza Strip.
14. Khoury, 'Rethinking the *Nakba*', p. 251.
15. Ibid. p. 254.
16. Kanafani, *Rijal fi al-Shams*, pp. 108–9.
17. Kashua, '*Aravim Rokdim*, p. 72.
18. Ibid. p. 72.
19. Ibid. p. 72.
20. Grumberg, *Place and Ideology*, p. 134.
21. Kristeva, *Strangers to Ourselves*, p. 15.
22. Ibid. p. 1.
23. Derrida, *Monolingualism of the Other*, p. 54.
24. Ibid. p. 55.
25. Ibid. p. 44.
26. Ibid. p. 49.
27. Kashua, ''Aravi, Daber 'Ivrit'.
28. Tawil-Souri, 'Qalandia Checkpoint as Space and Non-Place', p. 4.
29. Apter, 'Translation at the Checkpoint', p. 70.
30. Kilito, *Thou Shalt Not Speak My Language*, p. 94.
31. Kashua, ''Aravi, Daber 'Ivrit'.
32. Khalifeh, *al-Sabbar*, p. 10.
33. Grumberg, *Place and Ideology*, p. 134.
34. Ibid. p. 132.
35. See Habiby, *al-Waqa'i' al-Ghariba*.
36. Kashua, *Ve-Yehi Boker*, p. 93.
37. Ibid. p. 110.
38. Ibid. p. 94.
39. Apter, 'Translation at the Checkpoint', p. 71.
40. Kashua, *Ve-Yehi Boker*, p. 24.
41. Ibid. p. 24.
42. Ibid. p. 23.
43. Ibid. p. 24.
44. Ibid. p. 22.
45. Ibid. p. 48.
46. Ibid. p. 100.

47. The question of the border's relationship to both the idea of illusion and the concept of the mirror takes a very different form in other representations; see Chapter 6 for further exploration of these notions in connection to Elia Suleiman's film *Divine Intervention*.
48. This narrative device recalls Albert Camus' *The Plague*, in which an epidemic leads to a quarantine of Oran, Algeria, and the isolation forces a confrontation with the fractures and conflicts within the community.
49. Grumberg, *Place and Ideology*, p. 155.
50. Kashua, *Ve-Yehi Boker*, p. 20.
51. Ibid. p. 20.
52. Ibid. p. 29.
53. Ibid. p. 9.
54. Ibid. p. 148.
55. Ibid. p. 29.
56. Ibid. p. 29.
57. For instance, the phrase '*ata dafuk?*' is a common response to someone who makes a stupid comment, and roughly means 'have you lost your mind?'
58. Kashua, *Ve-Yehi Boker*, p. 124.
59. Ibid. p. 137.
60. Ibid. p. 140.
61. Kashua, *Second Person Singular*, p. 80.
62. Other types of borders, like walls, have more of a blocking effect, as we will see in Chapter 5.
63. 'East Jerusalem 2015: Facts and Figures Report'.
64. The main exception to this is the relatively new light rail line, which generated opposition from both Palestinians and Israelis for traversing the Green Line and for serving both Jewish and Palestinian areas. Sherwood, 'Jerusalem's Long-Awaited Light Railway Splits Opinions'.
65. Kashua, *Second Person Singular*, p. 79.
66. Kashua, *Guf Sheni Yahid*, p. 243.
67. Ibid. p. 267.
68. Ibid. p. 243.
69. Kashua, *Second Person Singular*, p. 265.
70. Kashua, *Guf Sheni Yahid*, pp. 251–3.
71. Ibid. p. 97.
72. Kashua, *Second Person Singular*, p. 129.
73. Kashua, *Guf Sheni Yahid*, p. 123.

74. Kashua, *Second Person Singular*, p. 129.
75. Ibid. p. 129.
76. Kashua, *Guf Sheni Yahid*, p. 180.
77. Benjamin, *The Arcades Project*, p. 10.
78. Kashua, *Guf Sheni Yahid*, p. 176.
79. Ibid. pp. 290–1.
80. Ibid. p. 290.
81. Hochberg, *In Spite of Partition*, p. 2.
82. Kashua, *Second Person Singular*, pp. 319–20.
83. Ibid. p. 320.
84. Ibid. p. 20.
85. See Abdel-Malek, *The Rhetoric of Violence*, p. 146, for a discussion of this aspect of Mansour's novel.
86. Kashua, *Guf Sheni Yahid*, p. 20.
87. Ibid. p. 32.
88. For instance, he picks up food at the 'most expensive sushi bar in the city'. Kashua, *Second Person Singular*, p. 24.
89. Often being a good citizen requires Palestinian complicity in Israeli security practices, whether within the territories or in Israel itself. See Cohen, *Good Arabs*.
90. Kashua, *Second Person Singular*, p. 28.
91. Ibid. p. 29.
92. Ibid. p. 345.
93. Levy, 'Exchanging Words', p. 111.
94. Echoes of his lost and hapless titular character can be found in many subsequent works of Palestinian literature, such as Anton Shammas' *Arabesques* and, more recently, Ibtisam Azem's *The Sleep Thief* (*Sariq al-Nawm*, 2011). Lital Levy argues that Habiby uses Said's misinterpretation and mistranslation of language to undermine official Israeli state discourse, thus giving his naivety a subversive purpose. Levy, 'Exchanging Words', pp. 111–12.
95. Sacks, *Iterations of Loss*, p. 182.
96. Kashua, *Second Person Singular*, p. 176.
97. Kashua, *Guf Sheni Yahid*, p. 155.
98. One example offered is its treatment of women. Kashua, *Guf Sheni Yahid*, p. 155.

II
DECEPTIVE BORDERS

4

Border Crossings and Stray Narratives of Return

> For here, where we are, is the tent for wandering meanings and words gone astray and the orphaned light, scattered and banished from the center.
>
> Mahmoud Darwish, *Memory for Forgetfulness*
> (*Dhakira li-l-Nisyan*, 1987)[1]

One day, Walid Masoud disappears. The titular character of Palestinian author Jabra Ibrahim Jabra's novel *In Search of Walid Masoud* (*al-Bahth 'an Walid Mas'ud*, 1978) leaves Baghdad in his car and vanishes, never to be seen again. Walid, like Jabra, is a Palestinian intellectual and writer living in exile in Baghdad, and his car is found en route to the Iraqi–Syrian border. Through the narrator, a friend of Walid's who seeks to solve the mystery of his disappearance, the novel unearths a trail of conversations, memories, writings and tape recordings that Walid has left behind. Yet all of these traces provide no definite resolution of the central mystery: where did Walid Masoud go? Many theories, none of them definitive, are presented. In one, he has turned up dead in Beirut.[2] In another, he is living in a cave somewhere, or he became a monk in an Italian monastery.[3] Another friend, Wisal, becomes convinced that he returned to occupied Palestine to join the *fidā'iyyūn* (Palestinian resistance fighters) and fight the Israelis, and the novel concludes with her departure to join him.[4] While we are never sure, it is this theory that sticks out as most likely.[5]

If we take the prevalent theory as true, then Walid's disappearance is a narrative of return to Palestine. He has gone back to fight for his homeland, leaving the trappings of exile behind. To be sure, many writers have sought to tell their own version of the narrative of Palestinian return from exile, as we saw with Ghassan Kanafani in Chapter 2. It is perhaps the most prominent Palestinian literary trope of recent decades. Yet in this novel the return journey does not function as a starting point, as with Kanafani's *Returning to Haifa*, but as the unsolved mystery of the novel, a gaping absence in the centre of Jabra's work that never reaches resolution and is only told in uncertain bits and fragments. Indeed, Jabra's novel is not so much about the narrative of return as it is about its failure to be narrated.[6] Walid the exiled writer intellectual cannot or does not tell his story; he falls silent as he nears the border with Syria.

This chapter grapples with the problems posed by the border's role in producing silence and disruption within the return journey. While Jabra's novel illuminates the questions that propel my analysis, the chapter as a whole centres on a close reading of a more recent return narrative. This novel, entitled *The Lady from Tel Aviv* (*Al-Sayyida min Tall Abib*, 2009) by Rabaʿi al-Madhoun, functions in many ways as a coda to the interrupted and silent return of Jabra's Walid. It follows the return journey of another Walid – Walid Dahman, the protagonist of al-Madhoun's novel – to Palestine several decades later, under vastly different circumstances. However, like Jabra's novel, *The Lady from Tel Aviv* is concerned not only with the experience of return but the way in which it is and is not narrated. In addition to telling the story of a return from exile, it also probes the limits of the return narrative as a literary trope, albeit with different results. The silent, mysterious return of Jabra's character gives way to a splintered return narrative that produces a chaotic cacophony of voices in al-Madhoun's novel. If *Walid Masoud* refuses to narrate the return narrative, al-Madhoun's novel reveals the impossibility of narrating it in a singular, cohesive manner in an era in which Palestinian experiences of borders are no longer confined to various national borders but now encompass a veritable nesting doll of expanding checkpoints and walls. This impossibility is staged through successive border crossings which interrupt, shatter and redirect Walid's narratives, producing an experience of return that quickly spins out of the control of both the protagonist and the author.

The Lady from Tel Aviv, a 2010 finalist for the International Prize for Arabic Fiction (IPAF), with an English translation by Elliot Colla released in July 2013, was the debut novel for al-Madhoun, who has since published a follow-up novel called *Destinies: A Concerto of the Holocaust and the Nakba* (*Masa'ir: Kunshirtu al-Hulukust wa-al-Nakba*, 2015)[7] that won the IPAF in 2016. Also a journalist who writes for *al-Sharq al-Awsat* newspaper in London, al-Madhoun has lived in exile since the Israeli occupation of Gaza began in 1967. Following his forced exile, al-Madhoun played an active role in the Palestinian resistance in the 1970s until deciding to devote his full attention to writing.[8] His novel has been compared to novels by Jabra but also to works by Emile Habiby and Elias Khoury, a lineage that makes its presence known through the novel's intricate structure, which features *mise en abîme*, somewhat startling shifts of time and space, and multiple narrators.[9] *Masa'ir*, which is structured around several 'movements' along the lines of a classical music composition, also reflects al-Madhoun's interest in complex narrative structure. The main character of both novels, Walid Dahman, is an author and journalist whose biography closely resembles al-Madhoun's, and his sensibilities and experiences reflect those of a generation of exiled, male Palestinian intellectuals who came of age after 1948, experienced the defeat of 1967, and then witnessed the peak and then rapid decline of Palestinian resistance in the 1970s and 1980s.

The Lady from Tel Aviv begins conventionally enough for a return narrative; Walid, a Palestinian living in London like al-Madhoun himself, contemplates his childhood in Gaza and the events that forced him into exile in 1967, as he prepares to return for the first time nearly forty years later. On his flight from London to Tel Aviv, Walid meets Dana, an Israeli woman who captivates him, and the two form a quick bond. Once they part ways upon arrival in Tel Aviv, the novel continues to follow each character's journey by alternating between Dana's return to Tel Aviv and Walid's homecoming in Gaza. This narrative split adds an additional Israeli voice to Walid's previously univocal narrative of return, and this shift in narrative structure occurs at the border crossing.

Like many of the borders examined in earlier chapters, the primary border crossings in the novel – the first at Ben Gurion Airport and the second at the crossing between Israel and the Gaza Strip – partially resemble but are not identical to a national land border such as the one between Iraq and Syria where Walid Masoud falls silent (or, for that matter, the closed border between Syria and Israel, Walid's ultimate destination). As Karim Mattar notes, referring both to borders like the airport and those that control entry into the Palestinian territories, these points of entry into Palestine, which he terms 'national checkpoints', are crucial elements of return narratives that mark a moment of crossing from exile to home.[10] However, for Palestinians they are also sites of further negation of Palestine as a homeland and political entity, as they require encountering and submitting to an Israeli 'authority that denies their very existence'.[11] While the two borders in *The Lady from Tel Aviv* are also distinct from each other in important ways, in the novel both mark at once return and the impossibility of return, as the demarcation of inside and outside and belonging and non-belonging becomes blurred and produces disorientation.

Added to this primary narrative, with its splits and shifts at the border, is a *mise en abîme* in the form of Walid's own novel, *A House with Two Shadows*, which tells the story of a Palestinian German man named Adel who also returns to Gaza for the first time and meets an Israeli woman along the way. *The Lady from Tel Aviv* incorporates pieces of Walid's novel-in-progress along with the narrative voices of Walid and Dana. As the novel progresses, the stories of Walid and Adel seem to merge; in Gaza, Walid meets a 'real' version of his character Adel, and this Adel seeks to reconnect with an old lover named Layla, who herself is a distant relative of Walid. Walid becomes intricately involved in this saga during his time in Gaza, and distinguishing between Walid's experiences and those of the real Adel and the fictional Adel becomes increasingly difficult. Meanwhile, the novel continues to follow Dana's return to Tel Aviv and her attempts to negotiate the status of her relationship with a long-time Israeli boyfriend, as well as a scandalous secret affair that has entangled her with the son of an unnamed Arab leader. In the end, Walid returns to London, and he and Dana plan to meet, but the rendezvous never takes place.

Al-Madhoun's novel is an example of contemporary Palestinian literary attempts to refigure common tropes, such as the narrative of return, narratives of resistance, and depictions of historical events like the *Nakba*, in order to engage with and challenge the proliferation and increasing fragmentation of Palestinian physical and cultural space.¹² Faced with the dissolution of – and disillusionment with – paradigms of armed struggle and coexistence as seen in earlier chapters, works such as *The Lady from Tel Aviv* search for other modes of dissent through writing. In al-Madhoun, the border crossing, by repeatedly inserting itself and interfering in the narrative and the novel's structure, declares its constant intrusion into Palestinian lives and by extension into Palestinian writing. In this way we can see al-Madhoun's novel as a means of grappling with the implications of the overwhelming presence of borders and the ways in which this presence shapes Palestinian narratives.

In this chapter, I examine the ways in which border crossings and border encounters redirect Walid's return journey and unsettle the experience of return. I argue that *The Lady from Tel Aviv* uses border crossings to reimagine the return narrative by subverting and parodying its conventions, and that border crossings create repeated disruptions, diversions and detours of the return journey, spawning a series of split narratives and encounters that undermine the author's control of the novel. This produces an anarchic text that dethrones the writer from his position of privilege and heralds the demise of the return narrative as the domain of the exiled author. In its place, *The Lady from Tel Aviv* produces a stray narrative, an out of control text that emerges from the terror and chaos Walid encounters in Gaza to displace the authority of the exiled author-intellectual. I begin my analysis by exploring the Palestinian cultural and literary trope of return from exile, which provides the starting point to which *The Lady from Tel Aviv* repeatedly returns in order to unsettle it.

Reconfiguring the Return Narrative

Return is a well-established trope in Palestinian literature. This reflects the importance that return has occupied in Palestinian political and cultural discourse since the *Nakba* of 1948. The desire to return to lost homes, villages and homeland has been a constant and central Palestinian political and cultural imperative for the past seventy years. This desire is often imagined as a victorious return after a successful struggle to defeat Israel.¹³ Return is the end point of what Rashid Khalidi describes as the decades-long, epic-like Palestinian narrative of struggle to re-form itself after loss and expulsion.¹⁴ Yet the many representations – both fictional and non-fictional – of return in

Palestine and elsewhere reveal a considerably more complicated set of meanings surrounding this term. Marianne Hirsch describes the desire to return, particularly in contexts of national loss and trauma, as a 'fractured encounter between generations, between cultures, and between mutually imbricated histories occurring in a layered present'.[15] The idea of return, in other words, becomes a site of conflicting narratives that disrupts and fractures as it also heals and unifies.

Tracing the development of this concept in Palestinian culture and literature reveals a fair bit of slippage in the concept. It has undergone several significant shifts at the epistemological and political levels in the decades since 1948. Early articulations saw return as a 'logical and natural outcome of the completion of "liberation"'[16] and assumed that the Palestinians' Arab allies would lead them to victory. However, the defeat of 1967 placed a military victory further away than ever, and the Palestine Liberation Organisation (PLO) and other groups emerged as powerful political forces that began to take matters into their own hands. The PLO trained and deployed resistance fighters to stage guerrilla operations against Israel from Jordan and later Lebanon. It also began to approach the 'right of return' as an issue in its own right and began to draw heavily on the discourse of global human rights to articulate this claim. A change in preferred terminology for those who fled, from *lāji'ūn* (refugees) to *'ā'idūn* (returnees), in the 1970s reflects the emergence of return as a distinctive demand.[17] This articulation of a right of return, first enshrined in 1974, emerged at the beginning of a gradual shift in Palestinian strategy from armed struggle to negotiated settlement (the 'two-state solution').[18] A further shift occurred in the 1990s with the signing of the Oslo Accords and the establishment of the Palestinian Authority. In the on-again, off-again, currently stalled peace negotiations that have occurred in recent years, the Palestinian leadership has included the right of return as one of its demands for a final status settlement, albeit without defining the scope or meaning that return would take in a negotiated agreement. Yet many refugees have expressed a sense of betrayal as a result of the peace process because Palestinian leaders seemed willing to sign away or dilute the right of return.[19]

This fear of losing the right of return reflects a tension between political contingencies and popular imagination. For many Palestinian refugees, the desire to return more closely resembles a 'collective wish passed on from one generation to the next' than a concrete political platform.²⁰ Though meanings and definitions have evolved with generational and political changes, the imperative to return has remained salient among many Palestinians in the diaspora even as it receives less attention from political leaders. Immediately following 1948, many expected a quick return to Palestine and sought to imitate pre-1948 society in exile.²¹ When this did not occur, memory, both cultural and individual, became the primary vehicle through which the imperative to return remained relevant. As new generations appeared over the years, these memories became an inheritance by which knowledge of Palestine was preserved from afar.

Memory has played a particularly important role in this process of transmission, through which, according to Victoria Mason,

> Palestine was made tangible to an almost sensory level where children born in the diaspora could describe their family's house down to the texture of the bricks, the position of an olive tree in the yard or the scent from a decades-old lemon tree.²²

The centrality of memory has long been reflected in Palestinian fiction,²³ but in recent decades such memories, typically preserved orally, have begun to appear in new forms. These so-called 'village books' provide a vehicle both for the preservation of memories and the imperative to return, as the generation that fled has begun to die out. They combine histories, stories, maps, documents, genealogies and land records of destroyed villages and function as documentation of village histories and memories.²⁴ Describing one such book from the lost village of Sumahta, Rochelle Davis writes that these memories and histories, both oral and written, articulate and preserve the desire to return to Palestine, prompting a new generation 'to continue to fight and believe that Sumahta and Palestine can be returned'.²⁵ These village books demonstrate the means by which memory functions as a weapon to ensure continued fighting and resistance, preservation, and the possibility of national repair and renewal through return. In this formulation, memories of pre-1948 Palestine represent not only the past but also a model for the future as well. Removed from the political considerations of how to accomplish this goal, return is imagined culturally as a fantasy of reclaiming of the past in the future in a way that makes Palestine whole again.

Significantly, most literary works that engage with the question of return avoid imagining this future return. Instead, they tend to portray experiences of return under present conditions (that is, under Israeli rule), which are often temporary journeys and/or illicit infiltration. Their narratives are often realist,[26] and this type of return is, as Edward Said notes, a fraught act that merges the exile's ecstasy at returning to the land he remembers with the shock of finding that this place has acquired 'a new name, people, and identity that deny Palestine altogether'.[27] The present contrasts violently with both pre-exile memories and the type of return imagined in popular culture. These moments of rupture reveal the experience of return under Israeli rule to be, according to Said, one that 'reenacts exile rather than repatriation',[28] It serves, then, as a reminder of the original loss and its lack of resolution, and of the necessity of continued struggle and commitment.

This mode of return as a type of shock therapy or rupture that revives a dying political consciousness is evident in the reading in Chapter 2 of Ghassan Kanafani's *Returning to Haifa*, and it finds echoes in other literary works such as Sahar Khalifeh's *Wild Thorns (al-Sabbar,* 1976),[29] in which it serves as an indictment of a societal complacency that has befallen Palestinians after 1967. *Wild Thorns* uses the shock of return to critique the gap between resistance movements outside of Palestine and conditions within the West Bank and Israel. The main character Usama, an exile who returns to the West Bank to fight the occupation, finds himself dismayed by the reality of the occupation and lashes out, decrying the laziness and complacency of the Palestinians he meets. As in *Returning to Haifa*, return for Usama produces a shock, forcing him to grapple with the gap between his memories of Palestine and his present reality, between his idealised image of a society actively resisting the Israeli occupation and the complicit acquiescence he perceives upon his return, embodied by his cousin Adel who appears resigned to making the best of his situation under Israeli rule. Both characters' stories end in disaster, a conclusion that serves as an indictment both of Usama's refusal to countenance reality and of Adel's complacency, and of the divisions that plague Palestinian society. Khalifeh's novel harnesses the return narrative to show the gap between the realities of life under occupation and the idealism of those in exile, and to reveal the need for a critical re-examination of Palestinian political strategies. Like Kanafani, the return journey serves as a catalyst for new political resolve by means of critical self-examination. These are excellent examples of a liberational form of realism; as Bashir Abu-Manneh puts it, 'realism and emancipation are born together in the Palestinian novel'.[30] In Kanafani, Khalifeh and Jabra, we can see the trope of return first and foremost as a political discourse, in which return, enacted by the crossing of a national border, offers a means of performing and reinvigorating a commitment to the Palestinian cause, however it might be defined.

Where this political impetus begins to fade is in the period of the Oslo Accords, the signing of which opened the doors to the return of a limited number of refugees to the West Bank and Gaza and led to new autobiographical return narratives. Poet Mourid Barghouti's memoir *I Saw Ramallah* (*Ra'aytu Ramallah*, 1996) portrays a journey of return for Barghouti, who has lived in exile since 1967. Like the other works mentioned, he confronts the gap between his memories, his desires and the reality he encounters and uses this to stage a critique of prevailing orthodoxies. In this case, Barghouti's experience undermines the 'victory' of the Oslo Accords and the establishment of the Palestinian Authority as he arrives at the border crossing into the West Bank that remains under Israeli control and waits to cross and return after thirty years of absence, and instead of a triumphant return he finds himself unsettled by what he finds: 'Do I really want boundaries for Palestine? . . . Now I want borders that later I will come to hate.'[31] Unlike earlier representations, Barghouti finds not certainty and political commitment but ambivalence and a political void, as the incorporation of the formerly revolutionary Palestinian leadership into a complicit quasi-state that is dependent upon Israel denudes the return narrative of much of its political significance. Borders in the post-Oslo period no longer galvanise Palestinian political consciousness. Mattar characterises *I Saw Ramallah* in this way:

> [With its] constant and erratic scene-shifts from Ramallah to Cairo to Budapest to Beirut to Amman to London, its contractions and expansions of temporality, its overlapping of past and present, memory and lived experience, its rapid stylistic and tonal transitions, and its absolute resistance to continuous narrative, the memoir itself takes on the form of exile.[32]

In this reading, the post-Oslo return narrative is also, to return to Said, a 'reenactment of exile', but it offers no solution and no narrative of national liberation or political progress, no clear demarcation of inside and outside, or home and away, but rather only a continuation and reproduction of exile.

Indeed, the pivotal moment of the return narrative in *The Lady from Tel Aviv* – Walid's arrival in Palestine – also confounds the typical expectations of the genre. The moment he arrives and touches the ground, Walid says that he has returned 'in search of soil to kiss, but I find nothing except a paved walkway, and a crowded arrivals hall'.[33] The 'paved walkway' and 'crowded arrivals hall' of Walid's first steps in Palestine supplant the familiar rural landscape, lost home or even horrifying border crossing that narratives of return typically portray. Walid finds an alien and sterile space that does not conjure any of his memories of Palestine; instead, at the moment of his arrival, he thinks about a story he heard from a British Jewish friend who travelled to Israel and Palestine and was told to kiss the earth upon arrival. He recalls that she protested, saying that she is British and has no connection with this place. This then prompts Walid to think of Dana, the Israeli who sat next to him on the flight, and her return to the land she also claims as home, and to interrogate his own relationship with this place.[34] Arrival provokes neither fond nor traumatic memories, nor overwhelming emotion, but rather a moment of questioning and self-doubt mediated by the experiences of (non-Palestinian) others.

In both Barghouthi and al-Madhoun, we see the 'redemptive' realist narrative described by Abu-Manneh[35] falter, as narrative forward progress and cohesiveness give way to fragmentation and spatio-temporal shifts and distortions. Moreover, the border, where Barghouti questions his assumptions about what form a solution to the Palestine question might take, is a crucial site of this uncertainty, and it reflects what Anna Bernard describes as a tendency in partition literatures to privilege ambiguity and fragmentation over narrative and nationalism.[36] *The Lady from Tel Aviv*, in which a series of borders engenders repeated disruptions and encounters, reflects Walid Dahman's uncertainty, anxiety and confusion through a cacophonic, stray narrative and intricate structure that calls into question the possibility of a cathartic return in a post-Oslo world of ever present borders.

A Narrative of Encounter

Both the encounter between Walid and Dana and the space in which it occurs push the novel further from the conventions of the return narrative. There is a long history of Palestinian literary depictions of Arab–Jewish romantic encounters, beginning with *al-Warith* (*The Heir*) by Khalil Baydas, which is considered the first Palestinian novel and tells the story of a love affair between a Syrian man and a Jewish woman in Egypt.[37] Works by Atallah Mansour and others have depicted such relations between Arabs and Jews, and portrayals of the Jewish characters have ranged from highly stereotypical (Baydas)[38] to idealised (Mansour). However, such encounters have rarely occurred within narratives of return, which tend to stage more confrontational encounters between Palestinian and Jewish characters. While Dana and Walid's time together is fleeting and does not become sexual or romantic, there is a flirtatious undertone that alludes to this literary history of such encounters and injects it into the return narrative.

It is significant that the encounter between Walid and Dana occurs on an aeroplane, which itself is a type of border zone, an in-between space set apart from the everyday world. Marc Augé terms places like the aeroplane, the airport, border crossings and transit camps 'non-places'. While the term 'place' in anthropology refers to 'culture localized in time and space', non-places are space in which people or goods are in transit or are otherwise decoupled from the specificities of time and space.[39] The latter, suggest Augé and others such as Jean Baudrillard, form an ever-increasing proportion of contemporary spatial experiences, as societies have become more mobile and technology has revolutionised mobility and communication.[40] As a result, these types of 'non-places' have proliferated at an accelerated pace, much like the intensifying border zones in Palestine and Israel. These are tightly controlled spaces that are set apart from everyday life, and the means by which people interact with them are distinct, governed by texts and documents like passports and tickets.[41] These documents bring Walid and Dana together by assigning them adjacent seats. The non-place of the aeroplane, as a space that is neither home nor exile, creates the possibility of an encounter not possible in the traditional return narrative, which operates at the level of a binary opposition between exile and home. The aeroplane moves them outside of this binary and makes possible their encounter within a distinct (non-)place.

The encounter between the two begins slowly, with mutual suspicion, but in the course of the journey an extensive and emotionally revealing dialogue opens up between them. Walid's engagement with an Israeli woman on an analogous journey of return pushes this narrative to reach different conclusions than Kanafani and Khalifeh. This is not to say that al-Madhoun's novel does not articulate a claim of Palestinian rights or a critique of the occupation. Walid's frequent references to his birthplace of Asdud (now Ashdod, in present-day Israel) serves as a reminder of his belonging to this place, and he often notes the suffering and violence imposed by occupation. Yet this claim exists alongside Dana, who is a human, knowable, relatable other, showing that the two are not mutually exclusive. Dana's inclusion into the story, made possible by the long waits of air travel and borders, complicates and disrupts what might have been a straightforward narrative trajectory. While their conversation ends at border control at the Tel Aviv airport, Walid's airborne encounter with Dana echoes throughout the rest of his journey to Gaza and comes to define a journey redirected by this encounter.

The effects of the chance encounter reverberate through the novel's structure as well, as the story splits into narrations from the alternating perspectives of Walid and Dana. They recount their plane journey together in alternation, in which a chapter narrated by Walid and labelled 'he' (*huwa*) is followed by a chapter narrated by Dana labelled 'she' (*hiya*), emphasising the two separate narratives that come together in an encounter on the plane and then split upon arrival. Just as Walid's arrival in Palestine is mediated by the narratives of others, the juxtaposition of alternating narrators reminds the reader of the limits of each narrative, which exist in relation to other, distinct but intertwined narratives. The formerly unitary narrative of return is now one of several. In this sense it takes the possibly clichéd, gendered encounter and uses it to interrupt the chronological narrative cohesion of the return novel.

The use of multiple narrators in Palestinian literature is not a new literary technique. Its use in modern Arabic literature has been traced to the influence of William Faulkner, whose predilection toward multiple narrators and other techniques such as stream of consciousness inspired a number of Arab authors to begin to experiment formally by way of Jabra's Arabic translations.[42] One such author was Ghassan Kanafani, who has acknowledged Faulkner's influence on his novel *That's Left to You* (*Ma Tabaqqa Lakum*), which contains multiple narrators, including 'time' and 'the desert'.[43] Kanafani deploys a similar technique in *Men in the Sun* (*Rijal fi al-Shams*), which, as previously noted, follows three Palestinian refugees as they try to make their way from Iraq to Kuwait in search of employment.[44] However, al-Madhoun's use of this technique represents an important break from earlier deployments. *Men in the Sun* uses multiple perspectives to draw attention to the dispersal of the Palestinians after 1948 by following each character's journey to a rendezvous point to cross into Kuwait. In the end, the deaths of all three refugees serve as a reminder of the Palestinian people's shared fate (despite its fragmentation), as an indictment of Arab silence and duplicity towards the Palestinian cause, and as a call to action and solidarity.[45]

Kanafani harnesses his employment of multiple perspectives to arouse sympathy and anger towards the treatment of Palestinian refugees by giving several voices to a singular experience that come together at the border, but *The Lady from Tel Aviv* uses an Israeli voice to emphasise the inability of a singular experience to capture the complex reality of the place to which Walid returns. Dana's inclusion as a narrator creates a form of parity between the two, and the alternation between the Palestinian and the Israeli forges distinct but connected narrative trajectories out of perspectives that are often placed in diametric opposition. While Kanafani uses multiplicity in service of a single narrative – thereby maintaining what Stefan Meyer calls a 'formal cohesiveness'[46] – al-Madhoun uses multiple voices to question the possibility of a single, unifying experience of return.

On top of the multivocal nature of the narrative, there are multiple shifts in voice and structure as the novel progresses. In *The Lady from Tel Aviv*, the border is a space of fracture in which narratives strands diverge, appear and disappear. As Walid and Dana land in Tel Aviv, the alternation between their two narrative voices ends. After this point, Dana no longer narrates her story in first person; instead, a third person narrator labelled 'the narrator' (*al-rāwī*) tells the story of her angst-ridden homecoming in Tel Aviv. Then, later in the novel when Walid crosses the Gaza border, the third-person narrator telling Dana's story *also* disappears, leaving Walid as the sole narrator for this portion of the novel. Finally, as Walid leaves Gaza and returns to London in the novel's concluding chapters, Walid's first-person account of his return to London alternates with – and contradicts – that of the omniscient 'narrator'. These changing narrative voices create an unstable, and occasionally unreliable, narrative and they map almost perfectly onto the various border crossings that Walid encounters, reflecting the extent to which borders destabilise and confuse the return narrative.

A Novel of Shadows

Metaphorically and structurally, *The Lady from Tel Aviv* reflects and performs the disorientation of returning to – and narrating the return to – multiple border crossings. In her short story 'Out of Time', Adania Shibli describes the experience of returning to Palestine as one that stops time. As soon as she lands at the airport in Lydd near Tel Aviv, she writes that her watch 'suddenly enters into a coma, with which it becomes unable to count the time'.[47] In this rendering, the act of crossing the border places one outside of time; the normal parameters by which one's experiences are chronicled, narrated, regulated and understood no longer apply. The act of crossing into Palestine produces a disorienting effect. Shibli's story goes on to suggest that the stoppage of time reminds the traveller of the larger timeless exceptionality that renders 'normal' life impossible in Palestine. This disorienting effect of the airport is captured in Darwish's poem 'Athens Airport' ('Matar Athina', 1987), which depicts the limbo of Palestinian exiles who spend their lives ('years and years') waiting in airports.[48] Writing of the border crossing at Ben Gurion airport, Mattar likewise characterises this space as an 'inversion of time and space, a void between times and spaces, a screen that through its process of screening projects and enacts fantasies of possession'.[49]

Like Shibli, al-Madhoun's novel creates an ambivalent and unsteady narrative in which encounters with the spaces of airports and other borders blurs place, time and voice through moments of suspension, distortion and screening. The novel reflects this through its preoccupation with the concept of the shadow. This interest appears in the title of the novel Walid is writing, *A House with Two Shadows* (*Zillan li-Bayt Wahid*), which he explains to Dana as a reference to two people – Palestinian and Israeli – sharing one land. However, this is merely one of the title's many layers of meaning. A shadow, as Walid notes, cannot exist by itself, as 'it is not born except in the light, and does not die except in the darkness'.[50] It is an inherently unstable and fragile entity, one that constantly changes position and can disappear at any time with the passage of a cloud or a sunset. It is also a reflection, a representation of some other entity. The image of *two* shadows emanating from a single object suggests a division, a border, and a split representation of its source, but one that is unstable and can collapse at any time. It questions how these two shadows, singular in origin but born of a rupture that splits them, relate to each other and to the unstable border that separates them. In this formulation, Walid poses a dilemma of representation: how can he (or al-Madhoun) perceive and depict a reality that is fractured, multiple, and ever changing?

The novel's structure, it seems, provides an answer as it challenges many of the structural conventions that would allow it to tell a cohesive narrative of return. At one point, Walid declares:

> I found myself an author and a protagonist . . . tracing Adel's footsteps and searching – on behalf of him and myself – for Layla, in reality (*al-wāqiʿ*) and in the novel, in reality and in the shadow (*al-ẓill*).[51]

In this statement Walid establishes a series of binaries – 'author' and 'protagonist', 'reality' and 'novel', and 'reality' and 'shadow' – while also declaring his intention to unsettle them. He places them in opposition to each other but also binds them together, inhabits and engages both simultaneously. By juxtaposing 'reality' and 'shadow' (*al-ẓill*), Walid contests the link between the two. A shadow may be, but is not necessarily, bound by reality, just as a protagonist is not bound by its author, and a novel is not limited by the reality that produces it. The verb form of *ẓill*, *ẓalla*, means 'to spend time doing [something]', with the caveat that it only refers to activities during daylight hours.[52] The noun, *ẓill*, then, denotes a shadow, a form of darkness that can only occur in the light. Its existence is contingent upon the presence of another object that creates it. The shadow can thus only exist as a reflection, a darkened mirror image. Yet the original does not limit the shadow; the shadow can move, shift, change shape and refract back onto its source. The shadow is a representation but one that does not remain faithful to its origin. Instead, it takes on a life of its own, and in *The Lady from Tel Aviv* proves an apt metaphor for the relationship of the journey of return to its fractured and unstable representation in words.

In a literary context the metaphor of the shadow – an imitation that goes beyond the original that produced it – denotes a contested relationship to representation. Plato's 'Allegory of the Cave', also reformulated in Tawfiq al-Hakim's play *The People of the Cave* (*Ahl al-Kahf*, 1933), relates the story of prisoners who can only see shadows of objects reflected off a wall. Unable to see the original, they mistake the representation, the shadow, for the object itself.[53] Perhaps then we can read the invocation of the shadow in *The Lady from Tel Aviv* as an expression of the limits of representation, and its unpredictability. Like the cave people, Walid has only seen encountered representations of the return, not the return itself. During his flight he imagines the good and the bad that will greet him upon his arrival, the land of Palestine, his mother, but also the interrogation that awaits him at the border crossing. However, the shadow, and particularly the notion of two shadows, hints at multiple narratives, and that these narratives will diverge from the expectations of the return trope. If for Khalifeh's protagonist Usama and for Walid Masoud the return produces a kind of moral clarity and closure, the dual shadows presage the divergence of the story into multiple voices and storylines in a manner that precludes this kind of desired resolution.

The shadow as a commentary on both the act and the limits of representation reflects the metafictional bent to the novel, in which the text comments on its own construction and authorship. Patricia Waugh writes that metafiction 'self-consciously and systematically draws attention to its status as an artefact in order to pose questions about the relationship between fiction and reality'.[54] It questions the divides that separate author from text and fiction from reality by shifting the reader's attention from the events of a novel to the act of narrating them, thereby 'undermining the traditional coherence of the "fiction" itself'.[55] Metafiction has become more widespread in recent decades in Arabic literature, as seen in the works of Elias Khoury, Rabee Jaber and others, a trend that has been interpreted as a renewed interest in pre-modern narrative modes.[56] However, the significance of metafiction goes beyond a return to the 'pre-modern'. A move away from realist techniques possesses an added layer of significance in Palestinian literature specifically because of historical and ideological connections between literary realism and Palestinian literature of resistance.[57] This tendency reflects a common (but by no means universally held) belief that realism is the most effective means of contributing to the Palestinian political struggle through literature by serving as an artistic vehicle for the articulation of political arguments.[58] While earlier return narratives are indeed largely realist, the metafictional turn of *The Lady from Tel Aviv* is yet another way in which post-Oslo narratives diverge from the politically engaged modes of representation that preceded them.

Walid's commentary on his own novel frames this refiguring of the return narrative in a positive light, as a means to turn away from a stale, cliché narrative of return. After discussing the story of his character, he says to Dana: 'Your presence rescued me (*anqadhanī*) from a narrative that could have been limited to telling a traditional (*taqlīdiyya*) love story between Layla and Adel.'[59] He credits her with an act of salvation (*inqādh*), suggesting that a 'traditional' narrative – *taqlīdiyya* in Arabic, which also means 'copy', emphasising a lack of originality – is some form of trap, that he fears simply rehashing old tropes. Dana's presence renders a 'traditional' narrative – in this case, the narrative of return to Palestine in which the Israeli primarily appears as a stock character that carries out the violence of occupation – inaccessible. Instead, Dana prompts Walid to produce a more complex, multifaceted story for his characters that unfolds alongside his own trip to Gaza. In place of familiar tropes of return, Walid and Dana give birth to a new set of stories, dual narratives that emanate from the common origin of the airborne encounter.

Al-Madhoun's narrative(s) of return seek to reflexively comment upon and critique their own existence. To return to the statement made by Walid above, he declares that he is at once author and protagonist, unsettling the divide between writer and character as he assumes the role of both in pursuit of his novel's character, Adel. His narrative merges with that of Adel, which subverts the other juxtaposition in this statement, the contrast between reality (*al-wāqiʿ*, literally 'that which has befallen us') and the novel. Reality and the novel are neither entirely distinct entities nor identical. The notion of multiple shadows emanating from the same source becomes a metaphor for the novel itself; it is born of a particular reality but also transcends the conditions that produced it and reshapes our understanding of it. *The Lady from Tel Aviv* is a novel that produces multiple novels, and a narrative of return that spawns a number of such narratives. Through these multiplicities, the novel stages the border's rupturing effect through the text and its narratives, characters and authors, and reveals the difficulties of narrating the experiences (return or otherwise) of Palestine today.

Multiplying Return Narratives

The Lady from Tel Aviv identifies itself as a metafictional text, a shadow of the return narrative, with the appearance of its title page, which heralds the many narrative disruptions, detours and splits to come in the novel. The title page appears not at the beginning of the text but on page forty-five. Prior to the title's appearance, the novel sets the stage for Walid's return. It begins with Walid's conversation with his mother in which he informs her he is coming to Gaza for the first time in thirty-eight years and chronicles her preparations for his return amidst the Israeli settlements, checkpoints and bombs that dominate life there. Then, as the moment of return approaches, the novel journeys into the past to the last time Walid was in Gaza, when he left to continue his studies in Cairo and never returned. It lays the groundwork for a familiar return narrative in which the exile must reconcile his memories with the reality of the present.

However, the appearance of the title page disrupts this narrative trajectory. Its appearance *after* the reader learns of Walid's return to Gaza and his memories of his pre-exile life situates elements outside of the principle narrative. They are background and function as a preface, informative but not crucial to the story. The confrontation between past and present that lies at the core of the works of Kanafani, Khalifeh and Barghouti is relegated to the edges of al-Madhoun's novel. This oddly placed title page that marginalises these elements of the return narrative forms a type of border, a signifier of the shift to a new set of narratives that emerge like shadows of the originary return narrative. It marks the appearance of these shadow narratives as a form of simulacrum, a distorted copy of an inaccessible original.[60] They signify not only a different type of return narrative but one that emerges in a context in which the original no longer functions as an available model for narrating the experience of return.

The novel's title as it appears here, *Al-Sayyida min Tall Abib*, marks it as a narrative that emerges from the trope of return but does not faithfully reproduce it. Like *Returning to Haifa* and *I Saw Ramallah*, this novel's title references a city, but while these other works articulate claims to these places as Palestinian cities that have been usurped by Israeli conquest and occupation, this title references Tel Aviv – the first 'Jewish city', which came to signify quintessentially Israeli, Zionist space.[61] For Palestinians, the very existence of

Tel Aviv serves as a constant reminder of defeat, and it is typically viewed as a space to be forgotten or erased rather than to be reclaimed.[62] Al-Madhoun's inclusion of 'Tel Aviv' in the title thus distinguishes the novel both from those works that stage a return to the lost home(town) as a site of return and reclaiming, and from the rhetoric of future return, which is predicated on forgetting/erasing the Israeli presence and Israeli-built spaces such as the archetypical Jewish Israeli city, Tel Aviv. Furthermore, '*al-Sayyida*' denotes a form of respect, which indicates gravity and politeness as well as distance in the novel's initial evaluation of Dana. Together, these elements of the title mark 'the lady from Tel Aviv', a central character of the novel, as one that is at once foreign, intriguing and respected.

Another element of the title page confirms this expanded Israeli role in the story: below the name of the author and title in Arabic appears the name 'Dana Ahuva' printed in Hebrew characters. There is no immediate explanation of this, though we later learn it refers to the eponymous 'lady from Tel Aviv'. The insertion of her name in letters which are indecipherable to most readers of an Arabic novel but recognisable as Hebrew signifies a potentially disruptive Israeli presence in a narrative already defined as a Palestinian return journey. Finally, a rather cryptic dedication that accompanies the title page marks another narrative split, that of the relationship between author, character and text. The dedication thanks a number of the text's characters 'who lived with us for three whole years'.[63] The notion that an author's characters 'lived with' him indicates a blurring of the distinction between character and author, suggesting that these characters' stories cannot be confined to a fictional text but that they escape that text and inhabit the world of the author, particularly when read in light of the narrative that follows. As Walid begins his cross-border journey, the lines between fiction and reality become unclear.

Adding an additional layer of structural complication on top of this, a second title page appears as Walid arrives at Ben Gurion Airport (the border crossing into Israel), that of Walid's novel-within-a-novel. Using a layout identical to the title page of *The Lady from Tel Aviv*, this title page lists Walid Dahman as author, and the title as *A House with Two Shadows* (*Zillan li-Bayt Wahid*). Though referenced in the airborne conversation between Walid and Dana, this title page is the first indication that *A House with Two Shadows* is possibly incorporated into the novel itself. The novel offers no explanation for the appearance of these pages at this point, and what precisely it marks at this moment is not clear. As if to affirm the ambiguous and sometimes disorienting nature of al-Madhoun's metafictional story, the title page of Walid's novel does not clearly signify a shift to the novel-within-a-novel of Adel's story. Instead, the story picks up with Walid's journey right where it left off and even adheres to the previous chapter chronology, and Walid passes through border control in Tel Aviv.[64] This unexpected continuity exploits one of the many contradictory characteristics of the border: the complex and vital relationship between the interior and the exterior marked by any boundary. The spaces marked by the border exist in an uneasy dependence and inseparability: that which lies 'inside' the border relies upon and cannot exist without that which lies 'outside'. Just as the shadow cannot exist without its source, the inside of the border cannot exist without its exterior counterpart. This relativity of the border replicates itself in the narrative structure: while the title page signifies a new border, another layer of textual interiority and exteriority, what follows 'inside' the new text is only legible in relation to that which preceded it 'outside' of the new text, a reminder that borders can often exaggerate differences and obscure similarities.

Dethroning the Author

At multiple points, the novel returns to the metaphor of the shadow to complicate the relationship between the author and his text and to interrogate the meaning of authorship. While waiting to cross the Erez crossing point into Gaza, Walid describes the interminable wait at the cold, hostile border checkpoint: 'We shivered together, Adel and I, as if we were one entity of shadow and truth.'[65] By framing his wait at the Gaza border as an experience shared with his character Adel, Walid articulates an unorthodox understanding of the relationship between author and character. The character does not spring from the author but they are mutually dependent equals negotiating a formative experience together. In the merging of author and character, Walid proclaims a new model of authorship, one in which author does not exert control over his character but instead merges with him, becoming 'one entity of shadow and truth'.

Earlier in the novel, Walid presents and then critiques a more conventional understanding of the role of author, that of a master puppeteer, setting the stage for the emergence of the newly merged author-character. During his conversation with Dana, he tells her that the two of them are in fact characters in a novel being written by someone else:

> We are both characters in a novel the events of which are being formed now. An author who knows us better than we know ourselves is animating us, and I don't even know the name of the novel of which he has made me its hero.[66]

By revealing the existence of this heretofore hidden author-puppeteer, Walid calls attention to the fictional nature of the events to this point, and to the narrative of return as a construct. At this point, the metafictional bent of the novel serves not only to comment upon how the narrative is structured, but also its ability to represent the experience of return in a comprehensible, cohesive fashion.

This act of exposure subverts the power of the omniscient author. The coherence of the fictional narrative is contingent on the enforcement of a clear division between author and text, but once Walid and Dana become aware of their status as fiction it becomes possible for them to escape the limits of the text. Walid perceives the possibilities this awareness creates and suggests that they ask the author – who 'can cooperate with us and take us beyond the text' – to put her name on the novel's cover, written in Hebrew letters ('mysterious words'), exactly as we see in the title page discussed above.[67] In this way the characters shape and reshape the construction of their own story, and they wrest control from the all-knowing author, whose characters instead become his shadows, emerging from him but transcending his limits.

By the end of the flight, the contours of new narratives made possible by the dethroning of the author reveal themselves as Walid and Dana take control of the narrative and split it. Walid declares that the 'author' will follow Dana's story, while he will 'leave it to me to narrate the events of what remains of my trip and of Adel al-Bashity's trip . . . and all of that will take place in a separate text', a proto-novel that emerges from 'what is taking place right now', that is, the conversation between Walid and Dana.[68] The story overspills its bounds and dialectically re-writes itself, creating something resembling what Elias Khoury calls a 'text without limits'. Khoury argues, channelling Roland Barthes, that the age of the all-knowing author of the likes of Naguib Mahfouz and Kanafani is at an end, to be replaced by a turn to literature in which the author is absent or erased.[69] *The Lady from Tel Aviv* does not completely erase the author but it neuters him. In the shift from linear return narrative to a self-consciously ambiguous and fragmented story, the author as omniscient prophet and puppeteer is dethroned from his pedestal. No longer master of the text, he becomes one of many character-authors who writes his own narrative in conflict and dialogue with many others.

The rupture of the border, then, appears within the author himself, as he splits and fragments while passing through successive border crossings. The figure of the exile, like Usama in *Wild Thorns* or Said in *Returning to Haifa*, who returns heroically to save the nation from complacency or to inspire new forms of resistance, now collapses within himself at the border, as does the heroic author, like Kanafani, who famously fought with the pen and not the sword. The border produces a form of collective fragmentation – of narratives, of memory, of authors – as people are herded through the turnstiles of the checkpoint and passport control at the non-place of the international airport. In the process, a reflexive, multivocal, cacophonic form of narration emerges from this fragmentation and refraction at the border, a refigured form of the return narrative that the novel here represents. The border functions both within and outside of the text and is at once material and fictional, disrupting narratives and encounters as it appears again and again along Walid's journey to Gaza.

Conclusion: Stray Bullets and Stray Narratives

If the journeys of Dana, Walid and Walid's characters disrupt the relationship of author and text and thereby subvert the return narrative and the authority of the author, they also make room for a different type of narrative. The unpredictable chaos that Walid encounters upon arrival in Gaza offers the beginnings of an answer. Once in Gaza, events stemming from the constant bombing and blockade repeatedly disrupt Walid's efforts to construct and shape his experiences and narratives. An explosion that rocks his mother's house derails one attempt to correspond with Dana, which prompts him to meditate on the randomness and unpredictability that violence wreaks on Gaza. Between the bombing of the Israeli warplanes and the 'stray bullets' (*raṣāṣa ṭā'isha*) that killed Walid's best friend, life in Gaza is characterised by 'roving death that chooses its victims randomly' and strangles all plans and hopes for the future.[70] Life is constantly interrupted, rerouted and cut down in the violence.[71]

Walid's observations of life there foreground the violence and hardship he finds in Israeli-occupied Gaza between the horrors of blockade, checkpoints and the pervasive, sinister presence of Israeli settlements,[72] and the armed militias that wreak havoc on Gaza's streets. It is a place where people are forced to 'live for the death that has already come to pass, and the death that will come'.[73] The optimism of the new narratives that Walid and Dana imagine fades away under the black cloud of bombs and bullets falling over Gaza. In a parallel fashion, through the metafictional disruption of the hierarchies of author, text and character, the return narrative spins out of control in Gaza and begins to embody the 'random' (*'ashwā'ī*) and 'stray' (*ṭā'ish*) nature of life there. The adjective *ṭā'ish* not only carries the meaning of stray but also refers to someone who is reckless, unwise or mad, embodied in the phrase *shāb ṭā'ish*, a 'wayward' or 'delinquent' youth. We can read the stray, delinquent narratives of *The Lady from Tel Aviv* in a similar manner: in a place enclosed by borders and bombs, the narrative of return becomes infected with a form of unruliness that resists the efforts of any author to determine its course. It becomes an uncontrollable, 'delinquent' narrative that, through its myriad encounters and border crossings, subverts all limits of text and narrative and instead careens haphazardly like a stray bullet, striking anything in its path.

In its transformation into a stray, out of control set of narratives, *The Lady from Tel Aviv* stages the disintegration of the decisive and cohesive return narrative. The trope of return as articulated in the works of Khalifeh, Kanafani and others, is predicated on the ability of the returning exile-author to harness the fresh perspective of temporal and spatial distance to shed new light on the Palestinian plight and the steps needed to rectify it. In *The Lady from Tel Aviv*, however, the author finds his authority disrupted, subverted and ultimately decimated by the intervention of forces beyond his control. The experience of being in and writing in Gaza, then, comes to resemble Mahmoud Darwish's description of a similar sensation during the Israeli siege of Beirut in 1982: 'For here, where we are, is the tent for wandering meanings and words gone astray (*ḍālla*) and the orphaned light, scattered and banished from the center.'⁷⁴ The author and his words go astray, like a wayward son (*al-ibn al-ḍāll*) who becomes lost (*ḍālla*) during the return journey. They spin out of control in a place that defies description, where words are not enough.

The narration of the return, in its journey from outside to inside, is interrupted, rerouted and fractured at the border. The border renders the experiences of living as a Palestinian in exile and as a Palestinian in Gaza mutually unintelligible, as the attempt to narrate and represent the incomprehensibility of what he finds on the other side of the border falters. *The Lady from Tel Aviv* situates the ability to evaluate the present reality of Palestine not with those who reside in exile but with those who live a 'stray' life beneath the shadows and bombs of Gaza. Those looking from afar, Walid and even Dana can revel in the chance encounter and imagine new narratives, but such dreams unravel with the harsh realities of a land of borders.

The inability of the returning exile to narrate and interpret his experience further confirms *The Lady from Tel Aviv*'s place on the Palestinian literary map not simply as a parodic response to earlier narratives of return but also as a complement to Jabra's *In Search of Walid Masoud*, with which I began this chapter. Disillusioned with the position of the exiled Palestinian, Walid Masoud abandons a comfortable life in Baghdad to return and join the struggle, and in the process he falls silent. Walid Dahman, inhabiting a post-Oslo political and intellectual landscape vastly transformed from the milieu of 1970s Baghdad, does not join an armed resistance, but he, like Walid Masoud, abandons his authorial voice in search of Palestine and the meaning of return. Only then does the stray, anarchic narrative of the shocking, incomprehensible, disorienting experiences of Palestinian life under occupation emerge from the shadows.

Notes

1. Darwish, *Memory for Forgetfulness*, p. 11.
2. Jabra, *In Search of Walid Masoud*, p. 5.
3. Ibid. p. 286.
4. Ibid. p. 288.
5. Jabra, *al-Bahth ʿan Walid Masʿud*. Thank you to Zeina Halabi for pointing me towards the parallels between the novels of al-Madhoun and Jabra.

6. As Halabi notes, 'The disappearance of the Palestinian exile cannot be represented and shall remain coded in mystery.' Halabi, *The Unmaking of the Arab Intellectual*, p. 104.
7. Al-Madhoun, *Masa'ir*.
8. See al-Madhoun's autobiography: al-Madhoun, *Ta'm al-Furaq*.
9. Muhajerani, 'al-Sayyida min Tall Abib'.
10. Mattar, 'Mourid Barghouti's "Multiple Displacements"', p. 109.
11. Ibid. p. 109.
12. I would include in this category not only reconfigurations of narratives of return and resistance, but also a proliferation of historically focused novels, among them Ibrahim Nasrallah's *Palestinian Comedy*, a series of novels that excavate various moments in recent and distant Palestinian history.
13. Khalidi, 'Observations on the Right of Return', pp. 33–4.
14. Ibid. p. 29.
15. Hirsch, *The Generation of Postmemory*, p. 206.
16. Schulz, *The Palestinian Diaspora*, p. 141.
17. Ibid. p. 131.
18. Khalidi, 'Observations on the Right of Return', pp. 34–5.
19. Schulz, *The Palestinian Diaspora*, p. 230.
20. Ibid. p. 230.
21. Mason, 'Children of the "Idea of Palestine"', p. 273.
22. Ibid. p. 273.
23. Jayyusi, 'Palestinian Identity in Literature', pp. 168–9.
24. Davis, *Palestinian Village Histories*, pp. 28–9.
25. Ibid. p. 55
26. For more on the realism of authors such as Khalifeh and Kanafani, see Abu-Manneh, *The Palestinian Novel*.
27. Said, 'Foreward', p. viii.
28. Ibid. p. xi.
29. Khalifeh, *al-Sabbar*.
30. Abu-Manneh, 'Palestinian Trajectories', p. 526.
31. Barghouti, *I Saw Ramallah*, p. 38.
32. Mattar, 'Mourid Barghouti's "Multiple Displacements"', p. 108.
33. Al-Madhoun, *Al-Sayyida min Tall Abib*, p. 125.
34. Ibid. p. 127.
35. Abu-Manneh, 'Palestinian Trajectories', p. 527.
36. Bernard, 'Forms of Memory', p. 25.

37. See Baydas, *al-Warith*.
38. Abdel-Malek, *The Rhetoric of Violence*, p. 24.
39. Augé, *Non-Places*, p. 34.
40. See Baudrillard, *Simulacra and Simulation*; Relph, *Place and Placelessness*; Appadurai, *Modernity at Large*; and Harvey, *The Condition of Postmodernity*. Each of these theorists deploys distinct terms, definitions and evaluations of the contemporary era's changing relationship with space and time, but all suggest a transformative shift from previous time periods.
41. Augé, *Non-Places*, p. 94.
42. For more, see Yousef, 'The Reception of William Faulkner in the Arab World'; and Azouqa, 'Ghassan Kanafani and William Faulkner'.
43. Kanafani, *Ma Tabaqqa Lakum*.
44. Kanafani, *Rijal fi al-Shams*.
45. Siddiq, 'On Ropes of Memory', p. 95.
46. Meyer, *The Experimental Arabic Novel*, pp. 268–9.
47. Shibli, 'Out of Time'.
48. Darwish, 'Matar Athina', p. 23.
49. Mattar, 'Mourid Barghouti's "Multiple Displacements"', pp. 114–15.
50. Al-Madhoun, *al-Sayyida min Tall Abib*, p. 107.
51. Ibid. p. 265.
52. Ibn Manzur, *Lisan al-'Arab*, vol. 8, p. 259.
53. Plato, *Plato: 'The Republic'*, p. 220.
54. Waugh, *Metafiction*, p. 2.
55. Hutcheon, *Narcissistic Narrative*, p. 28.
56. Khoury, 'Mawt al-Mu'allif', pp. 72–3. Also, see Meyer, *The Experimental Arabic Novel*, p. 268.
57. Authors of Palestinian prose have been a bit slower to move away from realism than those in some Arab countries, where the challenge to realist 'commitment literature' is well documented. For example, see several essays in Abdel-Malek and Hallaq, *Tradition, Modernity, and Postmodernity in Arabic Literature*. Of course, this is not a uniform rule, and there are important counterexamples such as *The Pessoptimist* by Emile Habiby, which uses humour and fantasy to train a critical eye on the predicament of Palestinians who remained in Israel.
58. Ghassan Kanafani's own experiment with non-realist techniques in *All That's Left to You* provoked a significant amount of controversy for its stylistic innovations and a heated debate over its efficacy as a work of resistance literature. Azouqa, 'Ghassan Kanafani and William Faulkner', p. 147.

59. Al-Madhoun, *al-Sayyida min Tall Abib*, p. 104.
60. Baudrillard, *Simulacra and Simulation*, p. 6.
61. Mann, *A Place in History*, p. xi.
62. Suad Amiry expresses this sentiment in her desire to forget the 'Zionist capital Tel Aviv' in favour of Jaffa, her 'Arab hometown' that has been swallowed up by Tel Aviv's expansive sprawl. Amiry, *Nothing to Lose But Your Life*, p. 150.
63. Al-Madhoun, *al-Sayyida min Tall Abib*, p. 47.
64. Ibid. p. 125.
65. Ibid. p. 174.
66. Ibid. p. 104.
67. Ibid. p. 105.
68. Ibid. p. 105.
69. Khoury, 'Mawt al-Mu'allif', p. 73. Here we see *1001 Nights* as a model and as a precursor of the metafiction we find in *Lady from Tel Aviv*.
70. Al-Madhoun, *al-Sayyida min Tall Abib*, p. 308.
71. Ibid. p. 309.
72. The Israeli settlements in Gaza mentioned in the novel were destroyed with the Israeli withdrawal from Gaza in 2005. Though Israeli restrictions on movement within Gaza were lifted, a blockade has severely restricted the flow of people in and out of the territory, and incursions and air strikes remain commonplace.
73. Al-Madhoun, *al-Sayyida min Tall Abib*, p. 308.
74. Darwish, *Memory for Forgetfulness*, p. 11.

5

Does the Camera Lie? Or, How to Document the Wall

I filmed the burial of this land.
— Simone Bitton, director of *Mur*[1]

A scene from the 2009 documentary *City of Borders*, directed by Yun Suh, depicts a Palestinian man, along with a few of his friends, attempting to cross the concrete barrier that snakes through the West Bank illicitly, under the cover of darkness. They travel from Ramallah to Jerusalem, where their destination is a gay bar called the Shushan. According to the film, this bar offers a safe space for gay Israelis and Palestinians in the area. It is also depicted as one of the few places in this divided city in which Israelis and Palestinians intermingle and communicate. The act of climbing over the wall in this scene provides a metaphor for the aim of the film as a whole: to show how people get around the myriad barriers and borders that preclude interaction, movement and communication in Jerusalem by uncovering the gaps in these limits. The film illuminates areas of the wall where one can climb over to the other side, or a gay bar on a side street in a quiet Jerusalem neighbourhood that can provide refuge from the pressures of ethnic discrimination, religious bigotry and anti-gay animus that mark the outside world.

City of Borders is one of many increasingly common representations that depict the West Bank barrier in order to critique the separatist and segregationist policies that confine and limit Palestinian movement both within the West Bank and between the West Bank and Israel. Many such films, books and works of art seek glimmers of hope from within the grim concrete of the wall. Frequently, portrayals of the wall, motivated by a belief in coexistence and peace, search for reasons for optimism, whether in the form of a gay bar that caters to both Israelis and Palestinians, nonviolent protests, or politically motivated graffiti adorning the concrete wall. Yet the search for coexistence can be problematic and produce certain blind spots to systemic practices and unequal power relations. For instance, the possibility of an Israeli gay bar as a neutral meeting space is immediately complicated by the question of pinkwashing, in which Israel's relatively permissive stance on LGBT issues produces an image of a progressive, tolerant Israel that effaces, sanitises and deflects from the decidedly un-liberal practices of occupation.[2] Moreover, as in Suh's film, the optimism that motivates such depictions almost always falters;[3] by the end of the film, the Shushan has shut down for economic reasons, and the Palestinian man who crossed the wall has emigrated to the United States. The hope that provided the project's impetus breaks down against the limits of the borders of Jerusalem, for the film remains bound by the logic of 'documentation' contained within the documentary form, a claim of fealty to a 'reality' which, to this point, has dashed the hopes of many writers, activists and filmmakers. Such documentaries, it seems, contain little room for fantasies of coexistence when confronted with this reality, a revelation that is staged on screen.

While this failure of coexistence might seem to bring us back to Chapter 3 and Kashua's novels, there are a couple of documentaries that avoid this framing. They use an intensive focus on the border and its construction to interrogate the ability of the wall documentary to reveal truth and reality, much as al-Madhoun's novel questions the author's ability to narrate his characters' return to Palestine. This chapter examines two such films. One, *5 Broken Cameras* (2011), a film by Emad Burnat and Guy Davidi that received a nomination for best documentary in the Academy Awards,[4] largely relies on amateur footage stitched together after the fact. Burnat, a resident of the West Bank village of Bil'in, used hand-held video cameras to document weekly protests against the West Bank barrier being built through the town, and his footage began to spread through YouTube and other media, eventually catching the attention of the Israeli filmmaker Guy Davidi. Burnat and Davidi were both credited as the film's directors, and it was funded by *Greenhouse*, an Israeli and EU-supported foundation. Yael Friedman suggests that this transnational production reproduces colonial power dynamics of a subaltern, Palestinian other and an Israeli, western cultural superiority.[5] I argue that focusing on the wall itself as subject and object of representation in this film nevertheless allows us to see the film's very real critique of the spatiality of Israeli–Palestinian power relations. The title, *5 Broken Cameras*, refers to the repeated destruction of Burnat's cameras by Israeli forces, and the breaking of the camera lens functions as a metaphor for the violence of the wall, through which the film reproduces formally the fragmentation and disruption wrought by the wall upon the residents of Bilʿin.

The other film, *Mur* (2004), the French word for wall, was directed by the Moroccan-born French-Israeli filmmaker Simone Bitton, who has also made films about Mahmoud Darwish and the politician ʿAzmi Bishara.[6] While it has garnered a certain amount of international critical interest, *Mur* never received the accolades heaped upon *5 Broken Cameras*, which perhaps reflects *Mur*'s more subdued approach to its subject matter and its eschewal of certain narrative conventions of documentary filmmaking. While other documentaries about the wall have used a particular place or struggle to dramatise and narrativise the effects of the wall, *Mur* distinguishes itself by making the wall its primary subject and structuring device. This results in a documentary that avoids an explicit narrative and instead focuses on the physicality of the wall's concrete and barbed wire, and the film's structure reflects the meandering and disruptive nature of the wall itself. Much of it documents the wall's construction and the accompanying destruction of the land on which it is built. Bitton acknowledges this; in her words, she says 'I filmed the burial of this land'.[7] The film mourns the loss of the land caused by the wall's construction by documenting the process by which it was erected.

In this chapter, I consider the ways in which these two films, *Mur* and *5 Broken Cameras*, interrogate the implications of 'documenting' this space on screen and the possibility of doing so. Both films use the camera to portray the wall as a space that resists and disrupts representation. I show that these films do not simply depict the wall in order to challenge its existence or look for hopes of a potential solution. Instead, I argue that they show how the act of documenting the wall can itself function as a form of complicity by perpetuating the wall's mythic power and reinforcing the notion of its irreversible permanence. First, I consider *Mur* as a meta-documentary that comments upon the difficulties of representing the wall, and specifically the problem of claiming an unmediated or objective depiction of the barrier. Building off of this, I then show that *5 Broken Cameras* uses the tools of documentary, particularly the camera, to circumvent attempts to suppress and challenge its filming of the wall, while also calling into question the veracity and utility of typical documentary narratives. Together, these films show that it is not enough simply to document the wall, but that critiquing the wall entails an interrogation of documentary filmmaking itself. In order to contextualise this argument, I begin with a discussion of documentary filmmaking within the context of the two films' efforts to depict the wall.

Documenting the Wall

The 500-kilometer Israeli barrier in the West Bank, the building of which began in 2002 and continues to this day, has become a major factor in political and cultural discourse around the Israeli–Palestinian conflict. It has spawned a wave of literature, film and art devoted to the controversial project. Its rhetorical power and resonance undoubtedly stem in part from its tangibility, a physical embodiment of an occupation that is constantly evolving, in motion, and difficult to pin down. It also fits into existing schema whereby walls have played a central role in major conflicts, from the Berlin Wall to the so-called 'peace lines' that still divide Catholic and Protestant areas of Belfast, Northern Ireland, and the West Bank barrier today. Just as the Berlin Wall was a symbol of the Cold War, so too is the West Bank wall an object that metonymically represents a larger conflict. Interest in the wall, both within Palestine and Israel and from abroad, manifests itself culturally in the numerous books of all types, works of art such as graffiti on the wall by the British artist Banksy, and feature films such as Hany Abu-Assad's Academy Award-nominated film *Omar* (2013).

Yet, in many works, the wall has remained, as Anna Ball has argued, elusive, 'a site that cannot be grasped in its material, emotive and intellectual entirety'.[8] This elusiveness can be seen in films such as visual artist Khaled Jarrar's *Infiltrators* (2013), an intense, gritty and engaging depiction of people who attempt to sneak across the wall and those who assist them. Filmed on a hand-held camera, *Infiltrators* offers an important portrayal of resistance and persistence against the separation imposed by the wall. Yet the unavoidably fragmented nature of the film's imagery – it is often filmed in tight spaces, areas of limited visibility, and sometimes furtively – causes the power and brutality of the wall as a single, expansive entity to fade into the background as it focuses in a microcosmic fashion on attempts to cross it. The wall is perhaps the most extreme example of what Hamid Dabashi terms a 'mimetic crisis'[9] in Palestinian cinema and culture, as a stranger-than-fiction reality exceeds and problematises attempts to represent it. The wall produces a necessary and compulsive desire to represent its brutality, but at the same time stymies many such attempts.

It is perhaps this problematic of representing the wall that has caused the documentary, among these various media and genres, to rise to prominence as a fertile medium for critiques of the wall. While I have focused largely on literature up until now, and there are certainly works of literature that engage heavily with the wall, the wall's sheer visuality seems to lend itself to filmic representation. Further, if, as Dabashi argues, the need to produce an 'alternative record of a silenced crime'[10] provides the impulse for filming the wall, documentary would appear to be a fruitful mode of representation. Indeed, its construction has spawned a new genre of wall documentaries. In addition to the two films at hand and *City of Borders* and *Infiltrators*, other wall documentaries include the 2009 film *Budrus* (directed by Julia Bacha), *The Iron Wall* (Mohammed Alater, 2007), and numerous short films. This mini-wave of documentaries that chronicle and protest the wall's construction and its effects on both Palestinians and Israelis indicates a belief among filmmakers in the ability of the documentary genre to chronicle the wall's presence and impact. The wall is an imposing and undeniable monument to the military power and technologies of occupation that produced it.[11] The wall, which slices through the land like a scar and, to use Gloria Anzaldúa's description of a border, scrapes and wounds the land and people around it,[12] possesses an arresting and entrancing visuality. It is a spectacle that begs to be seen, filmed, documented, explained and protested.

The burdening of Palestinian documentary with the additional task of serving as an 'alternative record' further heightens the stakes of this dilemma. While more recent Palestinian film production has been largely auteur fiction, in earlier periods documentary was the primary mode of filmmaking. As Nadia Yaqub shows in her study of revolutionary Palestinian cinema, many of these works were short, low-budget documentaries produced by film units of the PLO and other revolutionary groups. These products of a 'national liberation in progress'[13] were motivated by an impulse to galvanise support for and to archive both the political struggle and the experiences of Palestinian refugees.[14] These films were very different from contemporary documentaries in many respects: they were almost exclusively made in exile, typically focused on refugees, and existed within larger ecosystems of Palestinian revolutionary movements and global Third Cinema that differ greatly from the transnational mechanisms of funding and production that prevail today. While the loss of many of these archives in the Israeli invasion of Beirut in 1982 produced a rupture that severed later Palestinian filmmaking from this cinematic heritage, efforts by filmmakers such as Annemarie Jacir have emerged to reincorporate aspects of this era into contemporary Palestinian film culture.[15] Perhaps, then, we can view the recent documentary (re)turn as a reinvigoration of filmmaking as archive and protest, in dialogue with this earlier era.

For contemporary documentaries, the wall and its elusiveness present a representational dilemma that stems from this genre's claim to represent a verifiable reality and truth in a way that a novel or a feature film does not.[16] The authoritative claim to truth that the documentary accrues for itself is deployed to protest the wall. To depict the reality of the wall, the thinking goes, is to reveal its indefensibility. However, as Bill Nichols has argued, the primary means by which documentaries construct such arguments is by constructing a particular narrative and then resolving said narrative.[17] In the case of the wall, this creates a desire not only for a critique of the wall, but also for a form of resolution that considers the potential for altering the status quo. This creates a problem that we see in *City of Borders* and other films, for they must both convincingly depict the wall's unbridled power and make room for the possibility of overcoming or circumventing it. The challenge is to document a visual space in a way that conveys its unrelenting power as an argument against its presence, while at the same time making the case that its power is not *so* insurmountable as to make change impossible. We could go as far as to say that this dilemma lies at the centre of many examples of the documentary form, particularly when it tackles ethically troubling exercises of power, and that the difficulty of documenting the wall highlights this contradiction.

The primary means by which the documentary makes its claim to truth is visual, through its use of images. Often, the documentary image begs to be read as what Barthes terms a 'message without a code', as a transmission (albeit in reduced form) of reality, rather than a transformation of it.[18] Viewers expect more than a resemblance, they expect a 'record', a direct connection between the image and the 'real' subject.[19] However, as Gil Hochberg argues in her work on visibility and invisibility in the Israeli–Palestinian conflict, the image in this context is highly contested ground, with little or no agreement as to what images signify.[20] The possibility of the image as a true, reliable representation is already foreclosed here, which suggests that a documentary that uncritically assumes an ability to represent faithfully the reality of the wall will fall short of its desire to contest its presence. If a documentary seeks to be a 'record' of reality, and to convey its overwhelming force as a spectacle and projection of power, the wall problematises this desire and the documentary risks replicating and affirming the power dynamics that produce and sustain the wall. The particularities of the wall as a space, then, have produced a genre of wall documentaries that in some instances seek to accomplish this task through a self-aware mode of filmmaking that has implications for how we understand the broader category of documentary.

The works that I examine, *Mur* and *5 Broken Cameras*, acknowledge, engage with, and circumnavigate this dilemma by engaging in a reflexive form of documentary filmmaking that questions the types of recording (*tasjīl*) and filming (*taṣwīr*) that constitute such films and distinguishes between these two concepts. They acknowledge the problematic of recording, documenting and representing this reality. They do not simply seek to create a documentary narrative, but also to consider critically the means by which such narratives are constructed. They depict the act of documenting as an interrupted process, one that is at risk of misrepresentation in *Mur* or of delusion in *5 Broken Cameras*. By foregrounding the uncertainties and interruptions within the representation of this space, they grapple with the problem of documenting a space they wish to tear down and allows us to see the discursive weaknesses in the wall itself. In the remainder of this chapter, I will show the ways in which *5 Broken Cameras* and *Mur* interrogate the meaning of filming the wall and by doing so articulate a mode of documenting such a space without succumbing to it.

The Wall Lies

The first film, *Mur*, was released in 2004 and is one of the earliest films about the wall. The film itself alternates between silent shots of the wall, its construction and the people who interact with it, as well as discussions between the filmmaker and those affected by the wall and an extensive interview with one of the main Israeli architects of the barrier. Crucially, it does not merely document the wall's existence, but also its coming into being. It portrays the birth of a space and the violence and destruction that comes with it. Remarkably, it accomplishes this task with few direct depictions of the violence of the wall's construction or enforcement. Ball characterises the documentary as 'contemplative', with long, slow shots that convey both the 'weight' of time and of the concrete segments of the wall.[21] Perhaps it is this eschewal of violent *events* (i.e. narrative), that brings the violence of spaces and processes to the forefront, even as it makes for a less dramatic narrative than might be expected in a documentary about Palestine and Israel.

As it captures the construction and impact of the wall in different places and moments, *Mur* emphasises that the wall's birth is not a singular, linear event. Instead, it is part of what Eyal Weizman calls 'the dynamic morphology of the frontier',[22] a border that is constantly rerouted and functions as a 'seismograph' of the political, legal and strategic consideration that shape its path.[23] This point will become more apparent in my discussion of *5 Broken Cameras*, but for now it suffices as a reminder that such a space of simultaneous construction and destruction creates dilemmas of representation that the film addresses at the intersection of the documentary's voice and its visual construction. The film deploys a self-referential voice to interrogate the means by which it represents and documents the wall by calling attention to the process of filming itself. *Mur* creates what I call an 'interrupted documentary' in which the film's attempts to chronicle the wall through a series of long, silent, shots are frequently disrupted and questioned. In this way, documentary reveals the impossibility of simply 'letting the wall speak for itself' and shows instead that the wall is a space in which representation itself is always suspect. Moreover, in this warning, the film offers a model for an emerging genre of wall documentaries.

The primary means by which *Mur* reflects on the act of filmmaking occurs by toying with the documentary genre's conventions of 'voice' and the means by which it constructs shots through editing and framing. The first of these, its use of voice, describes the means by which the documentary 'speaks' to the audience to make its point and encompasses a wide range of approaches.[24] Many documentaries include some form of direct address, in which a narrator and/or interview subjects speak directly to the audience, which tends to imbue the speaker with authority. Other documentaries may eschew direct address or any other sort of spoken narrative, with the aim of letting the events on screen speak for themselves, while yet other documentaries emphasise the participatory role of filmmaking, as in the *cinéma-vérité* style of documentary.[25] *Mur* modulates between multiple modes, creating moments of interruption and a hesitant ambivalence towards the possibility of documenting the wall on screen. Specifically, *Mur* features no form of direct address, but rather stages a series of mediated conversations between interlocutors and the director herself, who speaks but remains off screen. This technique marks *Mur* as a documentary that calls attention to its own status as representation and artefact. In other words, the film uses the voices of the director and her interlocutors to question its own attempts to represent the wall.

One section from early in the film will help illustrate this point. It begins with a five-minute sequence without commentary in which the camera films the assembly of the wall's building blocks. The view of the countryside gradually becomes more and more obscured as the pieces of the wall come together, eventually blocking any view of the land beyond the wall (figure 5.1). The clanging of metal against concrete and the sound of the bulldozers' engines at work drowns out the serene rural silence. Then, the film cuts to another shot in which the viewer can see the finished wall extending from one side of the screen to another, with green fields in the foreground. The camera begins fixed on a small section of the wall, and then, in the same shot, begins a slow pan to the right that depicts the barrier extending off into the horizon. The camera, using a single long take, reveals the stark contrast of an endless wall of grey concrete and watchtowers looming over lush farmland (figure 5.2). According to David MacDougall, the use of long shots is unusual in documentaries, which tend to use short takes to maintain viewer attention.[26] Long shots, by contrast, risk disrupting the flow of the narrative and therefore losing the attention of the viewer. However, they also provide a means of allowing the viewer to peruse the image, to soak up the details of the shot and draw his or her own conclusions

HOW TO DOCUMENT THE WALL | 143

Figure 5.1 A shot in *Mur* (2004) depicting the construction of a concrete segment of the wall.

Figure 5.2 A long shot of the wall is pictured during a conversation with a Palestinian farmer.

about the meaning of the image. In this scene, the long shot allows the scale and impact of slow, plodding, mechanical relentlessness of the wall's construction and its unending expanse into the horizon to sink in.

However, in this clip, the camera's attempt to allow the viewer to absorb and make sense of the wall's presence is complicated by the presence of people not seen in this shot. The long, silent shot is interrupted by a series of questions from an onlooker. A man, who we learn is a farmer and a resident of the area named Bilal Mansour, peppers Bitton with questions. The director remains off screen, but we hear her respond to his inquiries in Arabic. Mansour wants to know what the filmmaker is doing. 'Are you filming the wall?', he asks. 'What do you think of the wall?' At first he receives no response, as if the director is too focused on the visual image of the wall to be disturbed. So he continues speaking, answering his own questions to fill the void left by the director's lack of response. However, she finally answers the man when he asks her if the cameraman is filming the wall. '*Byiṣowwir?*' He asks in Arabic. 'Is he filming?' She responds by correcting him with a single word, '*Byisajjil*', which means 'He is recording.'

In this seemingly minor correction of terminology we can discern the director's particular vision for the film, as well as the limits of this vision that the visual and narrative construction of this sequence acknowledges. *Byiṣowwir*, the word that Mansour uses, means 'to film or to photograph'. It is derived from the word 'picture' (*ṣūra*) and literally means 'to make a picture' or, more broadly, 'to form'. It is also related to the word *yataṣawwar*, 'to imagine', which emphasises that *taṣwīr* (the nominal form of the verb) is an intentional act of representation, the formation of a particular image. Thus, for Bitton to classify her work as 'filming', as *taṣwīr*, would acknowledge the active role of the director in shaping the way in which the object of the film, in this case the wall, is represented. On the other hand, *byisajjil*, the word used by Bitton to mean record (*tasjīl*), is derived from the root of *sijil*, or 'chronicle', which indicates a claim to accurate and credible depiction. A chronicle is a factual account of events in the order that they occurred, ostensibly free of narrative manipulations, recalling Barthes' characterisation of the documentary's impulse to be a record. Thus, in her correction – Bitton's assertion that the cameraman is recording, *byisajjil* – the director reveals her aspiration to create an unmediated representation of the wall, a long, silent shot in which viewers are allowed to see the wall's raw power for themselves. Bitton's use of the long shot is an attempt to record the wall as it is, uninterrupted by cuts, editing or interpretation. Her use of *tasjīl* indicates a desire for a simplified documentation, a move away from the narrative qualities of documentary.

However, by calling attention to the act of filming, and acknowledging its status as representation, this sequence also reveals the impossibility of this desire and Bitton's consciousness of this impossibility. Though she claims she wishes to simply record, to faithfully chronicle the painful reality of the wall, by articulating this wish for *tasjīl* on camera, she reveals a certain amount of scepticism towards her own desire. By including the dialogue between Bitton and Mansour, *Mur* breaks the illusion of cohesiveness, of abstracting the physical power of the wall from the lived experience it creates for the thousands of people who, like Mansour, are affected by its presence. Mansour's interruption reminds us of the human element that remains invisible in the scene's long shots and, in this reminder, shows the true disruption created by the appearance of the wall. 'It's a prison,' Mansour says. Indeed, throughout *Mur*, Bitton fields several similar questions from onlookers and interviewees. What are you doing? they ask. Why are you filming? Who are you making this for? Who is going to watch the film? Frequently, as in the sequence above, they interrupt the film's long shots and call attention to the act of filming. By foregrounding the process of filmmaking, *Mur* demonstrates, through its interrupted attempts to 'record', the deception and danger of maintaining the illusion of direct representation of the wall, of 'letting it speak for itself'.

A second scene in the film will help clarify this last point by showing that an unmediated representation of the wall would, if possible, run the risk of allowing it to justify its existence. Several sections of the film feature Bitton's interview with retired Israeli general Amos Yaron, who spearheaded the building of the wall. The film frames the interview with the general sitting at his desk, flanked by an Israeli flag on each side. This frame makes it clear to the viewer that the encounter with the general is staged, unlike the apparently spontaneous conversation with Mansour that I discuss above. Yaron does not speak directly to the audience, but rather the presence of the director and her questions mediate his statements. Though she does not appear on screen, like other conversations in the documentary, her voice is heard from behind the camera. This mediation creates critical distance, allows the general to make his statements and assertions about the wall while refusing to accept them at face value. Though Bitton never challenges the general explicitly, her mediation imbues scepticism towards the technical jargon he deploys to describe the wall's purpose and function.

In one part of this interview, Yaron explains a number of technical aspects of the wall. He describes it as a technologically advanced system, one that is an electronic obstacle as well as a physical barrier. Anyone who touches it will set off an alarm in a control room, where military personnel keep the wall and its surroundings under constant surveillance. If someone approaches, he claims, cameras, radar and electronic signals allow soldiers to arrive within minutes. However, his words ring hollow on screen because immediately before Yaron makes these claims, the film depicts a man climbing across the barrier unmolested (figure 5.3). Thus, while Yaron's description of the wall's system of panoptic surveillance oozes with confidence and self-satisfaction at the technological achievements of the barrier, the viewer knows the falseness

Figure 5.3 A Palestinian sneaks through a section of the wall, as an Israeli general touts its impenetrability via voiceover.

of his claims, which transforms them into an exercise in hubris and self-deception. The contrast of the visual narrative of the camera and the spoken narrative of the general illuminates the rhetorical power of the documentary form at its peak.

This point returns us to the danger of letting the wall speak for itself. The wall does speak in its own way, according to Yaron, by making its presence known through barbed wire and fences. If someone approaches the wall, Yaron says that its physical infrastructure acts a warning, indicating to the person, '*Ata lo yakhol la' avor. Lekh mi-po.*' 'You may not cross. Go away.' In other words, the wall's message is one of impenetrability. It presents itself as a barrier that cannot be crossed. Thus, to let the wall speak for itself would allow it to accrue the impenetrable power it claims for itself. However, the juxtaposition of these words with the man crossing in the previous scene also shows the viewer that this self-representation is deceptive and suspect at best. The film makes its statement and casts doubt upon the general's claim by refusing to let him, and the wall, speak for itself. The film accomplishes this task through careful editing, by assembling the images and sounds in a particular way to highlight the contrast between the general's voice and the images Bitton captures at the wall. This scene suggests that Bitton has moved from simply recording (*tasjīl*) to filming and forming (*taṣwīr*) her representation of the wall. Indeed, this scene shows that filming, not simply recording, provides her critique with rhetorical power by unveiling the absurdity of the general's words.

As if to reflect this change, Bitton revises her terminology in later discussions with onlookers. During a long shot that parallels the one discussed above, this one of a watchtower near Jerusalem, a woman asks Bitton, 'Why are you filming?' Bitton responds, 'We're filming the wall.' (*Binṣowwir al-jidār.*) She no longer says that the cameraman is 'recording' the wall, but now that 'we' are 'filming' the barrier. By switching from third person 'he' to first person 'we', Bitton stakes a claim to her own role as director in mediating the wall's portrayal. Moreover, in this shift from 'recording' to 'filming', from *tasjīl* to *taṣwīr*, the documentary acknowledges the inaccessibility of a pure unadulterated chronicle, perhaps in any situation but particularly in the context of Israel and Palestine, where the same raw materials and events can spawn incompatible and conflicting narratives and claims. This awareness allows the film to interrogate itself and its assumptions about both the wall and the means by which it can be represented. This invites the viewer to do the same, to consider not simply the raw power of the wall but also the means by which its depiction can imbue it with such authority.

This acknowledgement and interrogation of representation brings its own power, as the conclusion of Bitton's interview with the general demonstrates. During the course of the interview, he becomes increasingly impatient with Bitton's persistent questioning, and he finally stands up, informs her that the interview is over, and storms out of his own office. The impetus for this abrupt end to their conversations is Bitton's words, but it also provides a metaphor for the ways in which the film as a whole interrogates the wall's claims of impenetrability. Bitton prods and probes the general but does not argue with him, she offers no counter to the narrative he provides. Instead, the deliberate yet critical pace of questioning the general causes him to exhaust his own deceptive talking points until they become unsustainable. Likewise, by persistently and quietly pushing the narrative of the wall's impenetrability to its breaking point, *Mur* demonstrates the potential potency of the modes of representation it uses, particularly *taṣwīr*, as a means of producing an alternative narrative of the wall. Moreover, the film's self-aware interrogation of the wall and its representation allows the documentary to function not only as a commentary on the wall but also as a commentary on the way in which such spaces can be represented. In this way, *Mur* provides a roadmap for a 'wall' genre of documentary cinema, a reflexive form of filmmaking that acknowledges the sheer power of this structure while also contesting it.

A 'Strong Camera'

If *Mur* stages the transition from *tasjīl* to *taṣwīr* in the documentary in order to demonstrate the problematic of documenting it, *5 Broken Cameras* interrogates the limitations of *taṣwīr* by placing the camera, the device by which documentaries are made and filmed, at the centre of its narrative. Unlike *Mur*, the film and filmmaker accept the idea that *5 Broken Cameras* is an act of *taṣwīr*, but instead interrogate the types of meaning and narrative it can produce. From the title itself – *5 Broken Cameras* – the film declares its intention to produce a narrative that will be fragmented (broken), uncertain and reflexive (about the camera). Moreover, in its inclusion of the word 'camera', the film transforms the often invisible, unmentioned tool of filmmaking into the documentary's primary subject and structuring device. Thus, the film is a meditation on the simultaneous power and impotence of the camera – the rhetorical power of the camera to expose and protest injustice alongside the fragility of the physical device that makes this power possible.

Emad Burnat, the Palestinian resident of Bilʿin who filmed the weekly protests with the five cameras, provides a narrative voiceover at various points throughout the film. He describes his decision to make films about the protests as happenstance, the result of purchasing a camera in order to document the infancy and childhood of his youngest son Jibreel, who was born in 2005, and whose birth and growth parallels the construction of the wall and the protests it spurs. He says, 'I film (*baṣawwir*) to hold on to memories,' yet the footage presented from his cameras are not the memories he expects when he begins to film. Alongside happy images of a child's first steps and words, Burnat captures the clashes, destruction and violence that envelopes his village. As Burnat makes this statement, the viewer sees blurry images, clearly filmed by a wildly shaking, erratic camera, as if the person filming is running or falling. This is the first of many instances in the film that depict the chaos and violence of the wall protests. These moments emphasise the amateur, raw nature of the footage through its shakiness, sounds of static, and flickering between colour and black and white (figure 5.4). However, as noted in the discussion of *Mur*, the use of the term *baṣawwir* (the first person present tense form of *taṣwīr*) indicates a form of intentionality. Burnat states early on that 'I decided to film' (*qarrartu uṣawwir*), though the form that this act of *taṣwīr* took defied his expectations. His filmmaking took on a life of its own, derailed by circumstances, to become something else entirely, a stray film that mimics the unpredictability of life under the shadow of the wall. However, the exceptional and unpredictable nature of the events Burnat films are precisely the reason we see them. Suffice it to say, if Burnat's films had remained home movies of Jibreel, they would not have made it onto screens across the globe. The emphasis on the camera in the film exposes this interplay between intentionality and unpredictability that animates documentary narratives. It makes this relationship explicit and allows the viewer to consider the ways in which it shapes the films we see on screen.

Figure 5.4   An injury suffered by Burnat in *5 Broken Cameras* (2009) is depicted with a shaky, flickering image.

At various points in the documentary, Burnat expands upon his reasons for filming the protests, and he focuses on the potential for his films to contribute to the struggle against the wall. He notes that his videos have started to appear on the internet, on sites like YouTube, and that this has motivated him to continue producing footage of the wall and its protests. In one instance, he travels to different villages in the West Bank and shows his videos in order to get the message out about the protests. His films, which he created gradually over many years, and their reception thus exist in a symbiotic relationship – the circulation of the films prompts Burnat to produce more films, which then circulate further. This relationship affirms Burnat's declaration that, 'I have to think that these images have some meaning', but with a caveat. The meaning that Burnat wills into being derives not simply from the images he captures, but through their distribution, reception and emulation, the 'films' they create through *taṣwīr*. The end result that we see – *5 Broken Cameras* – emerges from this mutually reinforcing relationship of creation and reception that creates a slow accumulation of images that become not simply a narrative created through *taṣwīr* but a story of *taṣwīr* itself. By telling this story, the film not only captures the events of the protests, but the necessity of presenting and representing the events in a certain way in order to achieve particular goals.

As Burnat provides a voiceover at the beginning of the documentary, the film shows the five 'broken cameras' assembled on a table (figure 5.5). However, at the same time, we are able to see these broken cameras assembled through the lens of an additional, perhaps sixth, camera that is *not* broken, and is distinguished by the use of a wider aspect ratio than the footage from Burnat's handheld camcorders. The camera producing the images we see depicts the multiple cameras that recorded the bulk of the film's footage. With the appearance of this image of shattered camcorders, we must shift our framework for analysing the film from *the camera*, the omnipresent, abstracted, all-seeing device that forms the core of most analyses of film[27], to a fragmented, fragile plurality of *cameras*, a set of broken, imperfect objects. By laying the cameras on the table before the viewer, the film builds its structure on the fragmentation that they reveal. The progression of the film is largely chronological, but it is segmented according to which camera was used, and each section or 'chapter' is made up of the footage of a single camera. Just as

Figure 5.5 The five cameras used by Burnat to document the Bilʻin protests.

the rupture and violence of the wall is inscribed into the cameras' shattered lenses, it is also captured on screen by the blank spots between the destruction of one camera and the purchase of another.

The footage from the broken cameras is not sufficient to create a film; it is 'raw', unedited, unstructured. Rather, an additional layer of structure is needed to make a narrative; not only more visual footage but also in this case narrative voiceovers by Burnat are superimposed to create a documentary. The 'documents' (*wathā'iq*) are not enough to create a 'documentary' (*film wathā'iqī*). By revealing the different 'pieces' or elements that constitute this film, *5 Broken Cameras* acknowledges the constructedness of its narrative. The film's production and marketing reflect this as well; the footage from the video cameras is Burnat's, but the overarching structure of the film is the result of a collaboration between Burnat and the Israeli director Guy Davidi, whose involvement and connections to transnational filmmaking shaped its production, funding and overarching message, which eventually prompted disagreement between Davidi and Burnat.[28] At one point, Burnat states that he needs a 'strong camera' to film these protests. This might at first glance seem like an odd statement. We have seen, after all, that these cameras are broken, fragile and imperfect. How can they also be strong? The footage these cameras capture is shaky, tenuous and improvised. The perspective they offer is narrow, limited by the restrictions on movement from the wall and the authorities that enforce its presence. Yet paradoxically, it is this very brokenness that gives these cameras their strength. By using the broken cameras as a structural device, he is able to make full use of the power of the camera to depict visually the unreal, the unimaginable, to make the abstract idea of a 'protest' against the 'wall' into a tangible experience of fragmentation.

Burnat also contemplates other forms of power that the camera and the films it produces can provide. He uses it as a form of protection by relying upon the effect that images can have in galvanising opposition to the occupation, but it also provides a form of personal security by threatening to expose to the world the actions of soldiers and settlers. Repeatedly throughout the film, Burnat is ordered to turn off the camera, despite his possession of credentials as a journalist. In one instance, the army comes to his house and Burnat seeks to film the encounter. The soldiers announce that the area has been declared a closed military zone, which gives them the authority to order

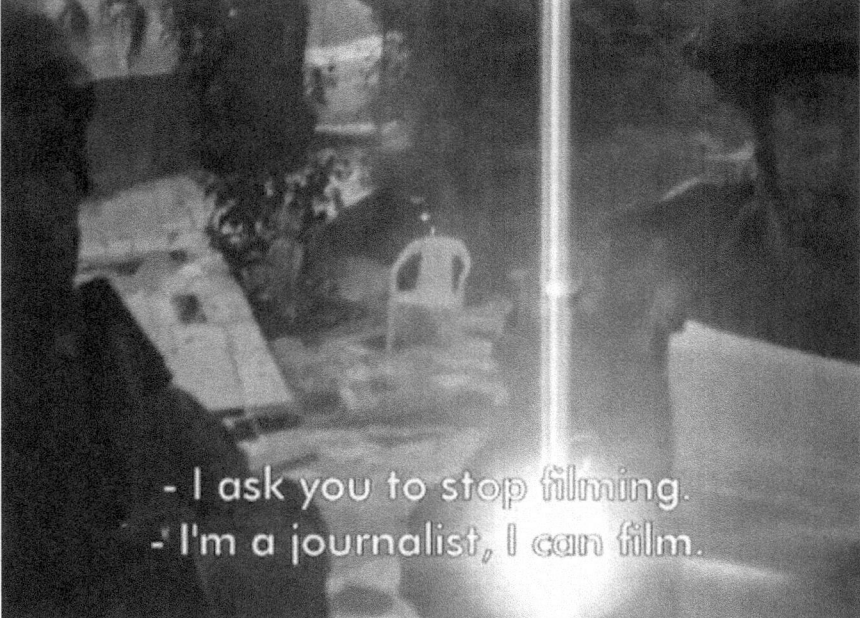

Figure 5.6 A soldier shines a flashlight into Burnat's camera to blind it.

him to stop filming. They stand close to his camera and shine a flashlight into the camera to disrupt the picture (figure 5.6). He argues with them and eventually sets the camera on the ground while the camera continues recording. For the viewer, the sudden blinding light and the jarring jerkiness of the camera's motion disrupts the flow of images expected from the camera. It visually recreates the shock of the surprise visit, during which Burnat is detained and placed under house arrest. Both Burnat and the military treat the camera as a powerful tool, and for the latter as a threat to its ability to act against the protests. This idea of the camera as protection is contained within the idea of the documentary genre, which claims for itself the potential to effect change through its images and narratives. The term in Arabic, *wathāʾiqī*, as stated above, indicates a form of confidence, *thiqqa*, something that is a reliable and permanent testament to a certain reality, but also something that ensures the continuity and protection of this reality. Just as a historical document preserves and safeguards knowledge, so the film footage attests to the veracity of the events narrated in the documentary.

One moment of intense fighting at a protest reveals both the power of the camera to protect and the limits of that power. As Burnat films a clash between soldiers and protestors, the deafening sound of shooting and exploding tear gas canisters causes Burnat to lose his ability to hear temporarily, and at that moment the viewer hears only a ringing sound as the images of chaos continue on screen. The sound effects mimic the physiological effects on Burnat, as the film's soundtrack represents the loss of hearing presumably experienced by the filmmaker. By anthropomorphising the audio, the film merges the perspectives of Burnat and his camera, and their sensory experiences become one. Then as Burnat (and the viewer) gradually regains hearing, the sounds of the fighting return. This technique allows the viewer to experience voyeuristically the disorientation, chaos and danger that the wall has brought. However, in merging the perspectives of Burnat and the camera through the sounds as Burnat hears them and the images as the camera records them, the film also calls into question the possibility of separating the two points of view. The documentary can protect its creator, but its broader protective power is unclear.

5 Broken Cameras interrogates the conceit of film as protection by taking it literally, by embedding this idea into the physical device of the camera. In the same scene, a few moments later, the camera is shot. A soldier fires at Burnat and the bullet lodges in the camera, and the screen goes blank. Here it appears that the camera provides not only symbolic protection but a form of physical protection as well, for if the camera had not caught the bullet Burnat could have been injured or perhaps killed, as he himself acknowledges. However, when Burnat states that when he films, 'I feel like the camera protects me, but it is an illusion', *5 Broken Cameras* questions its own ability as a documentary to provide the protection to which it aspires. The documentary can expose, sure, but can it do more? In this implicit question it acknowledges the limits of the documentary. It can represent in a particular way, to tell the story it wishes to tell, but it cannot determine the outcome. It performs and reveals the chaos and fragmentation of the wall but it cannot, as of yet, bring it down.

Conclusion: Beyond Reality

By problematising the act of documenting the wall, both *Mur* and *5 Broken Cameras* reveal distinct but interrelated aspects of the representational dilemma presented by border spaces, and which films from within the emergent wall documentary genre seek to address. While *Mur* reveals the deceptive quality of claiming the ability to record objective truth (*tasjīl*), *5 Broken Cameras* interrogates the claims of the power of representation (*taṣwīr*) in the documentary form. Together they show the risks of 'documenting' the border by revealing the ease with which the border's power can be uncritically reproduced even in a critique. Indeed, it this awareness of the limits of the documentary form that allow these two works to resist this type of uncritical reproduction. But through their intentionality, these documentaries also raise a larger question: how is it possible, visually or otherwise, to contest the border through cultural production? Many of the works examined in this and previous chapters have exposed, negotiated, lived with, crossed and challenged the borders they encounter frequently in the practice of everyday life in Palestine. Yet these borders remain intact. The wall marches relentlessly forward, with slight modification, protests spark worldwide interest but produce few tangible results, and new borders produce entrapment and disillusionment.

In both this chapter and the last we see the prominence of reflexivity to literary and filmic engagements with the border. This approach, it seems, allows these works to engage both with the meanings of border spaces and with the meanings that are created by representing them. This consciousness permits a form of engagement with the border that is absent in many works even as they take borders of various types as their subjects. Films like *Mur* and *5 Broken Cameras*, and literary works like al-Madhoun's, show that not only spatial but also discursive realities are determined by the authorities that impose borders in the first place. The wall in *Mur* is cloaked in military jargon. Crossing the wall and other borders is permitted through documents issued by the builders of the wall. Yet these documents do not so much reflect a pre-existing truth about their holder, but rather establish their own truths and realities (categories of identity that determine who may cross and who may not).[29] These truths and realities that the border's power creates then assert control over the power to document, to shoot a camera or tell a filmmaker to stop recording, to seize and destroy records, to render narratives incomplete and unreliable. The response that we see in these films is not simply to record the 'real', a category that has for all intents and purposes ceased to have meaning in such spaces, but rather to expose the constructed and contingent nature of these realities that are formed at and by the border. In this sense, these films represent not only a distinct genre of wall documentaries, but a mode of filmmaking that places them in conversation with other genres that emerge at and through the border.

Notes

1. El Fassed, 'Documentary Film Review: "Mur" (Wall)'.
2. Jasbir Puar cites Israel as a pioneer in the deployment of what she has termed homonationalism, in which certain queer bodies are incorporated into the nation (and nationalist forms of exceptionalism and imperialism), to the exclusion of racialised others. Puar, *Terrorist Assemblages*, p. 38.
3. The debate over pinkwashing, moreover, demonstrates that the notion of an Israeli gay bar as a space of Israeli–Palestinian encounters is in no way politically neutral.
4. Ironically, Burnat had a difficult time entering the United States to attend the awards ceremony, showing how walls that confine Palestinians do not end when they leave the West Bank, but rather reverberate outwards in an international constellation of restriction that do not explicitly support the occupation but in practice reinforce its limits. Martinez, 'Oscar-Nominated Palestinian Filmmaker Detained Briefly at LAX'.
5. Friedman, 'Guises of transnationalism in Israel/Palestine', pp. 26–7.
6. Relatively little has been written about *Mur*. For a study of depictions of Palestinian landscapes and the West Bank wall in *Mur* and other works, see Fischer, 'Landscapes of Scripture and of Conflict'.
7. El Fassed, 'Documentary Film Review'.
8. Ball, 'Impossible Intimacies', p. 178.
9. Dabashi, 'Introduction', p. 11.
10. Ibid. p. 11.
11. Weizman offers an insightful analysis of the spatial, architectural and technological modes by which the construction of the wall creates vertical and horizontal spatial divisions. Weizman, *Hollow Land*, pp. 179–81.
12. Anzaldúa, *Borderlands*/La Frontera, p. 25.
13. Yaqub, *Palestinian Cinema in the Days of Revolution*, p. 49.
14. Ibid. pp. 59, 76.
15. Ibid. p. 198.
16. Spence and Navarro, *Crafting Truth*, p. 12.
17. Nichols, *Introduction to Documentary*, p. 132.

18. Barthes, 'Rhetoric of the Image', p. 17.
19. Spence and Navarro, *Crafting Truth*, p. 15.
20. Hochberg, *Visual Occupations*, p. 9.
21. Ball, 'Impossible Intimacies' p. 185.
22. Weizman, *Hollow Land*, p. 7.
23. Ibid. p. 7.
24. Nichols, *Introduction to Documentary*, pp. 67–8.
25. Ibid. p. 184.
26. MacDougall, 'When Less is Less', p. 293.
27. The camera, of course, is meant to be itself invisible, even as it makes visible the events on screen. Instances in which this practice of filmmaking is violated, so called 'breaking the fourth wall', has the effect of calling attention to the camera's presence.
28. Friedman, 'Guises of transnationalism in Israel/Palestine', p. 23.
29. See Berda, *Living Emergency*, for an in-depth study of the regime of permits, documents, regulations, and most importantly exceptions, that govern Palestinian life in the Occupied Territories.

6

The Illusion of the One-way Mirror: Filming the Checkpoint in *Divine Intervention*

In a scene from Palestinian director Elia Suleiman's film *Divine Intervention* (*Yadd Ilahiyya*, 2002), the main character drives through al-Ram checkpoint between Jerusalem and Ramallah. The character, named E. S. and played by the director himself, passes from the Jerusalem side to the Ramallah side, and then he turns and parks his car in a lot adjacent to the checkpoint, where he waits for his girlfriend to arrive from the direction of Ramallah. The scene provides a general overview of the characteristics of the checkpoint space, which is a crucial setting in the film (figure 6.1). We can see the watchtower, the concrete and plastic barriers that direct traffic, a group of Palestinians walking through the checkpoint, armed soldiers manning the checkpoint and military vehicles nearby. It demonstrates that E. S. is able to pass through the checkpoint, while his girlfriend cannot, but he stops there, as his destination is the border itself. He parks at a vantage point that allows him to focus his vision on the checkpoint and act as an observer and a documenter of this space.

The scene uses filming techniques such as framing to remind the viewers of the constructedness both of the space of the checkpoint and of its filmic representation. The camera captures the arrival of E. S. from within the car he drives, facing out and forward so that the camera reflects the perspective of E. S. or a passenger. The viewer makes the journey through the checkpoint along with E. S. The dashboard, sides and tops of the front windshield are visible at the edges of the frame, which, along with the moving car, reminds us that we as viewers possess a limited line of sight, that what we see was

FILMING THE CHECKPOINT IN *DIVINE INTERVENTION* | 159

Figure 6.1 E. S. enters the checkpoint in Elia Suleiman's *Divine Intervention* (2002).

carefully framed and shot. It also draws attention to the fact that the viewer sees the events through a screen (on film), as we watch from the other side of the windshield. This perspective presents the viewer with the temporary, haphazard nature of the checkpoint. The concrete barriers and plastic cones appear hastily erected, as if they could be removed at a moment's notice. As E. S. drives through, there is an improvised, corrugated-tin-roof shelter against which a soldier leans nonchalantly, and the watchtower looks like it could be disassembled in a few hours. Finally, the rear-view mirror is visible and shows the reflection of E. S.'s eyes, which reveals two connected levels on which to read this scene. It shows the presence of E. S. as the director of the film, reminding the viewer that the scene is a representation, on screen, of the checkpoint. However, seeing the eyes of E. S. also shows the checkpoint to be, as Eyal Weizman argues in *Hollow Land*, a space that is constructed through the dynamics of sight and vision.[1] The ability to see, and conversely to control and restrict lines of sight of those passing through the checkpoint, permits the establishment of authority via visual control. Thus, the manner in which the checkpoint as a space functions is intimately connected to what is seen and what remains unseen. In *Divine Intervention*, Suleiman deftly critiques this relationship between power and vision by using the camera to 'look back'.

The scene above is one of many in the film in which Suleiman trains his camera's eye on the checkpoint in a sustained, persistent manner. This scene, moreover, reveals some of the insights that examining borders through a cinematic lens can offer. *Divine Intervention*, by foregrounding the construction of the checkpoint both as a space and as a representation, exposes the fragility that the border conceals with its illusion of overwhelming power. We have seen borders fracture narratives in Chapter 4, and that their deceptive nature complicates the documentary's claim to truth in Chapter 5. Here Suleiman eschews both narrative progression and documentary realism in order to depict the checkpoint in a way that undermines its claim to invincibility and makes room for dissent, yet in an improvised and sometimes playful manner that differs from modes of resistance seen in earlier eras of Palestinian literature and film.

I examine the film's sustained attention to the border by further exploring the relationship between the checkpoint as a space and as a representation in *Divine Intervention*. I begin by positioning the film in relation to contemporary Palestinian cinema as a body of work that seeks to grapple with the presence of the border through film. I draw on works by Michel de Certeau and Eyal Weizman to theorise the checkpoint as a space that disrupts, channels and reroutes vision and lines of sight through constricted perspectives and one-way mirrors. I argue that the film uses the cinematic camera to create a representation of the checkpoint that is unstable and constructed through visual tricks and illusion. Suleiman uses camera positioning and movement, shot sequences and limited perspectives to tear at the seams of the film's fabric and call the viewer's attention to its status as film. Moreover, by emphasising the fragility of the checkpoint's representation through moments that remind the viewer of the overlap between director and actor and that depict the checkpoint as a series of staged set pieces, *Divine Intervention* also reveals the constructed and unstable nature of the checkpoint itself and raises the possibility of breaking it down. The genres that the border produces and reformulates – the narrative of return in *The Lady from Tel Aviv*, the wall documentary, and now the checkpoint film – also come to function as sites of dissent and transgression of the border's expanding presence. The border's ubiquity exposes its own fragility.

A Checkpoint Film/Filming the Checkpoint

Elia Suleiman is one of the most recognised Palestinian filmmakers working today. Originally from Nazareth and therefore a bearer of Israeli citizenship, Suleiman lived for twelve years in New York City before returning in the 1990s, at which point he began his feature film career.[2] Subsequently, Suleiman has alternated between Israel and abroad, living mostly in Paris. In addition to *Divine Intervention*, Suleiman has produced numerous short films and two other feature-length films. The first, *Chronicle of a Disappearance* (*Sijil Ikhtifa'*, 1996), tells the story of E. S.'s return to Nazareth from exile, while the most recent film, *The Time That Remains* (*al-Zaman al-Baqi*, 2009), excavates the history of Palestinians in Israel from 1948 to the present through the eyes of E. S. and his family. The result is a body of work that is not a cinema produced in exile, but one that nevertheless reflects a sensibility shaped both abroad and in Israel/Palestine. Suleiman is a prominent member of what Gertz and Khleifi call the 'fourth period' of Palestinian cinema. The films of the fourth period, in contrast to a previous era in which the Palestine Liberation Organisation (PLO) funded films in order to 'document and promote the national struggle', is defined by the works of individual auteur filmmakers, often under severe budget and logistical constraints, filmed in Israel/Palestine rather than abroad as before.[3] This era of filmmaking can thus be understood as a post-resistance period, not in the sense that the concept of resistance is not present, but in terms of a body of works that is produced outside of the paradigm of mutual support that marked earlier relationships between filmmakers and movements such as the PLO. The films of Michel Khleifi from the 1980s mark the beginning of this period, and in the 1990s, Khleifi was joined by other filmmakers, among them Rashid Masharawi, Hany Abu-Assad and Suleiman himself.[4]

Borders in general and checkpoints in particular feature prominently in a number of the films of this period. Nurith Gertz and George Khleifi identify an emerging genre of 'roadblock films', examples of which include Masharawi's *Ticket to Jerusalem* (2002), *Rana's Wedding* by Abu-Assad (2002), and of course *Divine Intervention*. Many of these films appear around the same time, toward the beginning of the Second Intifada, a period in which checkpoints were proliferating at a rapid pace. That the checkpoint features heavily in *Divine Intervention* is therefore not surprising, and the checkpoint's relationship to the various locations depicted and the chronological structure of the film are worth noting briefly. The film consists largely of vignettes that revolve loosely around the silent main character E. S., as well as his family and girlfriend, and takes place in a number of settings: the first part of the film offers a glimpse of life in Nazareth, the middle section centres on al-Ram checkpoint, which divides Jerusalem and Ramallah,[5] and the end of the film is largely set in Jerusalem. The checkpoint generally occupies both the chronological and spatial centres of the film, since al-Ram checkpoint lies between Nazareth and Jerusalem geographically. This reflects the outsized role played by the checkpoint at the particular historical moment (the Second Intifada) in which *Divine Intervention* was produced.[6] The checkpoint functions as the site of repeated encounters between E. S. and his girlfriend in the film. As a resident of Ramallah, this unnamed woman cannot proceed past the checkpoint into Jerusalem, so the couple meets under the watchful eyes of the soldiers manning the checkpoint. They spend hours sitting in a car parked near the roadblock watching the procedures at the checkpoint. The film repeatedly and insistently returns to the checkpoint. Yet the film also moves beyond the checkpoint by the end, as the two main characters play a trick on the soldiers and escape into Jerusalem, where the woman deploys Palestinian national symbols to attack and defeat a group of Israeli gunmen. The film thus teases the possibility of some kind of resistance to the blockage the checkpoint imposes, even as it stages it as absurd fantasy, or perhaps what Nadia Yaqub has described as a 'yearning for the Palestinian utopia'.[7]

Suleiman's larger body of work provides useful context to the reading of the checkpoint in *Divine Intervention*. In particular, *Chronicle of a Disappearance* and *The Time That Remains*, which some critics have read alongside *Divine Intervention* as a type of trilogy,[8] deploy many of the same techniques and cinematic language that are crucial to understanding the depiction of the checkpoint. The other two films also revolve around a main character named E. S. who is played by the director himself and remains silent throughout the film, marking this as one of the most distinguishing features of Suleiman's films. Gertz and Khleifi suggest that this reflects the effects of the traumatic events he witnesses, which 'render him mute'.[9] As I show later in this chapter, the silent director-character also engages in a form of voyeurism that permits forms of rebellion and contestation. Silence reveals even as it conceals and negates memory. Scholars have also attempted to reconcile the unusual humorous, absurd tone and amalgam of cinematic styles present in Suleiman's works with the gravity of the situation he depicts. Haim Bresheeth argues that Suleiman inverts fantasy and reality in order to comment on the absurdity of the 'reality' faced by Palestinians.[10] Hamid Dabashi approaches Suleiman's 'frivolity' as a means of 'creatively retrieving the forsaken layers of memory and re-arranging them stylistically' in a manner reminiscent of Tourette's Syndrome.[11] It is a testament to the rich complexity of Suleiman's works that they are characterised at once by both silence and uncontrollable outbursts.

Suleiman's inversions, rearrangements of memories and repetitive narratives produce a rich and complex engagement with the idea of time. For Kamran Rastegar, Suleiman's work reflects an emerging Palestinian aesthetic of fragmentation, negation and voids that reflects a Palestinian nation that exists in a state of unending catastrophe and 'traumatic suspension' and concerns itself with the 'aporias' (unanswered and unanswerable questions) of Palestinian life.[12] Suleiman's refusal of narrative closure reflects the 'irresolution' of traumas such as the *Nakba*,[13] and his use of techniques such as repetition of scenes and shots with only slight differences with no logical explanation reproduces the Palestinian experiences of temporal distortion and suspension. In this sense, Suleiman's films are more elaborate manifestations of a tendency to refuse narrative coherence seen in a number of the Palestinian works discussed previously in this book, from al-Madhoun's narrative splits and shifts and depiction of the 'stray life' led by Palestinians in Gaza to the near impossibility of cohesively narrating acts of protest and resistance in *5 Broken Cameras*.

Analyses that emphasise the checkpoint show how the distortion and suspension of time is crucial to the construction of this particular space. David Fieni points to Suleiman's use of speed differentials (in which Israelis speed through while Palestinians are stopped) as a means of indicating the absurd distortion of Palestinian time that it produces.[14] Gertz and Khleifi argue that films reveal the ways in which these spatial restrictions preclude the representation of any type of cohesive Palestinian space,[15] and Refqa Abu-Remaileh focuses on the 'anti-narratives' and narrative gaps that the border encounter produces.[16] Waiting and suspension of time is a frequent presence in Palestinian depictions of border spaces. Take, for instance, two works referenced in Chapter 4. Mahmoud Darwish's poem 'Athens Airport' describes the Palestinian condition as one of being in transit, with no destination, for an indefinite amount of time: 'In Athens Airport we waited for years and years.'[17] In Adania Shibli's 'Out of Time', time is suspended when, as the narrator lands at Ben Gurion Airport to face inevitable interrogation, her watch stops. Both works convey a sense of intense frustration, but one that is mixed with determination to persevere. Particularly in earlier representations, waiting is frequently read not as acquiescence to Israeli power but a form of defiance. Julie Peteet notes how Palestinians reframe the daily waits and mobility barriers as a 'challenge' or as a tactic in the sense used by de Certeau (discussed in Chapter 1, and to which I will return later). Anna Ball notes that E. S. evinces a similar form of steely determination through his facial expressions and demeanour in *Divine Intervention*,[18] representing a contemporary manifestation of *ṣumūd*, a mode of defiance and perseverance that reflects a Palestinian commitment to staying put on their land, a refusal to yield to Israeli occupation, and various forms of non-violent resistance. If waiting can function as a form of defiance, then the checkpoint, as the quintessential place where Palestinians wait, becomes a place in which to search for moments of rebellion and to consider the extent to which these moments can serve as critiques of the checkpoint itself.

Finally, there is a sense in which the checkpoint, like the wall, beckons to be filmed. Fieni argues that the checkpoint, as a 'quasi-automated apparatus of seeing', itself functions as a type of camera, but it also invites other cameras to film it. Thus, a critically engaged form of cinema can invert the sovereign gaze of the checkpoint back on itself, turning it into an object of filming and representation.[19] Yet filmic representations show that even as it invites filming, the checkpoint also seeks to restrict or control how it is depicted. An illustrative example found in Yoav Shamir's documentary *Checkpoint* shows a moment in which a soldier implores the director to make the Israel Defence Force and the checkpoint 'look good'. Shamir's inclusion of this moment, thereby breaking the 'fourth wall', is a tacit refusal to do so, and this scene makes a larger point about the challenge of filming the checkpoint: the question for the filmmaker is how to depict the checkpoint without accepting its terms of representation.

For the purposes of this chapter, I want to focus on the concept of turning the checkpoint's gaze against it. This focus preserves Fieni's crucial insight that the checkpoint is a location that is cinematic, but it places greater emphasis on the space itself – it becomes not only a setting but a set and a stage – even as it focuses on its intersecting temporal and spatial distortions. In this we can see a crucial way in which *Divine Intervention* pushes the checkpoint genre beyond depicting or documenting images of violence from within the constricted parameters of the checkpoint. By refusing to accept the terms of the checkpoint – its visual limits and its spatio-temporal distortions – Suleiman's film manages to contest and eventually escape the checkpoint's performance of overwhelming power and force, staging a transition from stasis to a form of movement and reconnection that has become a common trope in Palestinian film, despite the ubiquity of roadblocks.[20]

Constricted Vision at the Checkpoint

Building on this discussion of time, space and the checkpoint, we can see how filmic representation of this space, and specifically the deployment of the cinematic camera in particular ways, can exploit the suspension/interruption/distortion of time to scrutinise and destabilise the checkpoint space. The final scene from Hany Abu Assad's film *Rana's Wedding* (*al-Quds fi Yawm Akhar*, 2002) will help elucidate this point before I turn to *Divine Intervention* in earnest. The protagonist, Rana, is faced with an ultimatum: to get married or leave Jerusalem for Cairo with her father. She resolves to marry her fiancé on the day her father leaves, but the fiancé and the officiant of the wedding become stuck at roadblocks entering Jerusalem. At this point, the suspension of time at the checkpoint leads the film to focus its attention on the checkpoint itself. Desperate to complete the wedding on time, Rana and the rest of the wedding party rush to the checkpoint and conduct the ceremony there. The marriage takes place in a van in line at the checkpoint, in a brief, utilitarian ceremony. Then the wedding party exits the van to dance and ululate joyfully in front of the checkpoint, as the sounds of singing and drums intermingle with the honks of cars and the roar of truck engines as they pass through the roadblock.

Throughout this scene, the framing of the shots emphasises the manner in which the checkpoint constricts and controls vision. As the ceremony takes place in the limited space of the van, the camera, which takes the perspective of an onlooker, cannot capture the bride and groom in one frame. Instead it switches back and forth between the couple, creating a physical distance between them that contrasts with the expectation of the wedding as a ritual that unites and binds two people together. Then, as the wedding party leaves the vehicle to celebrate on the road next to the van, the camera slowly pans up and away, zooming out from the celebration to show the lines of cars waiting to cross the checkpoint and the apartment buildings and abandoned lots that surround the roadblock (figure 6.2). In its movement from the constricted, interior space of the vehicle to a comprehensive view of the checkpoint, the film establishes the fragmentation of vision and experience created by the checkpoint, and the camera's potential role in contextualising and perhaps even countering that fragmentation. While it celebrates the *ṣumūd* and resistance located within daily practice and ritual, it also reveals the limits of these acts as a political project, as they are quickly drowned out both visually and aurally by the much larger checkpoint space.

However, the film also proposes a role for the camera as a vehicle for revealing and critiquing this broader context. The use of the camera in *Rana's Wedding* reveals the constricted and fragmented vision of those subjected to

Figure 6.2 A post-wedding celebration at an Israeli military checkpoint in Hany Abu-Assad's *Rana's Wedding* (2002).

forms of the panopticism described by Foucault in *Discipline and Punish*. Foucault's notion of panoptic systems of discipline emphasises the importance of vision (optic) to the establishment and exercise of authority.[21] This principle clearly applies to situations like a prison, but it can also appear in myriad other forms such as surveillance cameras, a point that *Rana's Wedding* emphasises in an earlier unsettling scene in which surveillance cameras track the soon-to-be-married couple as they spend a carefree day wandering through Jerusalem's Old City. As a corollary to the panoptic authorities, the person subjected to surveillance and control is often deprived or constricted in their vision. The individual being watched by a surveillance camera cannot see who is watching, and the prisoner can only discern a very small portion of what the prison guard can see. This dynamic is at work in *Rana's Wedding*, in which the vision of the wedding party is highly circumscribed by the space of the checkpoint, both because it forces them into the enclosed space of the van and in the limited lines of sight it produces after they exit. However, the camera itself is not bound by the same restrictions, as seen in the final shot. It floats above the checkpoint and looks down upon it, opening up the vistas around it unavailable to those on the ground, pointing to the possibilities offered by film and the camera for engaging with the restricted vision created by the checkpoint. Here the camera provides a filmic mode of transgressing the disciplinary limits imposed by the checkpoint.[22]

Eyal Weizman describes a system of border crossings into Palestinian territories that were established by the Oslo Accords that rely upon an unusual form of visual control, which he terms 'passages'. At these border checkpoints, a traveller wishing to enter territory controlled by the Palestinian Authority hands his or her passport to a Palestinian border patrol officer. Instead of stamping it, as one would expect, the officer slips the passport through a drawer in the counter and passes it to Israeli security officers, who decide whether to permit or deny entry and pass it back so that the Palestinian officer can stamp it accordingly. The Israelis are situated behind one-way mirrors, which allow them to view the activities in the border checkpoint without being seen. This layout establishes what Weizman terms a 'prosthetic' system of sovereignty in which Israeli authority is exercised behind the illusion of Palestinian control.[23] However, Weizman points to two cracks that open up in this panoptic system of invisible authority. He notes that late in the afternoon, the angle of the sun 'makes the one-way mirror transparent enough to expose the silhouette of the Israeli security agents behind it, and with it the designed charade of prosthetic sovereignty'.[24] Weizman also relates the experience of a photographer in the border checkpoint who, while trying to take a photo of a Palestinian border policeman, suddenly heard a voice shout in Hebrew, '*Zuz!*' ('Move!'). Only then did he realise that there were Israelis behind the mirror, and when he tried to photograph the mirror he was removed from the checkpoint.[25] The presence of the camera, and the threat that it poses to Israeli practices at the checkpoint, exposes the illusion of the one-way mirror by causing the unseen Israelis to reveal themselves. The disembodied voice shouting in a foreign language produces a disconnect between the visual and the aural at the checkpoint, revealing the presence of the unseen in a way that beckons more scrutiny. These inconsistencies and gaps in the visual appearance of the checkpoint permit us to consider the camera not only as a way of moving above and beyond the visual constrictions of the checkpoint, but also as a means of peering at and through the glass of the one-way mirror to reveal the illusion that underpins its authority.

In *Divine Intervention*, the checkpoint depicted differs somewhat from the border checkpoint described by Weizman and Mattar. Here there is no immediate performance, transparent as it may be, of Palestinian control that pretends to obscure the power relations of occupation. Yet they remind us of this prosthetic sovereignty, as checkpoints often mark the limits of 'Area A', the parts of the West Bank under the control the Palestinian Authority. The practices and sensations, such as the use of mirrors and the disembodied voices barking commands, that Weizman describes are found at many Israeli checkpoints across the West Bank, recalling Kotef's observation that excessive noise and shouting (in an incomprehensible foreign language) serve not to educate but rather to silence.[26] It is also important to recall that *Divine Intervention* predates the emergence of more extensive, terminal-like internal checkpoints such as Qalandia, which deploy the technology and physical structure of border crossings such as Allenby Bridge. The film emphasises the presence of many of the same elements of the articulation of control at the checkpoint, albeit in a more improvised and less systematic fashion. The camera functions voyeuristically, allowing the viewer to discern the charade of the checkpoint's exercise of power, much as the sun exposes the soldiers behind the one-way mirror at a certain time of day.

In one of the film's many roadblock scenes, the checkpoint is filmed from the vantage point of E. S.'s car parked in the adjacent lot, adopting the viewpoint of E. S., as it frequently does. However, as Rastegar notes, this often occurs without the typical markers of a subjective perspective, so the viewer might take time to notice this convergence of points of view.[27] The camera remains static in this shot of the checkpoint, maintaining a single frame, with concrete barriers lining the road on the left, with the watchtower on the right manned by two soldiers. Underneath the watchtower is a Jeep with three men sprawled against the vehicle, their arms up as if they are surrendering to arrest or detainment, but the person detaining them is nowhere to be seen. Into this frame drives a car, and three soldiers emerge, wipe dirt off of their shoes on the road's curb in unison, in a choreographed fashion, and get back into the car and drive off (figure 6.3). This sequence of events is interspersed with two brief shots of E. S. and his girlfriend sitting in their car that depict them staring forward toward the checkpoint.

The fixed framing and the *mise en scène* in this sequence, in alternation with the shots of E. S. and his girlfriend, give the scene a theatrical quality,

Figure 6.3   Israeli soldiers move in choreographed unison as detained Palestinians wait at the checkpoint.

as if the pair is the audience for a dramatic performance for which the scene's framing is the stage, and the soldiers and detainees who remain unmoving throughout the scene and the physical structures of the checkpoint provide the set. The soldiers who drive up are the performers, and their choreographed dance of cleaning their shoes serves to reinforce the theatrical quality of this scene. Through this drama, the scene reveals the pieces with which the film is constructed and reminds the audience that the film is a representation. It also depicts the checkpoint itself as a stage for choreographed dramas and performances. However, the shots of E. S. and his girlfriend through the windshield of the car provide the perspective that allows this choreography to be revealed (figure 6.4). They remind the viewer that the camera's depiction of the checkpoint scene is also mediated by a screen. The use of screens is a frequent technique of Suleiman's, which Rastegar reads as an expression of distancing and alienation of E. S. from his surroundings.[28] The use of this technique at the checkpoint, however, makes room for another reading of the 'screen' of the car window. The window, a piece of glass, recalls the one-way mirror described by Weizman and the ability of the camera to expose and look through it. By looking through the window for a sustained period of time imposed by the stasis of the checkpoint, the camera can perform an analogous act of exposure, allowing the viewer to observe the checkpoint

Figure 6.4   E. S. and his girlfriend silently watch the checkpoint from the parking lot.

with a clarity often denied by the visual constriction of this space, in which filming and cameras are often forbidden or disrupted, as we saw in the previous chapter.

While both the scene from *Rana's Wedding* and this scene engage with the visual restrictions of the checkpoint, there is a crucial difference. The scene from *Rana's Wedding* uses the camera's shots, framing and movement to reveal but not necessarily contest the constriction of vision at the checkpoint. Indeed the imposition of the checkpoint onto the decidedly non-everyday wedding ritual might serve as a means of de-normalising the checkpoint along the lines described by Anna Ball, in which films refuse to 'perform the expected trajectories of either subversive transgression or total subjection'.[29] By contrast, this scene and others in *Divine Intervention* consider how the camera might contest and circumvent more quotidian constrictions. The camera, unexpectedly steady, kept still by the suspension of time, interminable waiting and moments of *ṣumūd* at the checkpoint, allows a sustained contemplation of both the checkpoint space and the means by which the film itself is constructed. This attention allows the incongruities and contradictions of both to become more visible, as both the film and the checkpoint space feature the juxtaposition of tonally jarring and distinct pieces. In this sense, the form and structure of the film flaunts the 'seamlessness' that the viewer expects from a film in order to reveal and trace the instability of the checkpoint on screen.

Unsettling the Checkpoint

In many checkpoint scenes from *Divine Intervention*, the camera, the *mise en scène* and other visual and aural elements unsettle the (pan)optic control of the checkpoint, beginning with the first scene that the film stages in this space. This scene begins with the checkpoint as a chaotic space: soldiers have closed the checkpoint, forcing cars to turn around and head back to Ramallah. Tempers have flared, people are honking and shouting, and a soldier fires his weapon into the air to restore calm and control. Then the camera sweeps to a close-up of the bottom of a car door. As the camera moves away from the chaos of the checkpoint to the car, the noisy chaos of the roadblock is swept away by the sound of a whoosh of wind and then an eerie silence. The car door opens, a woman's high heel steps onto the road, and the woman we later learn to be E. S.'s girlfriend emerges from the vehicle. Instead of turning around like the others, she walks determinedly towards the closed roadblock. Well-dressed in heels, a dress and sunglasses, a white-collar professional who stands out in stark contrast to the dusty and chaotic checkpoint, she ignores the soldiers' warnings to turn back in badly accented Arabic, and instead keeps walking. As she walks towards the checkpoint, a song begins to play in the background.[30] The song 'Joi', by the British-Bangladeshi dance group Fingers, feels out of place; it is a song one might expect to find on a dance floor, not at a military checkpoint, but here it provides a new soundtrack that competes with the military soundtrack of static, of commands, of weapons being cocked to open fire. As she ignores their order to halt, they aim their weapons and hone in on her, as seen through the eyes of a soldier looking through his gun's scope with her face in its crosshairs. Yet the woman raises her sunglasses and stares the soldiers down as she continues to walk, and they raise their weapons, unable to shoot. She continues walking and crosses through the checkpoint unmolested. As she passes, the checkpoint's watchtower – the most tangible symbol of its authority and control – falls down (figure 6.5). Her beauty stuns the soldiers but also knocks down the checkpoint, producing a moment of paralysis. Her captivating act of crossing shakes the foundations of the exercise of power at the checkpoint. However, the seeming triumphant collapse of the checkpoint

Figure 6.5 The checkpoint watchtower collapses as the woman passes through.

as the woman passes through is followed immediately by another checkpoint scene that depicts the watchtower intact, revealing the fantastic nature of the collapse that preceded it.

The fantasy sequence of the collapse and reconstitution of the watchtower signals a rejection of realism, a mode of filmmaking that has predominated not only in documentary but in Palestinian fiction film as well. Yet despite this surrealism, the film also deploys certain techniques reminiscent of documentary. Several shots depict the woman as seen through the viewfinder of the soldier's gun as he contemplates shooting her, and her face appears in the crosshairs. This shot alternates with one from the perspective of her view as she walks towards the checkpoint, conveyed through the slightly unsteady movement of the camera. These unsteady shots recall the style of filmmaking most often used in documentaries to show events as they unfold in real time. Yet this pair of shots is interspersed with a slow-motion side shot of the woman walking with poise and determination toward the checkpoint, a technique often used in action films. The result is a scene that juxtaposes many dissonant filmic elements from different genres, from the slow motion of action movies to the unsteady shots of documentaries.[31] This formal dissonance suggests an uncertainty towards how to depict the checkpoint, an attempt to test out different modes and genres. In this scene, the camera searches for a means of adequately representing this space that is, as Mattar notes, overburdened with political meaning.[32] It distorts and fragments Palestinian space and time and signifies the attempted negation of political agency by subsuming Palestinian agency to the arbitrary whims of Israeli soldiers. It is a space of Kafka-esque visual and bureaucratic sleights of hand that lend themselves to absurd, surreal representations, but it is also the site of daily violence, threats and humiliation that is undeniably real. Suleiman's experimentation with different techniques and genres, which creates a dizzying and often humorous form of dissonance, serves as a means of acknowledging but not resolving these contradictions.

The instability within the representation of the checkpoint also allows us to consider how it shapes the film's commentary upon the checkpoint as a space and the significance of filming it. In another checkpoint scene, the camera functions as a means of communication from within the silent space of the checkpoint. The encounters between E. S. and his girlfriend occur frequently at the checkpoint, since the unnamed girlfriend's West Bank residency precludes her from entering Jerusalem, where E. S. resides. Their encounters are highly circumscribed. The only noticeable display of affection between the two is a very methodical type of hand-holding, in which the two hands slowly feel the other. The camera alternates between shots of the pair's upper bodies from in front of the car, looking through the windshield, and shots from the back seat, in which only the couple's hands are visible. The front shots show the sides and top of the car, framing the vehicle as a type of limit, only within the confines of which can the two be together. It portrays their encounter in a fragmented and disembodied fashion, the vision of both the characters and the viewers circumscribed by the panopticism of the checkpoint.

In addition to the physically confined space of their encounters, these scenes are characterised by long periods of silence, as the two sit and watch the checkpoint but do not comment upon it. The film thus presents the checkpoint itself as a largely silent space. In contrast to the noise of passing cars and celebration at the checkpoint in *Rana's Wedding*, such sounds are largely absent here. The only people who speak at the checkpoint are the soldiers, either over a walkie talkie or shouting commands in the broken language that Sayed Kashua describes as the 'army Arabic' of the checkpoint.[33] Like the command from the other side of the one-way mirror described by Weizman, these disembodied sounds often take the form of the imperative. It reflects a tendency for speech, which Suleiman uses sparingly in all of his films, to function in a unidirectional fashion as a mode of control rather than communication. In his earlier film *Chronicle of a Disappearance*, a Palestinian character gains possession of an Israeli police radio and uses it to comedic effect to eavesdrop, to dispatch police on absurd missions, and at one point to broadcast a sinister-sounding rendition of the Israeli national anthem, turning the state's agents and symbols against it. In *Divine Intervention*, by contrast, the film turns to visuality and the camera as a means of rebelling against the disembodied commands barked across walkie talkies and loudspeakers as the characters communicate silently in the vehicle.

Instead, the camera offers a means of non-verbal communication. In one of their encounters, the two meet in the parking lot off to the side of the checkpoint, where they are able to sit together, unnoticed by the soldiers, in E. S.'s car, where they exchange glances but stay silent (figures 6.6 and 6.7). It also creates a form of communication through a shot/reverse shot sequence

Figures 6.6 and 6.7   E. S. and his girlfriend exchange glances in a shot/reverse shot sequence.

that alternates between the two, creating an 'implied conversation'.[34] The act of looking at each other produces a form of communication that is non-verbal, expressive and intimate. It uses closes shots to establish the proximity of the two and then cuts to a shot looking into the car, which reminds us of the circumscribed space in which their conversation occurs. This renders their visual communication a furtive and surreptitious act.

Michel de Certeau's concept of the 'pedestrian speech act' is useful for reading this unseen communication, which is reflected in the movement of the camera's shot/reverse shot progression. Certeau describes a form of transgressive practice in which people reuse and move through spaces, typically planned in a utopian fashion and produced through the exercise of state power, for their own purposes.[35] Certeau contrasts the abstracted, birds-eye view from above, which makes an authoritative claim to omniscience,[36] with micro acts of rebellion on the ground enacted through unauthorised movements across and within these spaces that create both ambiguity and political agency. While Certeau's planned urban spaces are utopian in their aspirations, the proliferation of borders such as checkpoints are decidedly non-utopian.[37] As I suggest in Chapter 1, their purpose is not to produce a modern subjectivity in the Foucauldian sense, but to seek to herd, control and subjugate undisciplinable and unruly Palestinian bodies. In this sense, as Fieni briefly suggests,[38] the checkpoint can be read as a heterotopia, which as discussed in Chapter 1 is a real space, often one of deviance and abnormality such as a prison or hospital, partitioned from everyday spaces yet perceived as natural.[39]

In *Divine Intervention*, the surreptitious communication between the pair of lovers denaturalises the checkpoint by reminding the viewer of its peculiarity as a space that circumscribes and limits interpersonal encounters. If through much of the film, the silence of E. S. appears self-imposed and voluntary, here the viewer, having become accustomed to his silence, begins to see it as compulsory, at least for the time that he spends at the checkpoint. Additionally, by staging it in the vehicle to the side of the checkpoint, beneath but away from the focus of the soldiers manning the roadblock, it opens up a gap in the visual control articulated by the checkpoint by positioning their communication as unseen by the soldiers. While the panopticism of the checkpoint relies upon the seamlessness of the perspective it provides and the all-knowing and all-seeing form of visual domination it engenders, the camera turns its attention to the ruptures in the space in order to pierce through the checkpoint's control and to denaturalise it. The visual 'speech act' in this scene marks the camera as a device of subversive communication, one that, as we will see in the following scenes, can open up cracks in the panopticism of the checkpoint, and therefore in the cohesiveness of the space itself.

The notion of the camera as a vehicle for exposing the limits in the checkpoint's panopticism brings us to the next scene of interest, in which *Divine*

Intervention uses the intertwined acts of filming and watching to establish the camera as an entity that can control and destabilise the checkpoint. In this scene, E. S. has been sitting at the checkpoint for hours and night has fallen. He watches the checkpoint silently from his car, and the checkpoint is framed in the same manner as the 'stage' scene discussed above, with the watchtower on the right and a line of cars on the left. A soldier arrives in a jeep and tells the other soldiers to stop checking the vehicles waiting to cross, and he takes over. He walks among the cars waiting to cross and shouts commands at them through a megaphone, as the camera cuts to a closer shot that follows him as he walks back and forth. He begins shouting commands to those waiting in their cars to cross the checkpoint into Jerusalem. First, he tells them in Hebrew and Arabic to take out their ID cards and singles out one individual for ridicule, mocking him in a mean-spirited fashion. He forces passengers to switch cars, and he pulls a man out of his car and forces him to join him in a Hasidic Jewish dance as he chants the words "*Am Yisra'el Ḥai*' ('the people of Israel live'). Finally, the soldier allows the man to return to his car and waves the line of waiting vehicles through the checkpoint. While the soldier plays his games, the scene is interspersed with shots of E. S. in his car, observing the events at the checkpoint, which once again merges the viewer's vantage point with that of E. S.

This scene can be interpreted on two interrelated levels. First, we can read E. S. as a character, watching intently as the events unfold before him. The camera moving back and forth replicates his experience observing the soldier's shouts and dances. Moreover, the staging of the scene at night, in darkness, as the other soldiers disappear from the scene, suggests an illicitness to the soldier's activities, or at the least, a desire not to be seen. The presence of E. S. as an observer makes something visible that is intended to remain unseen, a means of looking through the one-way mirror. However, the framing and *mise en scène* also reveal glimpses of the scene's staging, as in the sequence discussed earlier. All of the events take place on the 'set' established by the initial frame, and the choreographed performance of "*Am Yisra'el Ḥai*' recalls the theatrical nature of the earlier scene. Through these devices, the film gives the viewer a glimpse of the staging and constructedness of the events at the checkpoint.

If we approach this scene as a staged and acted performance, then we can interpret the presence of E. S. not only as an observer, but also as the director of this performance, this film. By viewing the observations of E. S. in this way, we become aware that we are seeing the filming of the checkpoint from the perspective of the director. The camera replicates his perspective as he follows the performance of the choreography he set in motion. In this move from observer to director, moreover, we can interpret E. S.'s presence as an inversion of the one-way mirror at the checkpoint described by Weizman. While soldiers watch from behind the glass as Weizman films, here E. S. as director films the soldiers unseen from behind the glass of the windshield. He plays the voyeur, watching a series of events that he put into motion. Thus, the checkpoint with its set, choreography and dances is a charade, a staged performance of its functions, and the director is the person behind the mirror. By going behind the checkpoint, the one-way mirror, the camera can expose the farce that this space represents. It reveals the perspective that is intended to remain unseen and by doing so denaturalises the checkpoint space. This allows the camera's role to go beyond a means of creating furtive communication as a visual speech act beneath the panopticon of the checkpoint, but rather to unsettle the panopticism of the checkpoint, allowing the camera to claim the position of visual control that choreographs the events of the checkpoint and to reuse it for its own purposes.

Fantasies of Escape

In a particularly humorous scene at the checkpoint, the film uses this unsettling to toy with the visual restrictions of the checkpoint. In this scene, E. S. and his girlfriend sit silently in E. S.'s car. A quiet soundtrack begins playing, breaking the silence of the checkpoint, and with an expression of mischievous bemusement on his face, E. S. pulls out a balloon and inflates it. The balloon bears a drawing of Palestinian leader Yasser Arafat's face with a goofy grin, clad in his trademark *kūfiyya*, and he releases it through the sunroof. It floats toward the checkpoint, and the Israeli soldiers spot it but are confused, unsure how to react. One soldier trains his binoculars on the balloon and follows its path as it floats towards the checkpoint. One of them cocks his weapon in preparation to shoot, but his colleague restrains him and calls in a radio alert that warns that 'there's a balloon trying to get through' the checkpoint. He asks for permission to shoot it down but is told to wait for instructions. Instructions never come, and the grinning face of Arafat stares back into the soldier's binoculars as it floats closer and closer to the checkpoint through a shot/reverse shot between the soldier's perspective and the balloon's. As the balloon crosses, E. S. and his girlfriend capitalise on the ensuing commotion and drive through the checkpoint unnoticed, finally allowing them to enter Jerusalem together. After the couple and the balloon cross the checkpoint, the balloon continues its journey, passing into Jerusalem. It passes by a series of panoramic shots of Jerusalem, and crosses the walls of the Old City. There it passes Jerusalem landmarks such the Church of the Holy Sepulchre, and finally, it spins around the golden Dome of the Rock and comes to rest.

The film uses the balloon as a distraction for the characters to stage an illicit crossing of the checkpoint. As the balloon floats towards the checkpoint, the camera alternates between the perspective of a soldier looking through his binoculars and the perspective of the balloon itself looking towards the checkpoint, paralleling the earlier scene in which the woman crosses through the checkpoint but functioning in a different manner. As the soldier trains his binoculars on the approaching balloon, the viewer sees the pair of circles that mark the edge of the binocular's field of vision. Like the viewfinder in the earlier scene, this frame makes us aware of the limits of the soldier's vision (figure 6.8). Despite his vantage point atop the watchtower and the panorama it affords him, he can only see a small portion of the landscape around the checkpoint, a portion that quickly fills with the red of the approaching

Figure 6.8 An Israeli soldier follows the balloon as it approaches the checkpoint.

balloon. This framing also reveals the constructedness of the film itself. By showing the edges of the field of vision, it reminds the viewer that the view from the camera is a representation, staged and framed in a particular way. However, the shots from the perspective of the balloon show that this representation can unsettle the checkpoint's visual power. As seen from the vantage point of the balloon, the camera floats up above the checkpoint's watchtower, looking back down and inverting the panoptic vision of this space as the soldiers look up helplessly and constricted by their binoculars, as the camera denudes the checkpoint of visual control over the space around it.

The moment of crossing, in which the couple and the balloon move past and away from the checkpoint, stages a shift that opens up new spaces and new camera techniques. Up until this point, the trajectories and movements of both the balloon and E. S. and his girlfriend are staged from an interior and limited perspective: the viewer sees what the couple sees from inside the car, as well as the vantage points of the balloon itself and the soldiers looking at it, and the origin of each perspective is identified. However, after the crossing, the camera shows both the car and the balloon from an exterior, elevated angle (figure 6.9). The camera moves unbound to an identifiable object or perspective, and unmediated by the glass of the car's vehicle, and it opens up wide panoramic shots

Figure 6.9 The camera captures both the balloon and the car as they move towards Jerusalem.

of Jerusalem as the balloon makes its journey. The act of crossing, then, stages the escape of the camera and the film from the confines of the checkpoint, unleashing a distinct set of shots and perspectives, and newly available spaces outside of the stage-like set piece of the checkpoint. Through its camerawork and framing, the film works within the visual limitations of the checkpoint space to make possible an escape into wider spaces and vistas.

The shift in framing and perspective produced by the act of crossing the border points to a form of mimicking that appears repeatedly throughout the film's checkpoint scenes, in which the film reproduces or performs the visual effects of the checkpoint. The close shots from within the vehicle reproduce the constricted space of the checkpoint. E. S.'s observation of the soldier's performance from behind the windshield replicates the one-way surveillance upon which the checkpoint relies to function. The balloon floating above the checkpoint parallels the height advantage the checkpoint's watchtower offers to the soldiers watching the road below. However, this mimicry also allows the film to comment upon the checkpoint as a visual space. By emphasising unsteady shots, limited perspective and flimsiness, *Divine Intervention* reveals the checkpoint itself to be a highly unstable space.

This instability, of course, is present from the very first checkpoint scene, in which the watchtower collapses. The moment of crossing is one of distortion that entails the suspension of disbelief, physics and time in a manner reminiscent of Suad Amiry's narrative of crossing the wall described in Chapter 1. In both instances, fantasy facilitates the illicit crossing of a border. Yet while the initial presentation of the tower collapse is enigmatic and offers few clues as to its meaning, the film's subsequent set pieces, performances, constricted perspectives and modes of framing prove illuminating. In retrospect, we come to view the initial moment of collapse, then, not only as one that shows the instability of the checkpoint's filmic representation, but one that also reveals the fragility of the checkpoint itself. The film performs this task by turning the camera on the checkpoint and by destabilising the panopticism of this space. It calls into question the checkpoint's permanence and impenetrability and shows it to be a projection much like the images the viewer sees on screen. The checkpoint's claims to power, much like that of the wall in the previous chapter, possess rhetorical potency but are ultimately two dimensional, much like the backdrop of a movie set. If viewed from the particular, limited angle intended by the set designer, the backdrop looks fully formed and real, but if the angle changes even a little it can be seen as constructed and fragile, like a film set's painted backdrop of cardboard. *Divine Intervention* uses moments of subterfuge and even fantasy to shift perspective, to expose the 'set' of the checkpoint, and to view it from another angle (primarily that of E. S.). Through this act of unsettling the border, the film points to the possibility, even if fleeting, of tearing the checkpoint down, or at least of moving past it into the wider vistas of Jerusalem.

Conclusion: Beyond the Checkpoint

If the film's exposure of the illusion of the checkpoint is evident, it leaves the question of its effect, and the escape into Jerusalem that it permits, ambiguous. Suleiman, per usual, does not offer easy answers, and indeed the film juxtaposes contradictory possibilities without resolving the tension between them. Consider the two characters who stage the escape. E. S. goes about his life much as before; he visits his mother and father, silently observes the absurd and unexplainable actions of others, and yes, goes to the checkpoint and waits, but now alone and mostly in the dark. For E. S. the escape is a momentary diversion, followed up by the return to his quotidian routine, of which the checkpoint is a significant component. The repetitive, compulsive return to the checkpoint is a symptom of an obsession, someone who lives in limbo and is unable to move beyond waiting at the border.

The woman, by contrast, continues her journey further into the absurd and fantastical, as she transforms into a gravity-defying ninja who stages an attack on a group of Israelis conducting military training. In a David-and-Goliath-worthy feat, she flies, jumps, throws boomerangs and spears, and fells the entire group despite being outmanned and outgunned. It is as if, once the logic and myth of the checkpoint is broken, she is freed from the laws of gravity. So, we see a fissure in the film post checkpoint: earnest and melancholic quotidian realism for E. S. against escapist fantasy for his girlfriend, the inescapability of the checkpoint versus liberation. And it is clear which is more thrilling, for one is a calm, almost mournful perseverance, while the other is an excessive explosion of Palestinian revenge that has been building all through the hours, days, weeks and months spent waiting in silent suspended animation.

Finally, one must note that the film's fantastical turn, perhaps ironically, is also a symbolic turn. The couple escape the checkpoint by means of a balloon festooned with an iconic image of the Palestinian resistance movement: the image of Yasser Arafat, the long-time leader of the PLO, wearing a *kūfiyya*.[40] The Arafat balloon floats above the utilitarian space of the checkpoint towards the symbolically overdetermined city of Jerusalem and lands on that city's most iconic structure, the Dome of the Rock. The ninja attack is similarly burdened with a set of symbols that border on cliché. The woman disarms her opponents with the help of a *kūfiyya*, which, as the adornment of choice of many freedom fighters, is a signifier of Palestinian culture and resistance. She also possesses a map of (non-partitioned) Palestine that she uses as a boomerang and as a knife. Fantasy here serves as a means of weaponising symbols, of refiguring them from abstract markers of unrealised nationhood to tangible tools that are used to wage battle. If the proliferation of borders, as we have seen in earlier chapters, is a harbinger of the decline of certain forms of Palestinian political ideology and practice, perhaps then the long overdue escape from the border space in *Divine Intervention*, staged through fantasy and transgression, permits a reinvigoration of the political through cultural representation. Fantasy, then, is a unique contribution of *Divine Intervention* to the checkpoint genre. It is not only a means, following Ball, of looking askance at the checkpoint, of revealing its Kafka-esque absurdity and refusing to accept its performance of power and logic[41] as an overwhelming and inescapable presence in Palestinian life. It also allows a return to – and reimagination of – the political realm of resistance and contestation that has, as we have seen through much of this book, been depleted by the border's utilitarian, post-utopian quality and the removal of the question of national liberation from post-Oslo discourse. Intensive engagement with the border is not an end in itself. It is a means of escape from certain physical, discursive and political constraints.

Notes

1. Weizman, *Hollow Land*, p. 139.
2. Gertz and Khleifi, *Palestinian Cinema*, pp. 40–1.
3. Alexander, 'Is There a Palestinian Cinema', p. 154.
4. Gertz and Khleifi, *Palestinian Cinema*, pp. 31–2.

5. This checkpoint used to divide Jerusalem and Ramallah. Since the film was made, al-Ram has been closed, and those travelling to Jerusalem now must travel through the nearby but more inconvenient and congested Qalandia checkpoint.
6. As noted earlier, Helga Tawil-Souri has called the checkpoint 'the center of Palestinian life'. Tawil-Souri, 'Qalandia Checkpoint: The Historical Geography of a Non-Place', p. 36.
7. Yaqub, 'Utopia and Dystopia in Palestinian Circular Journeys from Ghassān Kanafānī to Contemporary Film', p. 317.
8. Rastegar, *Surviving Images*, p. 103.
9. Gertz and Khleifi, *Palestinian Cinema*, p. 41.
10. Bresheeth, 'Segell Ikhtifa = Chronicle of a Disappearance', p. 76.
11. Dabashi, 'In Praise of Frivolity', p. 142.
12. Rastegar, *Surviving Images,* p. 96.
13. Ibid. p. 97.
14. Fieni, 'Cinematic Checkpoints and Sovereign Time,' p. 13.
15. Gertz and Khleifi, *Palestinian Cinema*, pp. 152–3.
16. Abu-Remaileh, 'Palestinian Anti-Narratives in the Films of Elia Suleiman', p. 14.
17. Darwish, 'Matar Athina', p. 23.
18. Ball, *Palestinian Literature and Film in Postcolonial Feminist Perspective*, p. 85.
19. Fieni, 'Cinematic Checkpoints and Sovereign Time', p. 7.
20. Yaqub, 'Utopia and Dystopia in Palestinian Circular Journeys from Ghassān Kanafānī to Contemporary Film', p. 306.
21. Foucault, *Discipline and Punish*, pp. 195–203.
22. The notion of transgressing disciplinary limits as delineated or imposed by the border finds many theoretical articulations, among them Michel de Certeau, *The Practice of Everyday Life.*
23. Weizman, *Hollow Land*, pp. 139–41.
24. Ibid. p. 159.
25. Ibid. p. 138.
26. Kotef, *Movement and the Ordering of Freedom*, pp. 38 and 46. See Chapter 1 for more discussion of this notion.
27. Rastegar, *Surviving Images*, p. 112.
28. Ibid. p. 113.
29. Ball, 'Kafka at the West Bank Checkpoint', p. 84.
30. Suleiman's films are notable for their idiosyncratic soundtracks, which typically include an amalgam of musical styles from across the world.

31. Scholars such as Haim Bresheeth have noted Suleiman's use of a mélange of cinematic styles. See Bresheeth, 'Segell Ikhtifa = Chronicle of a Disappearance'.
32. Mattar, 'Mourid Barghouti's "Multiple Displacements"', p. 111.
33. Kashua, '"Aravi, Daber 'Ivrit'. See Chapter 3 for more on Kashua's engagement with language.
34. Abu-Remaileh, 'Palestinian Anti-Narratives in the Films of Elia Suleiman', pp. 4–5.
35. De Certeau, *The Practice of Everyday Life*, p. 98.
36. De Certeau, *The Practice of Everyday Life*, pp. 91–3.
37. For the relationship of borders to utopia, see Chapter 2.
38. Fieni, 'Cinematic Checkpoints and Sovereign Time', pp. 7–8.
39. See Lefebvre, *The Urban Revolution*, and Foucault and Miskowiec, 'Of Other Spaces'.
40. Arafat almost always wore a *kūfiyya* in public, which is itself an important signifier of Palestinian culture and resistance, typically paired with a military uniform.
41. Ball, 'Kafka at the West Bank Checkpoint', p. 81.

7

Conclusion: Physical and Fictional Borders

In 2005, the globally active British graffiti artist known as Banksy painted several murals on the wall in the West Bank. These murals, referenced in Suad Amiry's passage on crossing the wall in *Nothing to Lose But Your Life* discussed in Chapter 1, depict various means of passing through the barrier, either by cracking it open, peering through it, or climbing over it with a ladder. The murals use the material space of this barrier as a canvas to critique its construction and presence and to imagine alternatives to it. Yet this type of transformation of the cold concrete of the wall into a dissident political statement does not in itself produce a tangible means of contesting the border's physical presence. Banksy later wrote on his website about his experience painting the murals, and he described an encounter with an old Palestinian man who said his painting made the wall look beautiful. Banksy responded to this compliment with a thank you. But then the man continued and said to Banksy, 'We don't want it to be beautiful, we hate this wall. Go home.'[1] This man feared that utilising the wall for aesthetic purposes would at best distract from the desire to tear it down and at worst actually render it more tolerable and therefore more durable. For him, the aestheticisation of the wall would obscure the basic, ugly fact that it is an unwanted monstrosity imposed by an occupying power in order to control and prevent Palestinian movement. Responses to Banksy's most recent West Bank project – a fully operational, wall-adjacent hotel in Bethlehem with the 'worst views in the world' named 'The Walled Off Hotel' (a word play with the luxury Waldorf Hotel chain) – echo the Palestinian man's earlier comments on the murals, with Banksy facing criticism for promoting conflict tourism and for profiting from Palestinian suffering.[2]

I begin my concluding chapter with this anecdote because it is a further example, seen repeatedly throughout this book, of anxiety over the representation of borders. The Banksy example likely provoked a more strenuous response than most, by virtue of his reputation as a splashy artist who comments on controversial situations across the world. Yet it also illustrates fear of the possible role of art in beautifying, aestheticising or normalising borders, even when the artist possesses the political awareness to recognise this possibility. Much of this anxiety stems, quite reasonably as Anna Ball notes,[3] from a desire to resist the normalisation of oppressive border practices such as the ones we see in Palestine. At the same time, as the title of this book suggests, my analyses focus very clearly on representation, which by definition engage with metaphor, fiction, allegory and fantasy in ways that could be critiqued as trivialising, mocking or aestheticising borders. Even Chapter 5, which examines documentaries, a genre premised on its truth claims, centres on films that interrogate their own ability to tell the truth about the wall. Repeatedly, the more closely a work engages with the border, the more indistinct the line between real and unreal becomes, a tendency most noticeable in my readings of Raba'i al-Madhoun's *The Lady from Tel Aviv* and Elia Suleiman's *Divine Intervention*; in the former, I show that repeated border crossings produce narratives that spin out of the control of the author and unsettle distinctions of fictional/real and author/text, while the latter stages the checkpoint as a site of fantasy and a theatre of the absurd. While it might be tempting to evaluate border representations on the basis of their relative ability to convey the brutal reality of restricted movement in Israel and Palestine, in some instances a greater focus on the physical spaces of borders seems to take us even further into the realm of the metaphorical, unreal and fantastical. As we see in the Banksy example, an intensive focus on the border in representation does not resolve but rather amplifies this tension, as if the distortions and contradictions of borders themselves are inescapable in their representation.

However, my study of representations has sought to hew closely to physical borders by emphasising literary and filmic engagements with border spaces, from checkpoints and walls to the divided city of Jerusalem and the present-absent Green Line. Each chapter features readings of works in which borders are present as settings, narrative structuring devices, or both. In Part I, one effect of these borders, particularly the Green Line, the roadblock and the divided city of Jerusalem, is to stage the failure of certain literary-political-ideological paradigms and to reveal the role of expanding borders in refiguring the relationship of cultural production to political engagement. In Part II, which focuses more specifically on the emergent forms of post-Oslo border spaces, we see how the proliferation of such sites shapes narrative, structure and genre. The border crossings at Ben Gurion airport and the Gaza strip provide *The Lady from Tel Aviv* with a multi-vocal structure that supplants the political commitment of earlier Palestinian novels of return with a chaotic and ambivalent narrative. The selective and anxiety inducing crossings in al-Madhoun give way to the imposing physical barrier of the wall in *Five Broken Cameras* and *Mur*, both of which push the limits of the wall documentary genre in order to expose the illusion of impenetrability that the space projects. In *Divine Intervention*, the mind-numbing stasis of waiting at the checkpoint produces a transgressive and playful example of the roadblock film that reimagines the parameters and meaning of political engagement in the post-Oslo era.

I would like to close by considering how these two elements – the border as a physical setting/structure and the border as a fictional space – in addition to existing in tension can also work in tandem to interrogate the deceptions of borders and to imagine politically liberating responses to them. Indeed, the moments of fantasy, of merging author and text, of interrogating the possibility of documentary truth – all of which perhaps make border spaces beautiful, humorous or absurd – also depict borders in tangible and literal forms. In the works examined in this book, the border is frequently embodied physically, in diegetic or extra-diegetic fashion. In Chapter 4, border crossings are reflected in the physical, printed form of the book, as title pages of novels-within-novels and narrative breaks appear in unexpected places to reflect the act of crossing the border. In Chapter 5, a metaphorical notion of the border as 'speaking for itself' is literalised, as the border is anthropomorphised with the ability to speak to those crossing it. In *Divine Intervention*, the abstract, and indeed at present non-existent, borders of Palestine are embodied physically as a weapon used to slice and dice the ninja's Israeli opponents. In both *Second Person Singular* (Chapter 3) and *Doves in Trafalgar* (Chapter 2), coexistence is not merely an abstract notion but rather is embodied by characters who are respectively buried and shot, a human manifestation of this ideology's failure in contemporary Israel and Palestine. While we can of course read these characters as allegorical stand-ins for concepts and ideologies, they also provide physical embodiments of sometimes abstract notions of border crossing and border straddling.

Thus, even as the border is treated through representation and metaphor in ever more fantastical and innovative fashion, it is also in some ways made more literal and tangible. Here I think we can see glimmers of an artistic return to the political, and even to resistance, but in a manner distinct from the types enacted by Ghassan Kanafani and Mahmoud Darwish in an earlier era of revolutionary national commitment. Perhaps the most famous line from Kanafani's *Returning to Haifa*, examined in Chapter 2 of this book, is the one in which Said declares that 'Man is a cause.'[4] In this statement, Kanafani expresses a collective, universalist ethos in which the individual becomes an abstracted, symbolic tool in the struggle for liberation and homeland. However, by Chapter 6 of this book, in *Divine Intervention*, this relationship is reversed. Here, an intensive focus on the border permits its subversion and escape to a ninja fight scene, where the abstract symbols of nation and resistance are reconstituted as physical weapons used to fight Israelis. In the arms of the ninja, the map of Palestine becomes a lethal boomerang and the *kūfiyya* disarms her Israeli opponents. Rather than an abstract end in itself, the nation as a concept and a set of borders becomes a physical tool, a means to the end of liberation, in the hands of an individual who has been freed from the checkpoint that confined her for so long. If, in the heyday of the Palestinian liberation movement the individual became a weapon of the nation, here we see the nation as a weapon wielded by the individual.

Of course, one must ask: to what end? To offer one possible answer, I return, one last time, to one of the central claims of this book, which has been that borders are deceptive and illusory. From the present/absent Green Line in *Doves in Trafalgar* and the fabricated notion of a unified Jerusalem in *Second Person Singular* to the illusions of impenetrability produced by the wall in *Mur* and *5 Broken Cameras* and the staged performances of power and control of *Divine Intervention*, borders seek to conform physical reality to a particular narrative of power and authority, even as they naturalise themselves and obscure the processes by which they are constructed and produced.⁵ By turning to fiction and interrogating the realities that these borders produce, the works I examine perform a kind of denaturalisation of these borders. The balloon that floats above the checkpoint, the ninja who flies, the men and women who jump over the wall in *Mur*, they are not defying gravity but rather revealing the extent to which reality has been distorted and suspended. We can see the fantastical moments, the climbing up and over, as a corrective moment that reveals the border's deception.

At the border, the sense that things are not as they seem at times produces an indeterminant effect as described by Rancière, which I discuss in Chapter 1 as beckoning a closer look and different angles of viewing. These sustained closer looks in turn unsettle the deception in various ways. A passage in Raja Shehadeh's *Palestinian Walks* will help illustrate this point. Shehadeh describes a fraying during the late Oslo period of the elaborate system of one-way mirrors and prosthetic sovereignty described by Weizman in *Hollow Land*. In Shehadeh's telling, related by his friend Mustafa who had recently crossed the Allenby border checkpoint, the paint on the one-way mirror that conceals the Israeli border officials, who make entry decisions that are then implemented by the visible Palestinian officials, has faded. The Palestinian flag outside above the border checkpoint has disappeared, both of which he views as symbolic of the deception of the Oslo Accords.⁶ When the now-visible Israeli soldier delays Mustafa's entry, Mustafa refuses to leave until the Israeli comes out from behind the glass and admits that the whole thing is a 'stupid charade'.⁷ Shehadeh concludes that if everyone who crossed the border 'resisted these practices, we would get somewhere'.⁸ This passage shows both the slow disintegration of the illusion, and that close viewing and reading can, over time, help produce such a disintegration. It withers and fades under the sustained views of the observer, the protester, the worker who crosses daily, the camera, the critical eye of the artist, or even the bystander who sits quietly watching the checkpoint. Much as a magician can only perform a trick so many times before it loses its effectiveness, so too do the deceptions of these borders grow stale and unconvincing under sustained scrutiny. It also makes the case for the importance of looking at borders and how they are depicted, photographed, written about, and represented in as many ways as possible, from a variety of media, subject positions and perspectives.

Looking beyond Israel/Palestine, there are other borders where once the illusion has worn off, the charade becomes unsustainable. The most obvious recent example is the Berlin Wall, where a seemingly stable, decades-long status quo collapsed nearly overnight, bringing down the physical symbol of brutal forced separation. In other places like Northern Ireland, a less transformational and more uneasy peace has created a type of tentative equilibrium, in which the so-called 'peace lines' that divide Catholic and Protestant areas of Belfast still exist but their removal is an oft-stated goal.[9] In both instances, these current and past borders have remained dynamically present in cultural representations, so even as borders disappear or the conflict that produced them becomes less contentious, their cultural afterlives remain. There is no way to know when – or if – any such changes will happen in Israel and Palestine, so even as we acknowledge the power of representation to critique borders, this power should not be overstated. The works I have analysed prompt us to read borders outside of a teleology of permanence and impenetrability and to question the illusion that they are inevitable or invincible. But neither should we assume that they are fragile and prone to collapse at any moment. These types of physical structures, like the structures of power that undergird them, sustained by inertia and the indifference of a region and world that has lost interest in the Israeli–Palestinian conflict, are lamentably durable. The story of these borders is far from over.

Notes

1. Jones, 'Spray Can Prankster Tackles Israel's Security Barrier'.
2. Khader, 'The Walled-Off Hotel Controversy'.
3. Ball, 'Kafka at the West Bank Checkpoint', p. 79.
4. Kanafani, *Returning to Haifa*, p. 181.
5. Boer, *Uncertain Territories*, p. 4.
6. Shehadeh, *Palestinian Walks*, p. 174.
7. Ibid. p. 175.
8. Ibid. p. 175.
9. There is occasional talk of dismantling some of these walls, but so far progress is slow. Geoghegan, 'Will Belfast Ever Have a Berlin Wall Moment and Tear Down Its "Peace Walls?"'

Bibliography

Abdel-Malek, Kamal, *The Rhetoric of Violence: Arab-Jewish Encounters in Contemporary Palestinian Literature and Film* (New York: Palgrave Macmillan, 2005).

Abdel-Malek, Kamal, and Wael B. Hallaq (eds), *Tradition, Modernity, and Postmodernity in Arabic Literature: Essays in Honor of Professor Issa J. Boullata* (Leiden: Brill, 2000).

Abowd, Thomas, 'Present and Absent: Historical Invention and the Politics of Place in Colonial Jerusalem', in Mark LeVine and Sandy Sufian (eds), *Reapproaching Borders: New Perspectives on the Study of Israel-Palestine* (London: Rowman & Littlefield Publishers, 2007), pp. 243–65.

Abu-Manneh, Bashir, *The Palestinian Novel: From 1948 to the Present* (Cambridge: Cambridge University Press, 2016).

_____, 'Palestinian Trajectories: Novel and Politics since 1948', *Modern Language Quarterly* 75, no. 4 (2014), pp. 511–39.

Abu-Remaileh, Refqa, 'Palestinian Anti-narratives in the Films of Elia Suleiman', *Arab Media and Society* 5 (2008), pp. 1–29.

Alexander, Livia, 'Is There a Palestinian Cinema: The National and Transnational in Palestinian Film Production', in Rebecca L. Stein and Ted Swedenberg (eds), *Palestine, Israel, and the Politics of Popular Culture* (Durham, NC: Duke University Press, 2005), pp. 150–72.

Althusser, Louis, *Lenin and Philosophy, and Other Essays*, trans. Ben Brewster (New York: Monthly Review Press, 1972).

Amiry, Suad, *Nothing to Lose But Your Life: An 18-Hour Journey with Murad* (Doha: Bloomsbury Qatar, 2010).

Anderson, Benedict, *Imagined Communities: Reflections on the Origins and Spread of Nationalism* (London: Verso, 2006).

Anzaldúa, Gloria, *Borderlands/La Frontera: The New Mestiza* (San Francisco: Aunt Lute Books, 2007).

Appadurai, Arjun, *Modernity at Large: Cultural Dimensions of Globalization* (Minneapolis: University of Minnesota Press, 1996).

Apter, Emily, *Against World Literature: On the Politics of Untranslatability* (New York: Verso, 2013).

_____, 'Translation at the Checkpoint', *Journal of Postcolonial Writing* 50, no. 1 (2014), pp. 56–74.

Augé, Marc, *Non-Places: An Introduction to Supermodernity*, trans. John Howe (London: Verso, 2009).

Azem, Ibtisam, *Sariq al-Nawm: Gharib Hayfawi* (Beirut: Manshurat al-Jamal, 2011).

al-ʿAzm, Sadiq Jalal, *al-Naqd al-Dhati baʿd al-Hazima* (Beirut: Dar al-Taliʿa, 1969).

Azouqa, Aida, 'Ghassan Kanafani and William Faulkner: Kanafani's Achievement in "All That's Left to You"', *Journal of Arabic Literature* 31, no. 2 (1 January 2000), pp. 147–70.

Badr, Liana, 'Matar', in L. Badr, *Jahim Dhahabi* (Beirut: Dar al-Adab, 1991).

Ball, Anna, 'Impossible Intimacies: Towards a Visual Politics of "Touch" at the Israeli-Palestinian Border', *Journal for Cultural Research* 16, no. 2–3 (2012), pp. 175–95.

_____, 'Kafka at the West Bank Checkpoint: De-normalizing the Palestinian Encounter Before the Law', *Journal of Postcolonial Writing* 50, no. 1 (2014), pp. 75–6.

_____, *Palestinian Literature and Film in Postcolonial Feminist Perspective* (London: Routledge, 2012).

Barakat, Huda, *Rasaʾil al-Ghariba* (Beirut: Dar al-Nahar, 2004).

Bardenstein, Carol B., 'Trees, Forests, and the Shaping of Palestinian and Israeli Collective Memory', in Mieke Bal, Jonathan Crewe and Leo Spitzer (eds), *Acts of Memory: Cultural Recall in the Present* (Hanover: Dartmouth University Press, 1999), pp. 148–68.

Barghouti, Mourid, *I Saw Ramallah*, trans. Ahdaf Soueif (New York: American University in Cairo Press, 2000).

_____, *Raʾaytu Ramallah* (Beirut: al-Markaz al-Thaqafi al-ʿArabi, 1998).

Barthes, Roland, 'Rhetoric of the Image', in *Image Music Text*, trans. Stephen Heath (London: Fontana Press, 1977), pp. 32–51.

Bashkin, Orit, 'When the Safras Met the Dajānīs: Arabic in Hebrew and the Rethinking of National Ideology', *Journal of Arabic Literature* 47, no. 1–2 (2016), pp. 138–68.

Baudrillard, Jean, *Simulacra and Simulation*, trans. Sheila Faria Glaser (Ann Arbor: University of Michigan Press, 1994).

Baumgarten, Helga, 'The Three Faces/Phases of Palestinian Nationalism, 1948–2005', *Journal of Palestine Studies* 34, no. 4 (2005), pp. 25–48.

Baydas, Khalil, *al-Warith* (Ramallah: al-Raqamia for Publishing and Digital Distribution, 2011).

Ben-Ami, Yuval, 'The Round Trip, Part 1: In a Thorny Labyrinth', *+972 Magazine*, 6 April 2012, https://972mag.com/the-round-trip-part-1-in-a-thorny-labyrinth/40082/ (last accessed 11 December 2018).

Benhabib, Doli, 'Mi She-Einenu Karish – 'Al Gorelo Shel Ma She-Nintash be-1948 lefi Girsat Sami Michael', *Jerusalem Studies in Hebrew Literature* (2011), pp. 223–39.

Benjamin, Walter, *The Arcades Project*, trans. Howard Eiland and Kevin McLaughlin (Cambridge, MA: Belknap Press of the Harvard University Press, 1999).

Berda, Yael, *Living Emergency: Israel's Permit Regime in the Occupied Territories* (Stanford: Stanford University Press, 2018).

Bernard, Anna, 'Forms of Memory: Partition as a Literary Paradigm', *Alif: A Journal of Comparative Poetics* 30 (2010), pp. 9–33.

―――, *Rhetorics of Belonging: Nation, Narration, and Israel/Palestine* (Oxford: Oxford University Press, 2013).

Bhabha, Homi, *The Location of Culture* (London: Routledge, 1994).

Bishara, 'Azmi, *al-Hajiz: Shazaya Riwaya* (Beirut: Riyad al-Rayyis lil-Kutub wa-l-Nashr, 2004).

Boer, Inge, *Uncertain Territories: Boundaries in Cultural Analysis* (Amsterdam: Ropodi, 2006).

Boianjiu, Shani, *The People of Forever are Not Afraid* (London: Hogarth, 2012).

Brenner, Rachel Feldhay, *Inextricably Bonded: Israeli Arab and Jewish Writers Re-Visioning Culture* (Madison: University of Wisconsin Press, 2004).

Bresheeth, Haim, 'Segell Ikhtifa = Chronicle of a Disappearance', in Gönül Dönmez-Colin (ed.), *The Cinema of North Africa and the Middle East* (New York: Wallflower Press, 2007), pp. 169–80.

Brown, Alison P., 'The Immobile Mass: Movement Restrictions in the West Bank', *Social & Legal Studies* 13, no. 4 (2004), pp. 501–21.

Brown, Wendy, *Undoing the Demos: Neoliberalism's Stealth Revolution* (New York: Zone Books, 2015).

―――, *Walled States, Waning Sovereignty* (New York: Zone Books, 2014).

B'Tselem, *Restriction on Movement*, report for the Israeli Information Center for Human Rights in the Occupied Territories, 11 November 2017, https://www.btselem.org/freedom_of_movement (last accessed 8 December 2018).

_____, *The Separation Barrier*, report for the Israeli Information Center for Human Rights in the Occupied Territories, 1 January 2011, http://www.btselem.org/separation_barrier (last accessed 11 December 2018).

Campbell, Ian, 'Blindness to Blindness: Trauma, Vision and Political Consciousness in Ghassān Kanafānī's *Returning to Haifa*', *Journal of Arabic Literature* 32, no. 1 (2001), pp. 53–73.

Camus, Albert, *The Plague*, trans. Stuart Gilbert (New York: Vintage Books, 1991).

Certeau, Michel de, *The Practice of Everyday Life*, trans. Steven Rendall (Berkeley: University of California Press, 1984).

Cleary, Joe, *Literature, Partition and the Nation-State: Culture and Conflict in Ireland, Israel and Palestine* (Cambridge: Cambridge University Press, 2002).

Cohen, Hillel, *Good Arabs: The Israeli Security Agencies and the Israeli Arabs, 1948–1967*, trans. Haim Watzman (Berkeley: University of California Press, 2010).

Cresswell, Tim, *On the Move: Mobility in the Modern Western World* (New York: Routledge, 2006).

Dabashi, Hamid, 'In Praise of Frivolity: On the Cinema of Elia Suleiman,' in Hamid Dabashi (ed.), *Dreams of a Nation: On Palestinian Cinema* (New York: Verso, 2006), pp. 131–60.

_____, 'Introduction', in Hamid Dabashi (ed.), *Dreams of a Nation: On Palestinian Cinema* (New York: Verso, 2006), pp. 7–22.

Darwish, Mahmoud, 'Bitaqat Huwiyya', http://www.barghouti.com/poets/darwish/bitaqa.asp (last accessed 13 December 2018).

_____, *Jidariyya* (Beirut: Riyad al-Rayyis lil-Kutub wa-al-Nashr, 2001).

_____, 'Matar Athina', in M. Darwish, *Ward Aqall* (Beirut: al-Mu'assasa al-'Arabiya lil-Dirasat wa-al-Nashr, 1987).

_____, *Memory for Forgetfulness: August, Beirut, 1982*, trans. Ibrahim Muhawi (Berkeley: University of California Press, 1995).

_____, *State of Siege*, trans. Munir Akash and Daniel Abdel-hayy Moore (Syracuse: Syracuse University Press, 2010).

Davis, Rochelle, *Palestinian Village Histories: Geographies of the Displaced* (Stanford: Stanford University Press, 2010).

Dearden, Lizzie, 'Israel-Gaza Conflict: 50-Day War by Numbers', *The Independent*, 27 August 2014, http://www.independent.co.uk/news/world/middle-east/israel-gaza-conflict-50-day-war-by-numbers-9693310.html (last accessed 10 December 2018).

Debord, Guy, *Society of the Spectacle*, trans. Fredy Perlman (Detroit: Black and Red, 1977).

Deleuze, Gilles, and Félix Guattari, *Nomadology: The War Machine*, trans. Brian Massumi (New York: Semiotext(e), 1986).
Derrida, Jacques, *Monolingualism of the Other, or, The Prosthesis of Origin*, trans. Patrick Mensa (Stanford: Stanford University Press, 1998).
'East Jerusalem 2015: Facts and Figures Report', Report by the Association for Civil Rights in Israel, 12 May 2015, http://www.acri.org.il/en/wp-content/uploads/2015/05/EJ-Facts-and-Figures-2015.pdf (last accessed 13 December 2018).
Ehling, Holger, 'Monday Interview: Sami Michael (Israel)', 16 February 2015, http://www.ehlingmedia.com/blog/?p=4396 (last accessed 11 December 2018).
Elad-Bouskila, Ami, *Modern Palestinian Literature and Culture* (London: Frank Cass Publishers, 1999).
El-Ariss, Tarek, *Trials of Arab Modernity: Literary Affects and the New Political* (New York: Fordham University Press, 2013).
El Fassed, Arjan, 'Documentary Film Review: "Mur" (Wall)', *Electronic Intifada*, 21 November 2004, https://electronicintifada.net/content/documentary-film-review-mur-wall/3472 (last accessed 10 December 2018).
Farag, Joseph, *Politics and Palestinian Literature in Exile: Gender, Aesthetics and Resistance in the Short Story* (London: I. B. Taurus, 2017).
Fieni, David, 'Cinematic Checkpoints and Sovereign Time', *Journal of Postcolonial Writing* 50, no. 1 (2014), pp. 6–18.
Fieni, David, and Karim Mattar 'Introduction: Mapping the Global Checkpoint, *Journal of Postcolonial Writing* 50, no. 1 (2014), pp. 1–5.
Fischer, Nina, 'Landscapes of Scripture and of Conflict: Cultural Memories and the Israeli West Bank Barrier', *Landscapes* 15, no. 2 (2014), pp. 143–55.
Foucault, Michel, *Discipline and Punish: The Birth of the Prison*, trans. Alan Sheridan (New York: Vintage Books, 1995).
Foucault, Michel, and Jay Miskowiec, 'Of Other Spaces', *Diacritics* 16, no. 1 (1986), pp. 22–7.
Friedman, Yael, 'Guises of Transnationalism in Israel/Palestine: A Few Notes on *5 Broken Cameras*', *Transnational Cinemas* 6, no. 1 (2015), pp. 17–32.
Geoghegan, Peter, 'Will Belfast Ever Have a Berlin Wall Moment and Tear Down Its "Peace Walls?"', *The Guardian*, 29 September 2015, https://www.theguardian.com/cities/2015/sep/29/belfast-berlin-wall-moment-permanent-peace-walls (last accessed 8 December 2018).
Gertz, Nurith, and George Khleifi, *Palestinian Cinema: Landscape, Trauma and Memory* (Bloomington: Indiana University Press, 2008).

Ghanem, Asʿad, 'The Expanding Ethnocracy: Judaization of the Public Sphere', *Israel Studies Review* 26, no. 1 (2011), pp. 21–7.

Ghazoul, Ferial, 'Darwish's Mural: The Echo of an Epic Hymn', *Interventions* 14, no. 1 (2012), pp. 37–54.

Goldman, Lisa, 'Sami Michael: "Israel – Most racist state in the industrialized world"', *+972 Magazine*, 9 August 2012, https://972mag.com/author-sami-michael-israel-is-the-most-racist-state-in-the-industrialized-world/52602/ (last accessed 11 December 2018).

Grossman, David, *Isha Borahat Mi-Bsora* (Tel Aviv: Ha-Kibbutz Ha-Meʾuhad, 2008).

Grumberg, Karen, *Place and Ideology in Contemporary Hebrew Literature* (Syracuse: Syracuse University Press, 2011).

Habiby, Emile, *al-Waqaʾiʿ al-Ghariba fi Ikhtifaʾ Saʿid Abi al-Nahs al-Mutashaʾil* (Cairo: Dar al-Hilal, 1998).

Halabi, Zeina, *The Unmaking of the Arab Intellectual: Prophecy, Exile, and the Nation* (Edinburgh: Edinburgh University Press, 2017).

Harlow, Barbara, *Resistance Literature* (New York: Methuen, 1987).

⸺, 'Return to Haifa: "Opening the Borders" in Palestinian Literature', *Social Text* 13/14 (1 January 1986), pp. 3–23.

Harvey, David, *The Condition of Postmodernity: An Enquiry into the Origins of Cultural Change* (Cambridge: Wiley, 1992).

Herzl, Theodor, *Altneuland: Old-New Land*, trans. Paula Arnold (Haifa: Haifa Publishing Company, 1961).

Hever, Hannan, 'Hebrew in an Israeli Arab Hand: Six Miniatures on Anton Shammas's "Arabesques"', trans. Orin D. Gensler, *Cultural Critique* 7 (1 October 1987), pp. 47–76.

Hirsch, Marianne, *The Generation of Postmemory: Writing and Visual Culture After the Holocaust* (New York: Columbia University Press, 2012).

Hochberg, Gil, *In Spite of Partition: Jews, Arabs, and the Limits of Separatist Imagination* (Princeton: Princeton University Press, 2007).

⸺, 'To Be or Not to Be an Israeli Arab: Sayed Kashua and the Prospect of Minority Speech-Acts', *Comparative Literature* 62, no. 1 (1 January 2010), pp. 68–88.

⸺, *Visual Occupations: Violence and Visibility in a Conflict Zone* (Durham, NC: Duke University Press, 2015).

Hutcheon, Linda, *Narcissistic Narrative: The Metafictional Paradox* (Waterloo, ON: Wilfrid Laurier University Press, 1981).

Ibn Manzur, Muhammad, *Lisan al-'Arab*, vol. 8 (Beirut: Dar Ihya' al-Turath al-'Arabi, 1988).

Izikovitch, Gili, 'New Talent Unseats Old Favorites at Israeli TV Awards', *Haaretz*, 13 January 2013, http://www.haaretz.com/culture/new-talent-unseats-old-favorites-at-israeli-tv-awards.premium-1.493712 (last accessed 10 December 2018).

Jabra, Jabra Ibrahim, *al-Bahth 'an Walid Mas'ud* (Cairo: Dar al-Thaqafa al-Jadida, 1989).

_____, *In Search of Walid Masoud*, trans. Roger Allen and Adnan Haydar (Syracuse: Syracuse University Press, 2000).

Jameson, Frederic, *Archaeologies of the Future: The Desire Called Utopia and Other Science Fictions* (London: Verso, 2005).

_____, *Postmodernism, or, The Cultural Logic of Late Capitalism* (Durham, NC: Duke University Press, 1991).

Jayyusi, Salma Khadra, 'Introduction: Palestinian Literature in Modern Times', in Salma Khadra Jayyusi (ed.), *Anthology of Modern Palestinian Literature* (New York: Columbia University Press, 1992), pp. 1–80.

_____, 'Palestinian Identity in Literature', in Kamal Abdel-Malek and David C. Jacobson (eds), *Israeli and Palestinian Identities in History and Literature* (New York: St Martin's Press, 1999), pp. 167–78.

Jones, Sam, 'Spray Can Prankster Tackles Israel's Security Barrier', *The Guardian*, 5 August 2005, https://www.theguardian.com/world/2005/aug/05/israel.artsnews (last accessed 8 December 2018).

Kanafani, Ghassan, *'A'id Ila Hayfa* ('Iblin: Dar al-'Ilm wa al-Ma'arifa, 2011).

_____, *Ma Tabaqqa Lakum* (Beirut: Dar al-Tali'a, 1966).

_____, *Palestine's Children: Returning to Haifa and Other Stories*, trans. Barbara Harlow and Karen E. Riley (Boulder: Lynne Rienner Publishers, 2000).

_____, *Rijal fi al-Shams* (Cyprus: Dar Manshurat al-Ramal, 2013).

Karpel, Dalia, 'With Thanks to Ghassan Kanafani', *Ha'aretz*, 15 April 2005, https://www.haaretz.com/1.4850432 (last accessed 13 December 2018).

Kashua, Sayed, *'Arab Raqisun*, trans. Jamal al-Rifa'i (Cairo: Markaz al-Mahrusa, 2011).

_____, '"Aravi, Daber 'Ivrit: Sayed Kashua Mehapes Zihut', *Ha'aretz*, 5 September 2012, https://www.haaretz.co.il/magazine/sayed/1.1817934 (last accessed 11 December 2018).

_____, *'Aravim Rokdim* (Ben Shemen: Modan, 2002).

_____, *Guf Sheni Yahid* (Jerusalem: Keter, 2010).

_____, *Li-yakun Sabahan*, trans. Mara Tawq (Beirut: Dar al-Saqi, 2011).
_____, 'Sayed Kashua Bids Adieu: The Perils of Being an Israeli-Arab Writer', *Ha'aretz*, 17 November 2017, https://www.haaretz.com/opinion/.premium-the-perils-of-being-an-israeli-arab-writer-1.5466446 (last accessed 11 December 2018).
_____, *Second Person Singular*, trans. Mitch Ginsburg (New York: Grove Press, 2012).
_____, *Ve-Yehi Boker* (Jerusalem: Keter, 2004).
_____, 'Ze Nigmar', *Ha'aretz*, 3 July 2014, http://www.haaretz.co.il/magazine/sayed/.premium-1.2366140 (last accessed 10 December 2018).
Kershner, Isabel, 'Israeli Court Orders Barrier Rerouted', *The New York Times*, 5 September 2007, http://www.nytimes.com/2007/09/05/world/middleeast/05mideast.html/ (last accessed 11 December 2018).
Khader, Jamil, 'The Walled-Off Hotel Controversy: How Banksy Universalizes the Palestinian Struggle', *Middle East Research and Information Project*, 22 March 2017, http://www.merip.org/mero/mero032217 (last accessed 8 December 2018).
Khalidi, Rashid, 'Observations on the Right of Return', *Journal of Palestine Studies* 21, no. 2 (January 1992), pp. 29–40.
_____, *Palestinian Identity: The Construction of Modern National Consciousness* (New York: Columbia University Press, 2010).
Khalidi, Walid, *All That Remains: The Palestinian Villages Occupied and Depopulated by Israel in 1948* (Beirut: Institute for Palestine Studies, 1992).
Khalifeh, Sahar, *al-Sabbar* (Beirut: Dar al-Adab, 1999).
Khoury, Elias, *Bab al-Shams* (Beirut: Dar al-Adab, 1998).
_____, 'Lil-Dhikra al-Arba'in li-Ghiyab Ghassan Kanafani: Watan Yulid fi al-Hikaya', *Majallat al-Dirasat al-Filistiniyya* 92 (Fall 2012), pp. 7–12.
_____, 'Mawt al-Mu'allif', in E. Khoury, *al-Dhakira al-Mafquda: Dirasat Naqdiyya* (Beirut: Mu'assasat al-Abhath al-'Arabiyya, 1982), pp. 72–3.
_____, 'Rethinking the *Nakba*', *Critical Inquiry* 38, no. 2 (Winter 2012), pp. 250–66.
Kilito, Abdelfattah, *Thou Shalt Not Speak My Language*, trans. Waïl S. Hassan (Syracuse: Syracuse University Press, 2008).
Kotef, Hagar, *Movement and the Ordering of Freedom: On Liberal Governances of Mobility* (Durham, NC: Duke University Press, 2015).
Kristeva, Julia, *Strangers to Ourselves*, trans. Leon S. Roudiez (New York: Columbia University Press, 1994).

Lefebvre, Henri, *The Urban Revolution*, trans. Robert Bononno (Minneapolis: University of Minnesota Press, 2003).
LeVine, Mark, 'Modernity and Its Mirror', in Mark LeVine and Sandy Sufian (eds), *Reapproaching Borders: New Perspectives on the Study of Israel-Palestine* (London: Rowman & Littlefield Publishers, 2007), pp. 287–306.
Levitas, Ruth, *The Concept of Utopia* (Oxford: Peter Lang, 2010).
_____, *Utopia as Method: The Imaginary Reconstruction of Society* (New York: Palgrave Macmillan, 2013).
Levy, Lital, 'Exchanging Words: Thematizations of Translation in Arabic Writing from Israel', *Comparative Studies of South Asia, Africa, and the Middle East* 23, no. 1–2 (2003), pp. 106–27.
_____, 'Historicizing the concept of Arab Jews in the Mashriq', *Jewish Quarterly Review* 98, no. 4 (2008), pp. 452–69.
_____, *Poetic Trespass: Writing between Hebrew and Arabic in Israel/Palestine*, (Princeton: Princeton University Press, 2014).
Lowe, Josh, 'Austria "Ready" to Build Hungary Border Fence', *Newsweek*, 21 July 2016, http://www.newsweek.com/austria-hungary-border-fence-refugee-crisis-schengen-482631 (last accessed 13 December 2018).
MacDougall, David, 'When Less is Less: The Long Take in Documentary', in Brian Henderson and Ann Martin (eds), *Film Quarterly: Forty Years – A Selection* (Berkeley: University of California Press, 1999), pp. 291–304.
al-Madhoun, Rabaʿi, *Masaʾir: Kunshirtu al-Hulukust wa-al-Nakba* (Beirut: al-Muʾassasa al-ʿArabiya lil-Dirasat wa-al-Nashr, 2015).
_____, *al-Sayyida min Tall Abib* (Beirut: al-Muʾassasa al-ʿArabiya lil-Dirasat wa-al-Nashr, 2009).
_____, *Taʿm al-Furaq: Thalathat Ajyal Filistiniyya fi Dhakira* (Beirut: al-Muʾassasa al-ʿArabiya lil-Dirasat wa-al-Nashr, 2001).
Mann, Barbara E., *A Place in History: Modernism, Tel Aviv, and the Creation of Jewish Urban Space* (Stanford: Stanford University Press, 2006).
Mansour, Atallah, *In a New Light*, trans. Abraham Birman (London: Valentine, Mitchell & Co., 1969).
Marin, Louis, *Utopics: Spatial Play*, trans. Robert A. Vollrath (London: Macmillan, 1984).
Marrouchi, Mustapha, *Edward Said at the Limits* (Albany: State University of New York Press, 2004).
Martinez, Michael, 'Oscar-Nominated Palestinian Filmmaker Detained Briefly at LAX', *CNN*, 21 February 2013, http://www.cnn.com/2013/02/20/showbiz/palestinian-filmmaker-detained/ (last accessed 10 December 2018).

Mason, Victoria, 'Children of the "Idea of Palestine": Negotiating Identity, Belonging and Home in the Palestinian Diaspora', *Journal of Intercultural Studies* 28, no. 3 (2007), pp. 271–85.

Mattar, Karim, 'Mourid Barghouti's "Multiple Displacements": Exile and the National Checkpoint in Palestinian Literature', *Journal of Postcolonial Writing* 50, no. 1 (2014), pp. 103–15.

Meyer, Stefan G., *The Experimental Arabic Novel: Postcolonial Literary Modernism in the Levant* (Albany: State University of New York Press, 2001).

Michael, Sami, *Yonim be-Trafalgar* (Tel Aviv: 'Am 'Oved, 2005).

Moore, Jack, 'Netanyahu: We Will Surround Israel with Walls "To Defend Against Wild Beasts"', *Newsweek*, 9 February 2016, http://www.newsweek.com/netanyahu-we-will-surround-israel-walls-defend-against-wild-beasts-424566 (last accessed 13 December 2018).

Muhajerani, Atallah, 'al-Sayyida Min Tall Abib: Thulathiyyat al-Hubb wa-al-Hayaa wa-al-Mawt', *al-Sharq al-'Awsat*, 3 December 2009, http://archive.aawsat.com/details.asp?issueno=10992&article=546872#.XBJ5BBNKhsN (last accessed 10 December 2018).

Nichols, Bill, *Introduction to Documentary* (Bloomington: Indiana University Press, 2010).

Nolan, Dan, 'One Year On, Orban Plans Another Fence along Hungary's Border with Serbia', *DW*, 14 September 2016, http://www.dw.com/en/one-year-on-orban-plans-another-fence-along-hungarys-border-with-serbia/a-19549924 (last accessed 13 December 2018).

Oz, Amos, 'Nevadim va-Tsefa'', in A. Oz, *Artsot ha-Tan* (Tel Aviv: Agudat ha-Sofrim be-Yisrael Leyad Hotsa'at Masada, 1965).

Parker, Noel, and Nick Vaughan-Williams, 'Introduction', in Noel Parker and Nick Vaughan-Williams (eds), *Critical Border Studies: Broadening and Deepening the 'Lines in the Sand' Agenda* (London: Routledge, 2016), pp. 1–7.

Parmenter, Barbara, *Giving Voice to Stones: Place and Identity in Palestinian Literature* (Austin: University of Texas Press, 2004).

Paul, Drew, 'The Grandchildren of Yūnis: Palestinian Protest Camps, Infiltration, and Ilyās Khūrī's *Bāb al-shams*', *Journal of Arabic Literature* 48, no. 2 (2017), pp. 177–98.

Plato, *Plato: 'The Republic'*, ed. G. R. F. Ferrari, trans. Tom Griffith (Cambridge: Cambridge University Press, 2000).

Puar, Jasbir K., *Terrorist Assemblages: Homonationalism in Queer Times* (Durham, NC: Duke University Press, 2007).

Rancière, Jacques, *The Emancipated Spectator*, trans. Gregory Elliott (London: Verso, 2009).

Rastegar, Kamran, *Surviving Images: Cinema, War, and Cultural Memory in the Middle East* (Oxford: Oxford University Press, 2015).

Relph, Edward C., *Place and Placelessness* (London: Pion, 1976).

Sacks, Jeffrey, *Iterations of Loss: Mutilation and Aesthetic Form, al-Shidyaq to Darwish* (New York: Fordham University Press, 2015).

Said, Edward W., *After the Last Sky: Palestinian Lives* (New York: Columbia University Press, 1998).

_____, 'Foreward', in Mourid Barghouti, *I Saw Ramallah* (New York: American University in Cairo Press, 2000), pp. vii–xi.

Salih, Fakhri, 'al-Riwaya al-Filistiniyya fi al-Waqt al-Rahin: Isharat', *Majallat al-Dirasat al-Filistiniyya* 7, no. 22 (Spring 1995), pp. 157–68.

Salih, Tayeb, *Mawsim al-Hijra Ila al-Shamal* (Cairo: Dar al-Hilal, 1969).

Sazzad, Rehuma, 'The Voice of a Country Called "Forgetfulness": Mahmoud Darwish as Edward Said's "Amateur"', *Human Architecture: Journal of the Sociology of Self-Knowledge* XI, no. 1 (Fall 2013), pp. 115–26.

Schechla, Joseph, 'The Invisible People Come to Light: Israel's "Internally Displaced" and the "Unrecognized Villages"', *Journal of Palestine Studies* 31, no. 1 (Autumn 2001), pp. 20–31.

Schorske, Carl E., *Fin-De-Siecle Vienna: Politics and Culture* (New York: Vintage Books, 1981).

Schulz, Helena Lindholm, *The Palestinian Diaspora: Formation of Identities and Politics of Homeland* (New York: Routledge, 2003).

Senor, Dan, and Saul Singer, *Start-Up Nation: The Story of Israel's Economic Miracle* (New York: Twelve, Hatchette Book Group, 2009).

Sha'alan, Hassan, 'Kayfa Yuhajim Sayyid Qashu' al-Hujum 'ala Ghazza b-il-'Ibriyya?', *Panet.co.il*, 8 January 2009, http://www.panet.co.il/online/articles/1/2/S-171279,1,2.html (last accessed 11 December 2018).

Shafik, Viola, *Arab Cinema: History and Cultural Identity* (Cairo: American University in Cairo Press, 2008).

Shammas, Anton, *'Arabeskot* (Tel Aviv: 'Am 'Oved ve-Sifre Maikelmark, 1986).

Sheetrit, Ariel Moriah, 'Call Me Dov/Khaldūn/Ze'ev/Badīr: Issues of Language and Speech in Two Recent Israeli Re-workings of Ghassān Kanafānī's Returning to Haifa', *Middle Eastern Literatures* 13, no. 1 (2010), pp. 91–115.

Shehadeh, Raja, *Palestinian Walks: Forays into a Vanishing Landscape* (New York: Scribner, 2007).

Sherwood, Harriet, 'Jerusalem's Long-Awaited Light Railway Splits Opinions', *The Guardian*, 17 August 2011, https://www.theguardian.com/world/2011/aug/17/jerusalem-light-railway-opinion (last accessed 13 December 2018).

Shibli, Adania, 'Out of Time', *Drunken Boat*, 2007, http://www.drunkenboat.com/db13/2fic/shibli/out.php (last accessed 10 December 2018).

Shlaim, Avi, *The Iron Wall: Israel and the Arab World* (New York: W. W. Norton & Company, 2000).

Siddiq, Muhammad, *Man is a Cause: Political Consciousness and the Fiction of Ghassān Kanafānī* (Seattle: University of Washington Press, 1984).

―――, 'On Ropes of Memory: Narrating the Palestinian Refugees', in E. Valentine Daniel and John C. Knudsen (eds), *Mistrusting Refugees* (Berkeley: University of California Press, 1995), pp. 87–101.

Silberstein, Lawrence J., *The Postzionism Debates: Knowledge and Power in Israeli Culture* (New York: Routledge, 1999).

Slyomovics, Susan, *The Object of Memory: Arab and Jew Narrate the Palestinian Village* (Philadelphia: University of Pennsylvania Press, 1998).

Spence, Louise, and Vincent Navarro, *Crafting Truth: Documentary Form and Meaning* (New Brunswick: Rutgers University Press, 2011).

Sufyan, M., 'Mulahizat hawl Tabiʿat Adab al-Muqawama', *al-Hadaf*, 2 August 1969, pp. 18–19.

Tawil-Souri, Helga, 'Digital Occupation: Gaza's High-Tech Enclosure', *Journal of Palestine Studies* 41, no. 2 (2012), pp. 27–43.

―――, 'Qalandia: An Autopsy', *Jerusalem Quarterly* 45 (2011), pp. 73–81.

―――, 'Qalandia Checkpoint as Space and Nonplace', *Space and Culture* 14, no. 1 (2011), pp. 4–26.

―――, 'Qalandia Checkpoint: The Historical Geography of a Non-Place', *Jerusalem Quarterly* 42 (2010), pp. 26–48.

Twain, Mark, *The Innocents Abroad; or, The New Pilgrims' Progress* (New York: Hippocrene Books, 1869).

UNHCR, *Global Trends: Forced Displacement in 2015*, report by the UN High Commission on Refugees, 20 June 2016, http://www.unhcr.org/576408cd7 (last accessed 13 December 2018).

Wallach, Yair, 'Trapped in Mirror-Images: The Rhetoric of Maps in Israel/Palestine', *Political Geography* 30, no. 7 (2011), pp. 358–69.

Waugh, Patricia, *Metafiction: The Theory and Practice of Self-Conscious Fiction* (New York: Routledge, 2002).

Weizman, Eyal, *Hollow Land: Israel's Architecture of Occupation* (London: Verso, 2007).

Wilkinson, Tracy, 'Trump Says Walls Work: "Just Ask Israel"', *The Los Angeles Times*, 8 February 2017, http://www.latimes.com/nation/la-fg-trump-wall-israel-20170208-story.html (last accessed 13 December 2018).

Wirth-Nesher, Hana, *City Codes: Reading the Modern Urban Novel* (Cambridge: Cambridge University Press, 1996).

Yaqub, Nadia, *Palestinian Cinema in the Days of Revolution* (Austin: University of Texas Press, 2018).

———, 'Utopia and Dystopia in Palestinian Circular Journeys from Ghassān Kanafānī to Contemporary Film', *Middle Eastern Literatures* 15, no. 3 (2012), pp. 305–18.

Yehoshua, A. B., *Mul Ha-Yeʿarot: Sipurim* (Tel Aviv: Ha-Kibbutz Ha-Meʾuhad, 1968).

Yizhar, S., *Khirbet Khizeh*, trans. Nicholas de Lange and Yaacob Dweck (Jerusalem: Ibis Editions, 2008).

Yousef, Tawfiq, 'The Reception of William Faulkner in the Arab World', *American Studies International* 33, no. 2 (1 October 1995), pp. 41–8.

Filmography

Abu Assad, Hany, *Rana's Wedding*, 2002.
Abu Assad, Hany, *Omar*, 2013.
Alater, Mohammed, *The Iron Wall*, 2006.
Bacha, Julia, *Budrus*, 2009.
Bitton, Simone, *Mur*, 2004.
Burnat, Emad, and Guy Davidi, *5 Broken Cameras*, 2011.
Hawal, Kassem, *Return to Haifa*, 1982.
Jarrar, Khaled, *Infiltrators*, 2013.
Khleifi, Michel, *Wedding in Galilee*, 1987.
Saleh, Tewfik, *The Dupes*, 1973.
Samir, *Forget Baghdad: Jews and Arabs – The Iraqi Connection*, 2002.
Shamir, Yoav, *Checkpoint*, 2003.
Suleiman, Elia, *Chronicle of a Disappearance*, 1996.
Suleiman, Elia, *Divine Intervention*, 2002.
Suleiman, Elia, *The Time that Remains*, 2009.
Suh, Yun, *City of Borders*, 2009.

Index

Note: n indicates note, italic indicates figure

5 Broken Cameras (Burnat/Davidi, 2011), 35, 135–7, 140, 148–56, 188, 189
1967 *see* Six Day War

Abu-Assad, Hany, 137, 161, 165–7, 171
Abu-Manneh, Bashir, 14, 47, 115, 116
Abu-Remaileh, Refqa, 163
aeroplanes, 117–18
Akka, 9
Algeria, 14
Allenby Bridge, 11, 168
Amir, Eli, 49
Amiry, Suad, 28
    Nothing to Lose But Your Life: An 18-Hour Journey with Murad, 1–3, 4, 5, 186
Anzaldúa, Gloria, 19, 21, 138
Apter, Emily
    Against World Literature, 31
Arab Labor (Kashua, TV show), 80, 83–4
Arabic language, 20, 81, 83–4, 93, 95

Arabs, 13–14, 49–51, 99
    and Jewish romance, 116–20
    and Kashua, 86
    and Michael, 63–5
Arafat, Yasser, 58, 178–9, 183, 185n40
art, 1–2, 17
Augé, Marc, 117
Austria, 5
authors, 126–8
Azem, Ibtisam
    The Sleep Thief, 104n94

Badr, Liana
    'Airport', 13
Ball, Anna, 3–4, 26, 28, 137, 141
    and *Divine Intervention*, 164, 171, 183
Ballas, Shimon, 49
balloon, 178–81, 183, 190
Banksy, 2, 5, 137, 186–7
Barghouthi, Mourid, 4
    I Saw Ramallah, 115–16, 124
Barthes, Roland, 127, 140
Bashkin, Orit, 50

Baudrillard, Jean, 117
Baydas, Khalil
  The Heir, 117
Ben Gurion Airport, 9, 11, 120, 188
Benhabib, Doli, 51
Berlin Wall, 2, 27, 28, 137, 191
Bernard, Anna, 17, 31, 32, 116
Bethlehem, 8
Bil'in, 9, 35, 135, 149–54
Bishara, 'Azmi, 136
  Checkpoint: Fragments of a Novel, 20–1, 24
Bitton, Simone, 33, 35, 136, 144–6, 147–8
blockades *see* checkpoints; roadblocks
Boer, Inge, 4
Boianjiu, Shani
  The People of Forever Are Not Afraid, 18
border spaces, 1–5, 6–11
  and culture, 19–21
  and deception, 189–91
  and discipline, 23–4
  and film, 14–15
  and globalisation, 47–8
  and illusion, 27–33
  and internal, 11–13, 15–16
  and international, 13–14
  and Kanafani, 57–9, 61–2
  and Kashua, 78–9, 90–3, 95, 96–101
  and language, 24–5
  and al-Madhoun, 109–10, 119–20, 128
  and Michael, 65–6, 68–70
  and physicality, 188–9
  and power, 21–3
  and protection, 16–19
  and representations, 187–8
  and silence, 81–3
  and spatial restriction, 25–7
  and utopia, 54–5
  see also Green Line; wall, the; West Bank

Brenner, Rachel Feldhay, 17
Bresheeth, Haim, 163
Brown, Wendy, 4
  Walled States, Waning Sovereignty, 27–8
Budrus (Bacha, 2009), 138
Burnat, Emad, 33, 35, 135, 136, 149–54

cameras, 148–9, 151–4, 157n27, 166–7
  and *Divine Intervention*, 158–60, 168–9, 169–71, 173–5, 176–81
Castel-Bloom, Orly, 95
  Dolly City, 17
Certeau, Michel de, 21, 160, 164, 176
checkpoints, 3–4, 5, 6, 7–8, 10–11
  and *Divine Intervention*, 158–65, 168–83
  and film, 36
  and global, 31
  and Kashua, 82–3, 85–7, 88–90
  and language, 20–1, 84
  and protection, 18
  and *Rana's Wedding*, 165–7
  and 'tunnel road', 42n154
  and Weizman, 167–8
  see also Qalandia checkpoint
Chronicle of a Disappearance (Suleiman, 1996), 161, 162, 174
City of Borders (Suh, 2009), 134–5, 138, 139
city walls, 27
Cleary, Joe, 31
coexistence, 47, 51–2, 134–6, 188–9
  and Kashua, 77, 78–9, 89–90, 97–8, 100–1
  and Michael, 62–70
communication, 85–6
conquest, 57–8

Dabashi, Hamid, 138, 163
Dancing Arabs (Kashua), 79–80, 82–3, 84

Dancing Arabs (Riklis, 2013), 80
Darwish, Mahmoud, 11, 15–16, 18, 48, 129–30, 136
   'Athens Airport', 13, 120, 164
Davidi, Guy, 33, 35, 135, 152
Davis, Rochelle, 113
Debord, Guy, 29
deception, 91, 100, 146–7, 188, 189–90
defeat, 12–13, 57, 60
defiance (*ṣumūd*), 164, 166, 171
Deleuze, Gilles, 22, 55
Derrida, Jacques
   Monolingualism of the Other, 83, 94
diaspora *see* exile
discipline, 23–4, 25, 26, 167
displacement, 12–13
Divine Intervention (Suleiman, 2002), 36, 82, 158–65, 168–83, 187, 188–9
documentaries, 11, 134–5, 137–40; see also *5 Broken Cameras*; *Mur*
Doves in Trafalgar (Michael), 33–4, 46–7, 49, 50–3, 188–9
   and coexistence, 62–70
   and utopia, 55–6
Dupes, The (film, 1973), 15

Egypt, 6, 10
encounters, 116–20
estrangement, 79, 81, 83, 84–5, 86–8, 90–1, 93–4
ethnicity, 91, 97–8, 100–1
Europe, 5, 27–8
exile, 13–14, 18, 32, 109
   and return, 107–8, 115–16, 130

fantasy, 2–3, 4–5, 172–3, 178–83, 188
Farag, Joseph, 13
Fatah, 58
Faulkner, William, 118
fences, 9–10
fidā'iyyūn (freedom fighters), 22, 56–7, 61, 107–8

Fieni, David, 163, 164, 165, 176
film, 3, 11–12, 14–15
   and PLO, 139, 161
   see also *Divine Intervention*; documentaries; *Rana's Wedding*
Foucault, Michel, 22, 23, 26
   Discipline and Punish, 167
fragmentation, 4–5
framing, 158–9, 165–6, 169–71, 177, 178–81
freedom of movement, 9, 11
Friedman, Yael, 135–6

Galilee, 9
Gaza, 3, 6–7, 9, 133n72
   and Green Line, 45, 46
   and al-Madhoun, 128–30, 188
Gertz, Nurith, 19, 161, 162, 163
globalisation, 5, 47–8, 55
Golan Heights, 6, 10
'Good Fence' policy, 10
Gore, Al, 1, 2
graffiti, 1–2; *see also* Banksy
Green Line, 8, 33–4, 45–8, 70, 188
   and Kanafani, 52–3, 57, 59
   and Michael, 64
Greenhouse, 135
Grossman, David, 4
Grumberg, Karen, 17, 19, 88
Guattari, Félix, 22, 55

Haaretz (newspaper), 77, 78, 83–4
Habiby, Emile, 48, 49
   'The Mandelbaum Gate', 13
   The Pessoptimist, 13, 81, 85, 97, 98–9
al-Hadaf (newspaper), 48
Haifa, 9, 46, 49, 58–9
al-Hakim, Tawfiq
   The People of the Cave, 122
Halabi, Zeina, 12, 15
Hamas, 10, 77
Hawwal, Kassem, 15

Hebrew, 20, 25, 80–1, 125
  and Kashua, 78, 84, 92, 94, 95
Hezbollah, 10
Hirsch, Marianne, 112
Hochberg, Gil, 31, 50, 63, 95, 140
  In Spite of Partition, 20, 24, 26, 28
Holocaust, 49, 59
homeland (*al-waṭan*), 18–19, 60, 61
housing, 9
Hungary, 5

ID, 61, 85, 86, 91, 93, 96
identity, 87, 94–5
Infiltrators (Jarrar, 2013), 137–8
International Criminal Court (ICC), 9
Intifadas
  First, 7
  Second, 15, 47, 66, 70, 161
Iraq, 49, 72n19
Iron Wall, The (Alater, 2007), 138
isolation, 86, 88, 94
Israel, 1, 3, 5, 6–11, 77
  and Green Line, 45–6
  and utopia, 53–4
  see also Haifa; Jerusalem; Jews; Six Day War; Tel Aviv
al-Ittihad (newspaper), 49

Jaber, Rabih, 122
Jabra, Jabra Ibrahim, 11, 18
  In Search of Walid Masoud, 35, 81–2, 107–8, 130
Jacir, Annemarie, 139
Jaffa, 9, 17
Jameson, Frederic, 53
Jarrar, Khaled, 137
Jenin, 8
Jerusalem, 6, 7, 8, 54, 71n1
  and *Divine Intervention*, 162, 179, 181, 182, 183
  and Kashua, 90, 91–3, 94–5, 97–8
  and *Rana's Wedding*, 167

Jewish settlements, 7, 8, 10, 24, 92
Jews, 49–51, 63–5, 97, 116–20
'Joi' (song), 172
Jordan, 6, 92, 112
Judaisation, 9, 11

Kafr Qasim (Alaouié, 1975), 38n61
Kanafani, Ghassan, 11, 32, 128
  All That's Left to You, 18, 118–19
  Men in the Sun, 13–14, 81, 84, 119
  see also Returning to Haifa
Kashua, Sayed, 32, 77–85
  Let It Be Morning, 34, 78, 79, 85–90
  Second Person Singular, 34, 78, 79, 90–101, 188–9
Khalidi, Rashid, 3, 111
Khalidi, Walid
  All That Remains, 39n87
Khalifeh, Sahar
  Wild Thorns, 12–13, 14, 84, 114–15
Khleifi, George, 19, 161, 162, 163
Khleifi, Michel, 19, 161
Khoury, Elias, 81, 122, 127–8
  Gate of the Sun, 16
kibbutz, 17
Kilito, Abdelfattah, 84
Kotef, Hagar, 25, 26, 168
Kristeva, Julia, 82–3
kūfiyya (Palestinian scarf), 178, 183, 185n40

language, 20–1, 24–5, 89
  and checkpoints, 168
  and documentaries, 144–5, 147
  see also Arabic language; Hebrew
Lebanon, 6, 9–10, 22, 40n114, 112
Lefebvre, Henri, 21
Lemon Tree (Riklis, 2008), 18
Levitas, Ruth, 53
Levy, Lital, 20, 32, 50, 99
LGBT issues, 134–5, 156n2–3

literature, 11–14, 16; *see also* Amiry, Suad; Kanafani, Ghassan; Kashua, Sayed; al-Madhoun, Raba'i; Michael, Sami
long shots, 142, 144–5, 147

MacDougall, David, 142
al-Madhoun, Raba'i, 32
  Destinies: A Concerto of the Holocaust and the Nakba, 109
  The Lady from Tel Aviv, 34–5, 108–11, 116–18, 119–30, 187, 188
Mahfouz, Naguib, 128
Mandelbaum Gate, 52–3, 54
Mann, Barbara, 17
Mansour, 'Atallah, 117
  In a New Light, 80
  Samira Remained, 97
Marin, Louis
  Utopics: Spatial Play, 54–5
Masharawi, Rashid, 161
Mason, Victoria, 113
Mattar, Karim, 110, 120, 173
memory, 113
mestiza culture, 19
metafiction, 122, 124, 127
Mexico, 5, 19, 21
Meyer, Stefan, 119
Michael, Sami, 32
  A Trumpet in the Wadi, 49–50
  Victoria, 49
  see also *Doves in Trafalgar*
migrants, 5, 10
military, 7, 19, 24, 25, 112, 152–4
  and checkpoints, 8, 10, 27, 31
  and *Divine Intervention*, 158, 170, 172, 177–8, 179–80
  and documentaries, 152–3, 155
  and Green Line, 45, 70
  and Hamas, 77
  and Kashua, 87
  and language, 89
  and *Returning to Haifa*, 33, 49, 58, 60
  and the wall, 138, 146

mise en abîme, 109, 110, 125–6
mise en scène, 169–70, 171, 177
misreading, 98–9
Mizrahim, 49–50, 72n18
More, Thomas
  Utopia, 55
multiple narrators, 118–20
Mur (Bitton, 2004), 35, 136–7, 140–2, 143, 144–8, 154–6, 188–90
murals, 1–2

Nakba, 14, 50, 110, 163
Naqqash, Samir, 49
narrative, 124–9, 146–54
narrators, 118–20
nation states, 54, 55
Negev, 9
Netanyahu, Benjamin, 10
Nichols, Bill, 139
nomads, 22, 55
non-places, 117
Northern Ireland, 137, 191

Omar (Abu-Assad, 2013), 137
one-way mirrors, 167–8, 170, 178, 190
opening, 57–9
Oslo Accords (1993), 3, 6–7, 11, 15–16, 190
  and Green Line, 46, 70
  and return, 112, 115
Oz, Amos
  'Nomad and Viper', 17

Palestine, 5, 6–11, 79
  and border representations, 11–13, 31–2, 109–11
  and film, 14–15
  and Kanafani, 48–9, 56–61
  and Kashua, 85–90, 93–4
  and Kuwait, 40n114
  and literature, 15–16
  and Michael, 50–2
  and mobility, 71n6
  and refugees, 22–3

and return, 107–8, 111–16, 117–18, 120, 122–6
and time, 164–5
and utopia, 53–4
see also Arabs; Gaza; Jerusalem; West Bank
Palestine Liberation Organisation (PLO), 6, 14, 112, 139, 161
Palestinian Authority, 112, 115, 167, 168
panopticism, 167–8, 174, 176–7
Parmenter, Barbara, 18
Peteet, Julie, 164
photography, 17, 29
Plato
  'Allegory of the Cave', 122
PLO see Palestine Liberation Organisation
Popular Front for the Liberation of Palestine (PFLP), 48, 51
power, 21–3
protection, 16–19, 152–4

Qalandia checkpoint, 24, 27, 168, 184n5

al-Ram checkpoint, 158, 162, 184n5
Ramallah, 15, 61, 115, 134, 158, 162
Rana's Wedding (Abu-Assad, 2002), 161, 165–7, 171
Rancière, Jacques, 29, 190
Rastegar, Kamran, 163, 169, 170
realism, 2, 4, 114–15, 122–3; see also surrealism
reconciliation, 47, 63
refugees, 5, 14–15, 22–3, 40n114, 46, 119
  and return, 112–13, 115
resistance, 14, 48, 56–7; see also defiance
return, 107–8, 111–16, 117–18, 120, 122–6
Return to Haifa (Hawwal, 1982), 15

Returning to Haifa (Kanafani), 33, 46–7, 48–9, 51–3, 68, 124
  and borders, 13, 57–9, 61–2, 69
  and Palestine, 59–61
  and resistance, 56–7
  and return, 14, 114
  and symbolism, 189
  and utopia, 54, 55–6
roadblocks, 9, 161
romance, 116–20

Sacks, Jeffrey, 99
Said, Edward, 22, 114, 115
  After the Last Sky, 12
Saleh, Tewfik, 15
screens, 170–1
Screenwriter, The (Kashua, TV show), 80
security fence see wall, the
segregation, 9
separation barrier see wall, the
Serbia, 5
shadows, 120–3, 126
Shamir, Yoav
  Checkpoint, 164
Shammas, Anton
  Arabesques, 80, 81, 104n94
al-Sharq al-Awsat (newspaper), 109
Sheetrit, Ariel, 50–1
Shehadeh, Raja, 4
  Palestinian Walks, 190
Shibli, Adania
  'Out of Time', 120, 164
silence, 81–3, 85–6, 96, 162–3, 174–6
Sinai Peninsula, 6
Six Day War, 6, 45
soldiers see military
soundtracks, 154, 172, 178, 184n30
sovereignty, 21–2, 27–8, 190
Suh, Yun, 134–5
Suleiman, Elia, 32, 182, 184n30;
  see also *Divine Intervention*

surrealism, 2–3, 4, 172–3; *see also* fantasy
surveillance, 23, 24, 84, 146, 167, 181
symbolism, 189
Syria, 5, 6, 10, 14, 40n114

taṣwīr (forming), 147, 148, 149, 150–1
Tawil-Souri, Helga, 3, 27
Tel Aviv, 17, 124–5
television, 80
terrorism, 7, 8
Third Cinema movement, 14
Ticket to Jerusalem (Masharawi, 2002), 161
time, 163–4
Time That Remains, The (Suleiman, 2009), 161, 162
Trump, Donald, 5
Twain, Mark, 73n49
two-state solution, 71n4

United States of America (USA), 5, 19, 21
utopianism, 33–4, 47, 52–6, 176
and Michael, 66–8, 70

Vienna, 27
villages, 18–19, 85–90, 93–4, 113; *see also* Bil'in
voice, 141–2

wall, the, 1–3, 4, 5, 10
and *5 Broken Cameras*, 148–56
and Banksy, 186–7
and construction, 7, 8–9
and disguise, 41n118
and documentaries, 134–40
and film, 35–6
and *Mur*, 140–2, *143*, 144–8
see also checkpoints; roadblocks
walls, 27–8
wanderers, 22–3, 94–5
Waugh, Patricia, 122
Wedding in Galilee (Khleifi, 1987), 19
Weizman, Eyal, 5, 10, 15, 24, 25, 141
and *Divine Intervention*, 160
Hollow Land, 159, 190
and one-way mirrors, 167–8, 178
West Bank, 1–2, 3, 6–9, 168
and Banksy, 186–7
and documentaries, 134–6, 137
and Green Line, 45–6
and Jewish settlements, 24
and Kashua, 88–9
see also Ramallah
workers, 1–2, 18, 71n6, 86, 88–9

Yaqub, Nadia, 14–15, 138–9, 162
Yaron, Amos, 145–7
Yehoshua, A. B.
'Facing the Forests', 17, 81

Zionism, 17–18, 53, 58

EU representative:
Easy Access System Europe
Mustamäe tee 50, 10621 Tallinn, Estonia
Gpsr.requests@easproject.com

www.ingramcontent.com/pod-product-compliance
Lightning Source LLC
Chambersburg PA
CBHW070353240426
43671CB00013BA/2480